Maynooth College
reflects on
Facing Life's End
Perspectives on
Dying and Death

Published by Messenger Publications, 2022.

This volume was published with the financial support of
the Maynooth Scholastic Trust.

ISBN: 9781788125826

Cover image © Shutterstock
Typeset in Adobe Caslon Pro & Cormorant Garamond
Printed by Hussar Books

Messenger Publications,
37 Leeson Place, Dublin D02 E5V0
www.messenger.ie

Maynooth College Reflects on Facing Life's End
Perspectives on Dying and Death

Edited by
**Jeremy Corley, Aoife McGrath, Neil Xavier O'Donoghue
and Salvador Ryan**

CONTENTS

Foreword

Archbishop Dermot Farrell

The essays in this volume adopt a multifaceted approach to the subject of dying and death. For those who face its stark reality, and the loved ones who accompany them through its various stages, it can be a heartbreaking time, filled with a variety of emotions.

One of the essays discusses the *Ars Moriendi*, 'the art of dying well', which was a prominent theme in medieval literature. However, its concerns primarily revolved around spiritual preparation for death, and especially ensuring that a person's soul was in a fitting state to meet its Maker. In times past, there was often relatively little that could be done to ease the physical suffering of those in their final days. Thankfully, modern palliative care, with its advanced means of pain management, has made it possible for many to die with a level of dignity and specialist care that would have been unimaginable a couple of centuries ago.

As the essays here demonstrate, the care of the dying, and those who accompany them, extends beyond the management of physical pain. It involves seeing and hearing the other person, and attending to their needs in a holistic manner. Sometimes that involves having difficult conversations, and telling the truth to those we love, in order that we might face the reality of death together. Several essays show what it means to truly accompany a loved one on this journey: to listen to a person's 'sacred story'; to sit with them as they work through unresolved issues and to remain with them when all that can be shared are tears. The recent document, *Samaritanus Bonus*, reminds us that 'While essential and invaluable, palliative care in itself is not enough unless there is someone who "remains" at the bedside of the sick to bear witness to their unique and unrepeatable value.'[1]

Counterintuitively, for some, the stages of dying can be a life-affirming experience: an opportunity to look back on the past with gratitude; a time to reassess one's choices during life, and to make peace with them; sometimes, the chance to heal fractured relationships, or at least to let go of past hurts.

St Paul, in his letter to the Corinthians (1 Corinthians 12:4–5), speaks of the variety of gifts with which the community is entrusted. Treating our loved ones with dignity, whether in their final days, or in the rituals that follow their death, is not something that can be achieved alone; it involves communities of compassion and care. Healthcare workers, palliative care specialists, pastoral care teams and wide circles of friends each have their respective roles to play. And the same applies for the days after a person dies. One of the essays here highlights the importance of those who work behind the scenes in the context of the Irish wake – those who make the tea and scones, and those who stand at the roadside directing traffic. Each unique contribution forms a vital part of the fabric of accompaniment.

In the weeks and months following, there will also be the need to reflect on the significance of what happened. The search for meaning in the face of loss will often find those who are bereaved asking philosophical questions, even if they are not necessarily framed as such. They will sometimes find comfort in the written words of others who have reflected on bereavement, in a favourite passage of Scripture, or in the consolation offered by the words of the Christian liturgy, which assures us that death is not the end, and which offers the hope that

---

1   Congregation for the Doctrine of the Faith, *Samaritanus Bonus: On the Care of Persons in the critical and terminal phases of life*, II, https://www.vatican.va/roman_curia/congregations /cfaith/documents/rc_con_cfaith_doc_20200714_samaritanus-bonus_en.html.

we will one day be reunited with our loved ones where the suffering of our human condition will be no more.

I warmly welcome this book of reflections on dying and death and hope that its wide range of essays will prove thought-provoking for many.

Introduction

Jeremy Corley, Aoife McGrath, Neil Xavier
O'Donoghue and Salvador Ryan

Irish people have traditionally embraced death as part of life. The wake, the funeral, the month's mind, the anniversary Mass, the blessing of graves – all these rituals show that death has not been minimised here.[1] Yet, because of social changes, death is in some ways perhaps less familiar now than it was for our grandparents. The decline in infant mortality, coupled with longer lifespans, has meant that we may encounter death at close quarters less often. The general reduction in family size and the trend towards urban living, combined with developments in hospital treatment and hospice care, have meant that fewer people tend to encounter dying and death at home. While most funerals in Ireland involve the burial of the deceased, in some areas cremations are becoming more common.

Today many people find it difficult to speak about dying and death. While the experience is universal, and one of the few certainties of life, it is not easy to contemplate the prospect of the death of a loved one, or, indeed, one's own death. How should I set my affairs in order? What will those last few weeks or days be like? Will I experience much pain? Is there anything awaiting me beyond death and, if so, what?

---

1   See the essays in Salvador Ryan (ed.), *Death and the Irish: a Miscellany* (Dublin: Wordwell, 2016).

Similar questions are asked by those who are faced with the prospect of caring for a loved one in the final stages of their lives. What does he or she most need at this time? Who do they need to see? How can difficult conversations be had, while remaining sensitive to a person's vulnerability when faced with a terminal illness? How can a person be made most comfortable as they near the end? And does a stage come when further medical intervention becomes disproportionately burdensome?

In fact, the whole issue of dying and death has become a topic of current discussion. Various countries (including Ireland) have introduced legislation to allow for euthanasia in certain cases.[2] In the wider background, economic questions arise about the cost of care for the dying, yet the public often show great generosity to charities aiming to assist sufferers from cancer or other serious diseases. A recent issue of *Concilium* has noted 'that the end of life is anything but simple and that it requires multiple perspectives to do justice to the complex questions it raises'.[3]

This volume of essays on dying and death adopts, in a synodal style, a multifaceted approach to the topic. Each author speaks in her or his own voice, many giving witness to the voices of those they have accompanied in dying and bereavement. The contributions are diverse, and generally reflect the Irish Catholic tradition. The volume features contributions from those working within the areas of palliative medicine, hospital chaplaincy, pastoral care, philosophy and theology. The range of articles, each ending with a few questions for further discussion and reflection, will hopefully be of use to all who wish to think more deeply about issues surrounding death, dying and the care of the terminally ill.

The volume has four sections: Facing with Care, Facing Goodbye, Facing Challenging Questions, and Facing Suffering with Hope. The opening section on Facing with Care begins with spiritual care practitioner Dr April MacNeill's chapter on 'Spiritual Care at End of

---

2   See the themed issue, 'Dying with Dignity', *Studies* 110 (summer 2021).
3   Margareta Gruber, Linda Hogan and Stefanie Knauss, 'The End of Life: Framing and Complicating the Question', *Concilium* 2021/5, 7–13, at 12.

Life – Lessons from the Bedside'. Building on years of experience working with the dying, MacNeill gives examples of how spiritual care interventions have provided a safe space for individuals nearing death to express their feelings, facilitated the opportunity for them to 'tell their story', and supported them through the critical junctures of their illness. She notes that in creating space for people to express themselves at these difficult moments, we too are confronted by the realities of life, suffering and death, and, in our listening and caring, we too are transformed.

The chapter by palliative medicine registrar Dr Brendan Corkery, offering 'An Approach to the Challenge of Dying and Death', explores the meaning of palliative care, tracing it back to the work of Dame Cicely Saunders (1918–2005), founder of the modern hospice movement. Her crucial breakthrough was to develop the concept of 'total pain' – identifying the need to address the physical, emotional, social and spiritual aspects of distress. The adjective 'palliative' was taken up in 1974 by Canadian surgeon Balfour Mount to describe a specific model of holistic care – including body, mind and spirit – with the aim of being integrated within a healthcare system. This development sought to address the previously recognised relative neglect within the hospital system of focused care for the dying patient. Although the World Health Organization (WHO) now explicitly acknowledges access to palliative care as part of the human right to health, dedicated palliative care is still currently unavailable in more than 30 per cent of all countries.

In her chapter, Dr Anne Francis (practitioner in spiritual and psychological care) celebrates 'The Power of Story in Accompanying People Towards the End of Life'. Comparing each person's story to a flowing river, she explores the place of story in the pastoral accompaniment of adults who are nearing the end of life. Through listening to people's stories, pastoral care workers can assist the dying by accompanying them as they discover aspects of their life, relationships or memories that are taking away their well-being. By listening deeply, those providing pastoral care can avoid the temptation of hurrying towards a happy ending or offering answers to suffering without honouring the challenging realities of human experience. Appropriate pastoral care can offer the possibility of reintegration of the self or a journey to wholeness for the dying person.

Thereafter, Rev. Chris Hayden, Spiritual Director at the National Seminary, Maynooth, puts in a plea for the recognition of the need for 'Love in the Pastoral and Professional Care of the Dying'. He notes that our culture frequently operates on notions of quality, productivity, efficiency and use of resources. From such a perspective, contemporary culture may tend to see death as a problem with no possible solution. While professional medical treatment is a fundamental requirement, human beings always need something more than technically proper care. Hayden proposes that in the care of the dying, there may be scope for viewing love more explicitly and more intentionally, as part and parcel of the caring relationship.

Internal medicine specialist Dr Sinéad Donnelly's chapter focuses on 'The Transformative Power of Palliative Care'. Donnelly explores core aspects of palliative care, such as non-abandonment; being present and the mystery of what happens; dying in a 'healed' state; dignity; caring; and suffering. She explains that while palliative medicine affirms life, it regards dying as a normal process, and hence seeks neither to hasten nor to postpone death. Drawing on her experience as a doctor of palliative medicine, she gives stories exemplifying the holistic nature of palliative care, the healing power of the moment, and the importance of human dignity, right until the end of life. She describes witnessing the transformative power of palliative care at work when the physician sees not just a disease, nor even a patient, but the person herself or himself.

The section on caring concludes with moral theologian Rev. Dr Michael Shortall's contribution on 'The Art of Dying Well'. He begins by referring to the memoir of a neurosurgeon who was diagnosed with inoperable lung cancer, and comments on the need to find meaning in dying. He recalls the medieval European tradition of *Ars Moriendi* (the art of dying well), which has perhaps been lost because nearly half of all deaths in Ireland nowadays occur in hospital. He recounts a personal experience of a friend who exemplified the art of dying well. He reflects that meaning can be found in death through the willingness of the dying person to participate in the task of dying well (acceptance), the resources offered by the community (awareness), and the commitment of others to pay attention in a caring way to what the dying person is experiencing (accompaniment).

The volume's second section, Facing Goodbye, begins with the personal chapter by church historian Prof. Salvador Ryan, 'Memento Mori: Reflecting on the Music of my own Death'. Ryan recalls childhood experiences of serving requiem Masses at Moneygall church and being impressed by the emotion of the occasion, conveyed especially through the music. Accordingly, he explains the hymns that he has chosen for his own funeral liturgy, whenever this arrives. Such hymns will reflect his belonging to his local community, as well as aspects of his life.

Thereafter, retreat facilitator and author Bairbre Cahill describes 'Tea, Scones and Stories – the Liturgy of an Irish Wake'. She begins her chapter with the poignant childhood experience of the wake for her young brother. This experience underlines the reality of a wake, where we encounter the reality of death, our fear of dying and an awareness of our own mortality. She goes on to describe some of the customs at an Irish wake. She proposes the wake as one model for the synodal process as a particular liturgy of encounter, beginning with the ministry of welcome, formal or informal. She sees significance in the cups of tea and the homemade scones, because love is made real in the gathering and sharing of food. When wakes could not happen because of Covid-19 restrictions, people missed out on gathering, to talk over cups of tea and to remember and celebrate the life of the deceased. Lack of the wake left unfinished business, which stalled the process of grieving. The wake can be a sacred space, teaching us not only how to begin to grieve but also how to live.

Next Rev. Prof. Liam Tracey OSM considers: 'What happens when we die? Reflections on the *Order of Christian Funerals*'. Tracey notes that when a death occurs, the Church calls each member of Christ's Body to participate in the ministry of consolation. A parish funeral team can assist families in preparing the funerals of loved ones, while 'Bethany Groups' can offer a service of accompaniment for those who mourn. Tracey recognises that what we hope for beyond death impacts on how we minister at the time of death and its aftermath. He explores the *Order of Christian Funerals* (1991), the ritual book that gathers the various funeral rites from the prayers at the time of death till the person is buried or cremated. Besides praying for the deceased, the funeral rites provide the mourners with a ritual and supportive path through grief. At a time of death, the funeral rites proclaim that each person has been created for eternal life, and that by his dying and rising, Jesus has broken the chains of sin and death that bound humanity. The rites also recall that we are united in the communion of saints. While the living and the dead are now physically separated, we are one body of Christ, and in the new heaven and the new earth we will eventually be reunited where death is no more.

The section on Facing Goodbye concludes with a reflection on 'Children and Death' by Rev. Dr John-Paul Sheridan, a theologian with a specialism in religious education and catechesis. He notes that relationships are of vital importance when speaking to children about death or helping them to speak about it. Adults need to put aside their own fears around the subject of death and assist children during the grieving time, and to have a healthy and natural attitude to the reality of death. Within the primary school, the month of November provides a suitable time to talk about death without the immediacy of a bereavement in the family or community. It also gives the children an occasion to respond to death in prayer, and to remember all who have died, from families, the school and community, and even the wider world. Communal prayer for the dead in the school helps a child to realise that they are not alone in the grief they feel for a loved one that has died. It also helps them to realise that grief does not go away by forgetting about it or suppressing it, but that it will never be overwhelming when we express it.

The volume's third section, Facing Challenging Questions, opens with Scripture scholar Rev. Dr Jeremy Corley's chapter, offering 'Scriptural Perspectives on our Mortality'. The chapter begins with a poem by Gerard Manley Hopkins ('Spring and Fall') about a young girl who is feeling melancholy at the sight of golden leaves falling from the autumn trees. The poet reflects that in fact the girl is being confronted with decay and, ultimately, death, represented by the falling foliage. The chapter then considers passages on mortality from the Old and New Testaments. Whereas Job and Sirach focus on human mortality, the Book of Wisdom offers hope of immortality. John's Gospel offers wisdom for facing life's end in Christ's life and death, because Jesus traces a pattern of *exitus* and *reditus* – going out from the Father and then returning to him. The chapter ends by considering another Hopkins poem ('On the Comfort of the Resurrection').

In his contribution, healthcare chaplain Rev. Canon Dr Daniel Nuzum reflects on 'Perinatal Death: Complex and Nuanced Life, Love and Loss'. Drawing on his experience as a Church of Ireland chaplain and clinical pastoral education supervisor, he explores some of the complex ethical issues arising in difficult situations. While every expectant parent wants a healthy baby, a diagnosis of life-limiting uncertainty or a stillbirth intrudes as the most unwelcome of guests. In perinatal death, parents are forced to come to terms with the loss of hope, life and dreams for their expected child. Yet, despite the high incidence of pregnancy loss, it still remains a relatively silent area in public discourse, so that many bereaved parents experience a 'silent grief'. In heartrending cases of 'fatal foetal anomaly' or 'life-limiting condition', parents need somehow to come to terms with the reality of the impending loss of their pregnancy, or the death of their baby during pregnancy or shortly after birth. The increased provision in Ireland of pastoral resources, as well as training for hospital chaplains, can provide comfort and acknowledgement of this loss alongside a public recognition of the value of every life.

In the next chapter, moral theologian Rev. Dr Pádraig Corkery reflects on 'The Role of Prudential Judgements in End-of-life

Decision-making'. Cases of patients in a persistent vegetative state, and the debate on euthanasia in Ireland and across the globe, arise from the complexity of medical care and the ability of modern life-sustaining interventions to preserve life for many years. The theological tradition has taught that we are not obliged to go to extraordinary lengths to prolong our lives or the lives of those in our care, but it is not always agreed what means are extraordinary. The important question arises about who makes the decisions: the individual, the family, the medical profession or the courts? The tradition has weighed up the anticipated benefit of a particular medical intervention, balanced with the burdens that may accompany the intervention. While there is a presumption in favour of providing artificially administered nutrition and hydration to persons in a vegetative state, a prudential judgement may be needed in cases where continued intervention could be excessively burdensome.

The chapter by philosopher Dr Gaven Kerr discusses 'Death, Dying, and Dignity: A Philosophical Perspective'. The question of human dignity is an acute issue for medical treatment, particularly end-of-life care. Oftentimes it is felt that when an individual loses certain abilities previously possessed, dignity is lost. In such a context, advocacy is sometimes made to end such medical treatment or even take measures to bring about the patient's death. Kerr proposes a contrasting view of dignity, which is not a result of something that the individual can do, but is rather a feature of what the individual is. If someone is a being that is dignified, the individual has an intrinsic dignity, regardless of what he or she can do. This philosophical account of personal dignity views every human being as a subject of value, worthy of love. Palliative care of the dying is a witness to the fact that because of human dignity, no matter the situation, the person's life matters and deserves to be valued right up to the point of death.

The last chapter in the section on Facing Challenging Questions is the reflection by philosopher Dr Philip Gonzales about 'Being's Mystery: On Not Belonging to Ourselves'. He argues that in modern Western culture we seek to master death and suffering, instead of receiving them as events that are beyond our control. According to this modern outlook, each person has the 'right' to decide the manner and the hour of their death. To counter this view, Gonzales turns to two prophetic counter-cultural voices in the Western tradition: Plato and St Paul. Both the pagan sage and the Christian saint professed a wisdom of dispossession and a metaphysical humility that challenge our twenty-first-century world of possessive mastery and blinding pride. Both knew that being human entails understanding that we do not belong to ourselves, and without this knowledge one cannot die with dignity. The witness of Plato and St Paul can challenge the 'throw-away culture' prevalent in our twenty-first century society.

The volume's fourth section, 'Facing Suffering with Hope' begins with a chapter from Scripture scholar Rev. Dr Luke Macnamara OSB, entitled 'Raising the Victim of the Good Samaritan Parable: A Scriptural Reflection'. Like the robbery victim in Jesus' parable, many people suffering from severe illness share a sense of vulnerability and isolation, while their able-bodied neighbours are busy with everyday life. Such sufferers may have little quality of life and a meagre prospect of recovery, while, for prospective helpers, the sight of the victim may recall uncomfortably the fragility of their own lives. Nevertheless, the injured victim on the roadside prefigures Jesus' own destiny, and hence the experience of Jesus as a victim can be a source of comfort for all who find themselves suffering through serious illness. By freely choosing to go to Jerusalem and suffer there, Jesus willingly shares in the destiny of the roadside victim, and, indeed, in the destiny of all who face serious illness and death. The isolation of the seriously ill person is now transformed by the presence of Jesus, participating in the suffering. Moreover, because Jesus' journey to Jerusalem does not end with death but with resurrection, a victim's close association with Jesus is full of promise.

Systematic theologian and specialist in liturgy Rev. Dr Neil Xavier O'Donoghue's chapter explores 'The Sacrament of the Sick and its Role in a Christian's Sickness'. Because anyone facing serious sickness or debilitating old age is eligible to receive this rite of anointing, the Sacrament of the Sick is a more correct name than Extreme Unction, yet, unfortunately, many Irish people still consider this to be an 'extreme' sacrament. While it is good to call a priest when someone is dying, it would be better to request this sacrament at the onset of illness, and, indeed, at the onset of the debilitating effects of old age. Christians are not immune from suffering and death, nor are they immune from feelings of doubt and despair, but they are called to bear witness to Christ's conquest of death and the existence of heaven. Their faith assures them that God desires to bring to heaven any human person who desires to go there and cooperates with his redeeming grace. Since Christians are not necessarily strong people, the secret is to discover that Christ can strengthen us when we are facing trials and tribulations. Thus, the Sacrament of the Sick can be a great help during our sickness, both for the sick and for their relatives and friends.

Thereafter systematic theologian Dr Andrew Meszaros contributes a reflection entitled '"Go Forth, Christian Soul, from this World": A Theological Commentary on the *Proficiscere.*' The chapter explores the traditional prayer of commendation for the dying, beginning '*Proficiscere, anima Christiana*'. The prayer has become more widely known through John Henry Newman's epic poem, *The Dream of Gerontius* – later put to music by Edward Elgar. The chapter notes that earlier versions of the prayer included a more extensive litany, invoking not only Mary and Joseph, but also angels and archangels, patriarchs and prophets, apostles and evangelists, martyrs and confessors, holy monks, hermits and virgins. Since the liturgical reforms of Pope Paul VI, a shorter form has been used. The prayer invites the dying person to leave the present world of struggle and suffering, in order to journey to the next world of eternal peace and joy in the presence of our Creator. Amid widespread alternative or agnostic views on the afterlife, the prayer expresses faith in the clear Gospel promise of our heavenly Father's house with many rooms.

The chapter from philosopher Rev. Prof. Thomas Casey SJ explores the transition 'From Death to Eternal Happiness'. Because death robs us of so much, it is undesirable, and hence it might seem excessive to suggest we are destined to partake of a joy beyond any happiness we can possibly imagine. Even when we are intellectually aware of the grandeur of the Christian notion of paradise, the spontaneous images in our minds can lag far behind the truth. Some recent novels have visualised heaven as the intensification of earthly satisfactions, yet something in us wants to believe that eternal happiness is infinitely more wonderful than anything we experience in this life. Casey's wager is that our innate desire for eternal happiness corresponds to a state of bliss that really exists, even if heaven is always greater than any concept that we can form of it. The doctrine of bodily resurrection gives grounds for tremendous hope, since it emphasises the value of the body and promises that all of human existence will be renewed and transformed. Casey suggests that when it comes to eternity, we need to believe boldly that God promises this unimaginable gift of salvation to us, and to be confident enough in this hope, despite the disintegration of the body after death.

Appropriately, the volume ends with a chapter from systematic theologian Rev. Prof. Declan Marmion SM on 'The Life of the World to Come'. In a framework of hope, Christianity has traditionally spoken of 'four last things': death, judgement, heaven and hell. Christians live in the expectation of communion with God – beginning in this life and culminating in the next. Marmion recalls that Jesus' resurrection transformed his disciples, filling them with hope in the face of death. Nevertheless, the prospect of rendering an account of our lives after death has often filled Christians with a sense of fear, yet we trust that the loving mercy God shows us in this life will not cease in the next. Ultimately, the final judgement is not about appearing before a vengeful God, but a process of coming into the truth within the context of divine love. If purgatory is heaven's 'antechamber', eternal life completes our dynamic longing for God, who alone can bring about a definitive realisation of our deepest desires. If God is the goal of all human life, then, in heaven, all our desires for communion will be ultimately fulfilled within the contemplation of God.

At this point, the editors wish to express thanks to many people who have helped the volume reach completion. Thanks are due to the President of Maynooth College, Rev. Prof. Michael Mullaney, for supporting this book project, and to the college's Scholastic Trust for generous financial assistance. We are also grateful to the staff at Messenger Publications, especially Cecilia West (director), Donal Neary SJ (editor), Paula Nolan (art director) and Fiona Biggs (editor), for their professionalism and patience. Finally, we express our gratitude to all the contributors who provided chapters for this volume.

All these chapters are intended to stimulate reflection and discussion on the painful topic of dying and death. We hope this volume will be helpful to laypeople, religious and clergy who minister to the dying and bereaved, and, indeed, to every reader facing the difficult question of life's end in one way or another.

One: Facing with Care
1: Spiritual Care at End of Life –
Lessons from the Bedside

April MacNeill

Jesse,[1] they said, 'was a curious, chatty girl, who had so many questions ... and she never sat still'. She loved soccer, her dog, and practising hair braids with her friends. Jesse was nine years old when she jumped out of the car and ran across the road to pick up the fish and chips her mum had ordered. Excited, waving her chips in the air, she didn't see the oncoming car as it collided with her young body. For the staff in the ICU, stories and photos would be the only way we would get to know Jesse.

Jesse had suffered a catastrophic brain injury. Her body clung to life, and as her family confronted the reality of their daughter's impending death they raised the possibility of organ donation, desperately seeking to create meaning from her living and dying. I came on to the ward at the beginning of my shift as an ICU nurse to witness the first set of brain death testing. Undertaken by an intensive care specialist, the examination was to determine Jesse's brain function. These same tests were repeated eight hours later as I stood beside a second ICU specialist, watching ... waiting. In the final apnoeic test, however, Jesse

---

1   In this article, names have been changed to preserve anonymity.

took one breath.[2] She was unable to be an organ donor and she was dying. I walked into the treatment room overwhelmed, distraught, aware of the impact of the impending conversation with Jesse's family. The hopes, the needs of the family to make some sense of this catastrophic accident, to find meaning in their daughter's death, were dashed. In that moment it felt like death had come twice.

I was almost paralysed by my own sense of helplessness, not knowing what to do, or what to say, thinking, 'How in the hell can we do this ... how can I walk back into that room?' In that moment Steve, the ICU specialist, walked in. I quickly wiped away the tears, feeling embarrassed, aware my face was scarlet in colour. Approaching gently, he stood beside me. With his quiet, unassuming manner, he acknowledged the situation in front of us. He shared his heartbreak at what was unfolding for Jesse and her family. His honesty gave me permission to share mine. All my fears, confusion and doubts came tumbling out. His openness to sharing his vulnerability to provide a space for me to share mine, reminded me that I was not alone, that we were not alone, and that together we could find a way forward to care for Jesse and her family.

Not until many years later did I realise that I had received spiritual care that night. Steve had modelled to me a new way of being and a new way of doing as he taught me how to provide spiritual care at the end of life. In his words, in his actions, in the silence, he had invited me to consider another way of caring for people and their families, and of understanding my purpose as a healthcare professional. Steve had helped me find my courage. He inspired in me a desire to learn more, to do more, to become more.

Twenty-six years later, I'm still learning. As a spiritual care practitioner and educator, I have listened to thousands of stories. A traumatic event or a diagnosis of a life-limiting illness can involve a type

2   Three criteria need to be established for the neurological determination of death by clinical examination: absence of responsiveness; absence of brain stem reflexes; and absence of breathing. However, apparent spontaneous breathing may result from ventilator auto-triggering or auto-cycling, and this should be excluded. https://www.donatelife.gov.au/sites/default/files /anzics-statement-on-death-and-organ-donation-4.1.pdf, 15.

of death, where our understanding of our world, our beliefs, our relationships, and our personhood can be shredded. People can be left oscillating between anxiety and hope as they encounter the terrain in which they have found themselves confronted by illness and the reality of death. It is not a linear process, but rather a dynamic unfolding, as themes of connection, community, self-worth, shame, hope, peace, meaning, love, reconciliation, forgiveness and faith emerge. As people share their experience, new understandings can be discerned, beliefs and values explored, and wishes about end-of-life care declared.

Spiritual care practitioners and chaplains working in the healthcare context are at the forefront of providing bespoke spiritual care, recognising the uniqueness of every situation they confront. Expressed through the provision of attentive and reflective listening, practitioners seek to identify the individual's spiritual resources, hopes and needs.[3] In recognition of a diversity of spiritual perspectives, spiritual counselling, faith-based care and the provision of religious services, all contribute to the care provided to people and their families.[4] Gaining an understanding of another's reality, meeting people in their reality, is the essence of spiritual care. But when does end-of-life spiritual care begin? Is it in those last hours, days or weeks after one is told, 'There is no more that can be done'? Is it at the bedside when the chemotherapy is no longer effective, or when a husband is no longer able to return home to live with his wife because they are both too frail? Or perhaps it begins the moment one arrives at the emergency department and tells the nurse, 'They rang me and told me to come up.'

The following stories are a composite of thousands of hours of listening and learning at the bedside. They are the stories of those who have invited me to accompany them in their living and dying. The names and scenarios have been changed to honour the privacy of

---

3   Spiritual Health Victoria, *Spiritual Care in Victorian Health Services: Towards Best Practice Framework*: https://www.spiritualhealth.org.au/download/Guidelines-4-Qual-Spir-Care-Health -2020-5-310120-Web.pdf.
4   Ibid., 7.

the individuals and their families, yet the wisdom they share is universal. They are the true teachers of spiritual care, and these are some of their stories.

As I approached her door, I took a deep breath. I knocked, introduced myself and sought permission to enter. She sits before me in a chair, the bedside trolley with breakfast leftovers pushed to the side. As I enter the room, the sunlight streams through, creating an instant cosy, warm feeling on a cool autumn day. Her eyes were beaming brighter than ever before, her smile contagious. Tears were welling in her eyes, and I could feel the tears in my eyes. In that moment I instinctively knew the answer to the question I dared to ask, 'Was she in remission? Was she going home?'

We sat in that shared space quietly, silently, absorbing the new reality. Wow … she's got through, I thought, she's got through … and after a few minutes Stacie spoke. She delighted in telling me the medical staff had come in early, letting her know she was OK, she could go home. Her blood counts had climbed. After thirty-one long and very difficult days, she could go home. There had been so many conversations between us when she talked and I listened. We had laughed together, sometimes cried together, and always prayed together. On other occasions, sitting silently in the corner, providing a quiet companionship, was all she wanted. And now, here we were.

As a team we had all witnessed her anguish, the physical pain she had endured as her body imploded in response to the treatment delivered. Her heartbreak and confusion were palpable when her diagnosis was confirmed; her frustration immense with how 'the system ran'; her loneliness and isolation as she was disconnected from family and friends; and her childlike faith that had felt hollow when it appeared that all had been lost. After a lifetime of struggle, Stacie now had to fight for her life. In so many ways, she was not expected to survive, yet she did.

As we spoke, I invited her to share once more about her experience – I wanted to learn, to understand, to honour all that she had been through. So, I asked her, 'After all of this, what's most important for you?' Stacie sat up straight, her expression serious, looked me straight in the eye and said, 'I have found my voice, I know who I am now, I have found my voice.' Stacie's voice was clear and strong; her illness experience had been transforming. I was in awe, aware I was witnessing something sacred. In the ordinary moments of her day-to-day care, Stacie had rediscovered herself, and her sense of worth. I invited her to tell me more, and without a moment's hesitation she shared.

It had been in the moments when, at three in the morning, the nurse attending to her didn't yell or scream at her with her bed full of diarrhoea. 'He was so gentle,' she said. 'I never felt like I was judged.' These experiences were echoed in her contact with cleaning and catering staff, orderlies and the clerical team. It had been those moments of being invited to share her experience and contribute to her care, instead of being told what to do and what to think, that had been most powerful. She commented that it had given her time to step back and think about her life and what she wanted. Stacie had been freed from the shackles of shame and embarrassment that had haunted her all her life; they were now gone. Stacie had discovered, or one might argue, rediscovered her worth, her value and her place in the world. She commented: 'I know I may not survive this, I know I'm probably gonna die, but you see that doesn't matter any more because I know who I am. For the first time in my life I know who I am, and that's all I need to know.' In the most ordinary of days the power of care, community, trust, faith, hope and love was revealed.

'It is not just the act of listening and waiting with others that matters; it is how we do this that is most significant.'[5] Knowing when to stay and when to leave can be some of the hardest moments in providing care, regardless of our role. Discerning 'whose need is this?' in deliberating whether to stay or go, is crucial, and sometimes the choice is not always clear. Yet if we create space for the other to tell us what they need at this time, we can all find a way forward.

5   Ewan Kelly, *Personhood & Presence* (London: Bloomsbury, T&T Clark, 2012), 28.

We sat together, the room dark, watching, waiting. At nearly seventy years of age Peter never imagined that Tim would go first. Peter never thought it would be this way, watching ... waiting ... for his son to die. Tim's breath had become shallow; he no longer responded to a voice. Peter jumped up, pacing the room like a caged lion, his sense of powerlessness profound. I too felt profoundly powerless to ease Peter's pain. This was not the time for clever words, or empty clichés. I remained still, sitting next to the empty chair vacated by Peter. I was silently praying for all of us. Though I had known Tim well throughout his treatment, and he had shared deeply, his dad Peter had only recently arrived from interstate. Relationships with staff had yet to be fully formed, and Peter was unsure about 'that spiritual care stuff'.

I looked towards Tim, then glanced towards Peter, ever mindful of the bond between a parent and their child. This was a sacred time, private, personal. Quietly I commented, 'I wonder if you would prefer some time alone with your son?' Peter let out a huge sigh, his shoulders fell, he walked back and sat down in the chair. As he placed his face in his hands he stated, 'Yes ... I do ... yes, I do ... '. I gently nodded my head in acknowledgement of what was spoken and unspoken between us. He needed this time with Tim, with his son, alone, and I walked towards the door. As I pulled it open he asked, 'You be back tomorrow?' 'Yes,' I said, and began to walk away. Peter commented, 'See you then ... and thanks for understanding.' For the briefest of moments, he smiled. I never met Peter again. Tim died overnight. The staff had informed me that Peter remained with his son until after Tim's death and had left with other family members. 'Oh, and by the way,' they said, 'he said to say thanks for everything.'

For John, his faith beliefs and his relationships with his faith community were at the heart of his spiritual care; they were his sources of strength. An attentive listening presence was offered as John spoke of stories of adventure, freedom and love; comfort was offered as he grieved over 'mistakes we make' and the brutality of 'life inside'. He shared his disappointments, isolation and rejection as others became aware of his struggles with addiction and time spent in prison.

He told of his joy at finding 'a new place to belong' when he had first gone to his local church group. Like many people John remained 'hopeful for a cure, a miracle', as he transitioned from supportive to palliative care. In responding to his spiritual needs, spiritual resources, denominational support and prayer were provided. Then one day he commented, 'It's not like in the movies, is it? Sometimes it just remains as it is … shitty.' There was a deep sadness in his voice as he reconciled with his reality that some relationships would never be healed. He would remain separated from his family of old; distanced from those he had once loved. Though grateful for the community who now supported him, John's heart ached for what could have been. Acknowledging and sitting in the messiness of one's life can feel acutely more painful at the end of life. Informed by our own beliefs about 'closure' and 'a good death', do we all somehow seek a 'feel-good' ending, whether we are patients, family, friends or staff? What does 'a good death' look like, anyway?

Our living and our dying are as unique as each of us is individually. In our desire to 'do what's best', sometimes as healthcare teams we can quickly fall into 'knowing what's right' for the other. Our own personal values and beliefs, life experience, relationships and professional expertise shape how we hear and understand the patient experience. Giving voice to the individual's understanding of their experience, their values and beliefs, their needs, fears, hopes and wishes, is an essential component of spiritual care. For spiritual care practitioners, our role as patient advocates can bring another dimension to end-of-life care.

It had been nine years since Kellie's initial diagnosis and treatment. She was the mother of a ten-year-old boy. He was her everything. Together with her husband, she was proud of all she had achieved. 'Work had been busy,' she said, 'and getting Ollie to school, his cricket, catching up with family. Well, you notice something's not quite right, then you push it to the back of your mind.' She fell silent, and after a long pause she continued, 'The doctors said it's just so aggressive. A few weeks if I'm lucky.' She rubbed her stomach, which was enlarged and tight, looking down at her swollen ankles. Her skin was a light yellow hue. She looked exhausted. The medical team had already spoken to Kellie about the need to transition to palliative care: 'Go home,' they had said, 'spend some time with your boy.' But this was not what she wanted. For Kellie, 'fighting to my last breath is what I need to do'. 'I'm not leaving,' she said. I was a little stunned, not so much by her desire to live but by her choice to remain in hospital. Her family had spoken about the support they could offer Kellie, to 'bring her home'. But Kellie wasn't budging. As a team we were at an impasse. What were we missing? What had we failed to understand about Kellie's needs?

Over the following days Kellie continued to deteriorate. Her husband Ben and son Ollie were visiting every day. There was increasing distress amongst the staff, many of whom had known Kellie and her family since her initial treatment nine years ago. 'Why won't she go home?' one asked, 'I just don't understand it.' But understanding was the key to caring for Kellie. 'Don't you see that, as his mother, I need him to know I did everything to stay. That right up till my last breath I did everything to stay with him.' For Kellie, supporting her in her living and dying, in accordance with her beliefs about motherhood, was the most important thing we could offer. 'That's what I need, to do this my way.' In the remaining days of Kellie's life, she was cared for in hospital. Kellie agreed to treatment limitations with the medical team, as together we discussed her spiritual needs in preparation for her death. Witnessing Kellie dying with her family by her side was both heartbreaking and sublimely beautiful all at once. In our final conversation she expressed her thanks for all the care she had received from all the staff, and the comfort this gave her, and yet it was us who needed to thank her. We needed to thank her for challenging us when we became too comfortable in our 'knowing', and for her bravery in speaking and living her truth.

This snapshot of the patients' and families' experience and the provision of spiritual care at the end of life reinforces the uncertainty and suffering that individuals experience throughout their illness and in their transition to end-of-life care. The spiritual care interventions provided created a safe space for individuals to express their fear, uncertainty, frustration, anger, anguish, pain, hopes, joy and love. They facilitated them in 'telling their story', and supported them through the critical junctures of their illness as they sought to make meaning of their life, particularly in transition to end-of-life care. As noted by palliative care physician Christina Puchalski:

> healing is not a cure but a movement from the chaos often associated with illness and crisis to a place of groundedness and peace within that chaos. It is a restoration of relationships, meaning and purpose. The meaning is often a new meaning for the person who is affected by the experience of facing death and seeing oneself and others in a new and perhaps deeper light.[6]

Spiritual care requires more than skill sets or techniques.[7] As we create the space for people to tell their story, we too are confronted by the realities of life, illness, trauma and death. Theologians have often recognised that the onset of illness can be 'a transformative experience', a threshold moment. Thomas Merton suggests it is God who is present in our questioning, when we confront 'the value of our existence, the reality of our commitments, and the authenticity of our everyday lives'.[8] Identifying and working with our own complexities, contradictions and personal narrative is a crucial component of spiritual care practice. These personal reflections cannot be undertaken alone, and require the compassion, support and guidance provided by colleagues, managers, supervisors and spiritual directors. For it is in our listening, our caring, our learning and our loving, that we too are transformed.

---

6   Christina Puchalski, 'Spirituality and the Care of Patients at the End of Life: An Essential Component of Care', *OMEGA* 56:1 (2007–2008) 33–46, at 39.
7   Bruce Rumbold, 'Models of Spiritual Care', in *Oxford Textbook of Spirituality in Healthcare*, ed. Mark Cobb, Christina M. Puchalski, and Bruce D. Rumbold (Oxford: Oxford University Press, 2012), 177–83, at 181.
8   Thomas Merton, *Love and Living*, ed. Naomi Burton Stone and Brother Patrick Hart (New York, NY: Farrar, Straus & Giroux, 1979), 39.

As practical theology dares to consider new horizons in interdisciplinary care and research, it can potentially offer both healthcare and faith communities new insights into understanding the world in which we live and the expression of the sacred in this world. In the final chapter of *Method in Theology*, twentieth-century philosopher and theologian Bernard Lonergan reminds theologians that the Church 'exists not just for itself' but for humankind.[9] For it is our own awareness and experience of 'the gift of redemptive love' that enables individuals and communities to mediate this same love to another.[10] This experience of love can be a resource of strength in the search for clarity and truth in end-of-life care. As demonstrated, an experience of love can be transformational, opening into new insights of loving and being loved, a new awareness of our capacity for love and sacrifice, and an ability to make changes in the way we live our life.[11] In their courage to meet with us, share their stories and engage in an authentic relationship, a sacred space of trust and love is engendered between the individuals, families, spiritual care practitioners and healthcare communities in which the true face of God can be revealed.[12]

Questions for Reflection and Discussion

1. What thoughts/feelings arose for you as you read this chapter?
2. Which sentence and/or passage stood out for you? Why?
3. What insights did you gain about spiritual care?
4. How does this personal reflection support or challenge your own experiences of receiving or providing spiritual care?
5. What further questions does this chapter evoke for you in the provision of spiritual care at end of life?

9   Bernard Lonergan, *Method in Theology* (Toronto: University of Toronto Press, 1927), 363.
10   Robert Doran, *Theology and the Dialectics of History* (Toronto: University of Toronto Press, 1990), 245.
11   Elizabeth. J. Snedden, *The Eros of the Human Spirit – The Writings of Bernard Lonergan SJ* (New York, NY: Paulist Press, 2017), 99.
12   Edward Schillebeeckx, *Jesus: An Experiment in Christology* (trans. Hubert Hoskins) (London: Collins, 1979), 146.

2: An Approach to the Challenge of Dying and Death

Brendan Corkery

In a reflection on palliative care which focuses on dying and death, many people will think these terms are synonymous. In much the same way that society has developed an alternative lexicon for death, there is often a fear when the term palliative care is mentioned that there is an implicit message that the patient is dying, and the final days of life are near. This is certainly not necessarily the case. Of course, words matter. As a man once commented on his initial referral to a palliative care team I was working with, it is hardly a surprise that people think that palliative care must mean that death is imminent – he grew up in the Harold's Cross area of Dublin and in his youth frequently walked past the entrance to 'Our Lady's Hospice for the Dying'. It is important therefore to explore what is meant when we say palliative care.

While it can be true that referral to a palliative care team, either in hospital or in the community setting, may be prompted by the anticipated imminent death of the person, the introduction of the service – if explained clearly and introduced early – can often alleviate the initial barrier of fear and anxiety about their input into that person's care. This apprehension may be even more acute for family and friends.

Here I will briefly outline the background of what is meant by the modern palliative care movement, and suggest that it is not solely reserved for care at the very end of life. I hope to begin to explore the concept of dying and death from a palliative care perspective, and examine some of the goals of care for the person, their loved ones and their carers. It is crucial to acknowledge that the experiences of the journey towards dying and death are as individual as people themselves. Thus I hope to allow reflection on some of these issues and address common misperceptions, which lead to the barriers and stigma that are often encountered when palliative care is discussed.

Palliative care as a modern medical discipline is only decades old and has evolved even in this relatively brief period. It is important to be clear that there can be palliative care input at any stage of the journey for a person with an advanced life-limiting illness. It is not reserved for those with a diagnosis of incurable cancer, nor only for those at the end of life, to mention a couple of common perceptions. Specialist palliative care can include people with advanced cardiac, respiratory, neurological, or any other domain of illness that is anticipated sooner or later to lead to death, with symptoms needing specialist advice and support.

When faced with the diagnosis of an illness that we know will ultimately progress and – all other factors being equal – cause the death of the person, more complexities may arise than can be addressed in a short essay. Palliative care input to support and manage symptoms does not preclude other medical treatments that aim to control an advanced illness, such as chemotherapy in a metastatic (spread) cancer, or ongoing cardiology management of advanced heart failure, for example. As improving treatments in many of these illnesses can prolong the course of the illness for a period, there can be an increasing challenge over time (for patients, families and healthcare providers) in recognising when a person is approaching the end of life. Palliative care involvement is therefore based on an individual's needs, which often change over time.

The Modern Palliative Care Movement

The catalyst for the modern palliative care movement is largely credited to the work of the Hertfordshire-born Dame Cicely Saunders (1918–2005), particularly related to her experiences during and after the Second World War. Saunders was a remarkable person, with a remarkable career, including training as a social worker (or 'lady almoner'), as a nurse and as a doctor.[1] She pioneered the concept of 'total pain' – identifying the need to address the physical, emotional, social and spiritual aspects of distress. Crucially, Saunders founded Saint Christopher's Hospice in London in 1967 – the first modern hospice – with an approach that has been replicated in many other such units and which has helped establish the discipline of palliative medicine. There is the oft-quoted statement by Dame Saunders that summarises the approach that palliative care embraces: 'You matter because you are you, and you matter to the end of your life. We will do all we can not only to help you die peacefully, but also to live until you die.'[2]

Although it is a relative newcomer in modern medicine, palliative care is an approach with a much older heritage. In the original meaning, hospices were places of rest and refuge for travellers, as well as providers of free care for the ill and poor, and care for the dying. There were parallels between the growth of Christianity and care for the sick and the dying in many parts of the Roman Empire.[3] In subsequent centuries, we find the medieval practice of the seven corporal works of mercy – largely based on Jesus' parable of the sheep and the goats at the Last Judgement (Matthew 25:31–46) – in the Benedictines and other religious orders, which included care for the sick. Burial of the dead was also included as a work of mercy.

1   Caroline Richmond, 'Dame Cicely Saunders, founder of the modern hospice movement, dies', *British Medical Journal*, vol. 331, issue 7510 (23 July 2005), 238, https://www.bmj.com /content/suppl/2005/07/18/331.7509.DC1.

2   Quoted by Robert Twycross in 'A Tribute to Dame Cicely Saunders', Memorial Service, 8 March 2006, reported in *Church Times*, 2 November 2006.

3   William E. Phipps, 'The origin of hospices/hospitals', *Death Studies* 12/2 (1988), 91–99.

We can be proud that Ireland is among the countries with an established tradition in caring for the dying. In the nineteenth century, the Religious Sisters of Charity founded a hospital/hospice in Cork (1870) and in Harold's Cross in Dublin (1879), with a particular focus on care for the dying that was lacking in hospitals.[4] A home for the dying was set up in Paris in 1874 by an association known as the Sisters of Calvaire (Golgotha). Examples in the US included Rosary Hill Home (opened in 1901 by the Dominican Sisters of Hawthorne, New York), and Calvary Hospital in New York City (1899). These early examples of homes set up to care for the dying were all founded and run by religious orders. The motivation in establishing these institutions was generally as a living witness to their faith. The focus was mainly on supportive and nursing care rather than on the more interventional or invasive medical care that would be anticipated in the acute hospital setting.

Dame Cicely was documented as being devoutly Christian, and Phipps reports that she thought of herself as the reviver of the centuries-old monastic hospice tradition. Her conception was dedicated care for those at the end of life whose needs were not being met by the healthcare system at the time. This was generally referred to as 'hospice care'. Use of the term 'palliative care' is more recent still. The word palliative has its root in the Latin word *pallium*, meaning a cloak. In the context of medicine, this suggests the sense of mitigating the effects of illness on a person, without effecting a cure. The use of the adjective 'palliative' in modern medicine had some usage in surgical literature before it was co-opted in 1974 by Canadian surgeon Dr Balfour Mount to describe a specific philosophy of care.[5] Palliative care was then a novel term to describe a model of holistic care – including body, mind and spirit – with the aim of being integrated within a healthcare system. This was in order to address the

---

4   E. Bruera, I. Higginson, C. von Gunten and T. Morita (eds), *Textbook of Palliative Medicine and Supportive Care*, 2nd ed. (Boca Raton, FL: CRC Press, 2015), 3.
5   Devon Phillips, interview with Balfour Mount, accessed 16 January 2022. https://www.mcgill.ca/palliativecare/portraits-0/balfour-mount.

recognised relative neglect in the hospital system of focused care for the dying patient. Although overlap in definitions between *hospice* and *palliative* care is evident, part of the motivation for the adoption of this terminology was to make this philosophy of care more accessible to people of any background or belief system.

Barriers to Accessing Palliative Care

Access to palliative care is now explicitly recognised by the WHO under the human right to health. The WHO estimates that about 40 million people around the world need palliative care each year.[6] However, over three-quarters (78%) of these people live in middle- and low-income countries, where they may not be able to access high-quality palliative care. In one survey in 2019, the WHO found that palliative care was available in only 68% of countries, and 40% of countries reported that the services were available to at least half of the patients in need. There are many barriers to accessing palliative care services, which can include national health policies; limited or lack of training in or availability of healthcare professionals; and lack of awareness or misconceptions about palliative care. These can be cultural or societal perceptions.

Significant barriers to providing palliative care include misconceptions about the role of opiate analgesic (pain) medicines. There is the perception that improving access to opiate analgesia will lead to increased misuse. This is not the case when opiates are properly provided and used for patients with symptoms requiring this type of medicine for adequate symptom relief. Access to adequate opiate analgesia is crucial to providing high-quality palliative care; however, there is a global disparity in this provision. The WHO reported that in 2018, 87% of the morphine used for management of pain and symptoms was consumed by just 21% of the world's population.

---

6   World Health Organisation, *WHO Fact Sheets – Palliative Care* (2020). Accessed 31 July 2021. https://www.who.int/news-room/fact-sheets/detail/palliative-care.

Again, it was mostly people in low- and middle-income countries that suffered from this inequality.

A common concern amongst patients or their families is that using opiates will hasten death. In referring to the use of medications for symptom relief at the end of life, the *Catechism of the Catholic Church* succinctly summarises the approach that is recognised by palliative care providers (*CCC*, 2279):

> The use of painkillers to alleviate the sufferings of the dying, even at the risk of shortening their days, can be morally in conformity with human dignity if death is not willed as either an end or a means, but only foreseen and tolerated as inevitable.[7]

This is referred to as the ethical principle of double effect, whereby the desired effect or priority is the intention to treat, or, in this case, to relieve suffering. If there are secondary effects of this intervention, these can be ethically tolerable. The role of palliative care at the end of life is to relieve suffering, and not necessarily to prolong or shorten a person's natural life. The goal of maintaining the dignity and comfort of the person is paramount.

In his message for the World Day of the Sick in 2007, Pope Benedict XVI reflected on suffering due to illness.[8] He called for more support and improved care for the dying and those with incurable illnesses. He identified caring for the dying as essential to maintaining human dignity, feeling it necessary 'to stress once again the need for more palliative care centres which provide integral care, offering the sick the human assistance and spiritual accompaniment they need. This is a right belonging to every human being, one which we must all be committed to defend.'

---

7   *Catechism of the Catholic Church* (Dublin: Veritas Publications, 1995). Online: https://www.vatican.va/archive/ENG0015/__P7Z.HTM.
8   Pope Benedict XVI, *Message for the Fifteenth World Day of the Sick, 11/2/2007* (given 8 December 2006). https://www.vatican.va/content/benedict-xvi/en/messages/sick/documents/hf_ben-xvi_mes_20061208_world-day-of-the-sick-2007.html.

What Does End-of-Life Care Look Like?

Dr Kathryn Mannix, the well-known palliative medicine consultant and writer, has astutely observed that as a society we have often lost the familiarity of dealing directly with dying and death.[9] Clear exceptions to this are those parts of the world where wars and violent conflicts continue to traumatise generations of people, of which there are always too many examples. However, in the second half of the twentieth century, medical advances and improvements in standards of living have meant that people are living longer and are much less likely to die from illnesses that are often now seen as more chronic ailments. This is seen in increasing life expectancy in many countries and is also reflected in population trends in this period. Changes to the structure of society and healthcare mean that the two universal experiences of being born and dying have largely moved from the home to a healthcare setting. For some people, dying at home is a key wish, although it may not be possible for a variety of reasons. Hospice inpatient units and many hospitals can provide the care that a patient needs at the end of life. Additionally, one of the primary objectives of community palliative care teams and community-based services is to support those people who wish to die at home, and their families.

Supporting a person's wish to die at home is a multidisciplinary team effort in mobilising available community supports to ensure that the person can be cared for safely and comfortably. A common worry for a family when preparing for this eventuality can be that, while they have a strong desire to honour this wish, they may not have the experience or knowledge of what is involved in caring for a dying person. This may be a first experience of the dying process and the family are often unsure of what to expect. It is not unusual to see an unrealistic portrayal of dying on television or in the movies – although exceptions to this can be startlingly impactful for viewers. The dying

---

9   Dr Kathryn Mannix's book *With the End in Mind: Dying, Death and Wisdom in an Age of Denial* (London: Collins, 2017) is a powerful evocation of many of the issues that people confront at the end of life, told through stories. She speaks eloquently with great experience and insight.

process is one that can challenge and distress, especially if one is unprepared. While the end of each earthly life is as unique as the person themselves, there are common patterns of change that can guide how we manage in each situation; and with good support, people are able to deal with this most challenging of times.

When we talk about end-of-life care, this may refer to the last hours, days, weeks or short months of a person's life. Such care is a recognition of and support with issues around the final part of life. Recognising the approach of death is a time of great sadness and worry, and communicating to patients and their loved ones a sense of the process of dying can often relieve at least a little of this worry. While this may not be information that everyone will ask about, it is important to show a willingness to discuss any questions that may be troubling the person or their family.

While everyone's journey is their own, in general what we see when someone is dying is a gradual weakening of the body. This is reflected by the slowing down of body functions such as appetite and digestion. We expect the person to sleep more and have less energy for conversation and concentration during periods of wakefulness. At some point, the person will be unconscious most, or all, of the time. Changes in breathing will be seen, with more shallow and irregular breaths. Saliva and respiratory secretions can collect in the back of the throat and cause audible sounds that can be distressing to hear. At this stage, the person themselves is usually beyond being aware of this sound. Changes in circulation result in coolness and changes in skin colour. Common symptoms (which benefit from medicines to maintain comfort) include signs of pain, laboured breathing symptoms or respiratory secretions, and symptoms of worry or distress. Medicines can be given orally while a person can safely swallow. As the person gets weaker, so does the ability to swallow, and we can use alternative routes to give these types of medicine, such as subcutaneous (under the skin) injections or infusions if needed.

There are other ways in which a person who is dying (or anticipated to soon be so) may need support. There may be practical concerns, such as making a will or having one's affairs in order (matters that we should all consider regardless of our health), with which an ill person may need support from his or her family. Psychological and spiritual support can often be as crucial for a person's comfort as attending to practical issues. A person may have worries about a relationship with a loved one. There can be reflections on the past that stir unresolved anxieties or distress, for which offering support – if not the possibility of change – may be important. Patient help services, including counselling or psychology services, can have a significant benefit for people. Faith often assumes a particular or renewed focus for both patients and families, and spiritual support and chaplaincy form part of the multidisciplinary team approach to end-of-life care.

Providing support for relatives is an important part of helping them through this experience of loss. If they are planning to care for a person at home at the end of his or her life, thought should be given to preparing the physical environment that will facilitate safe caring. This can include consideration of what equipment may help as their care needs increase, and practical considerations such as a room with space for an appropriate bed, toilet facilities, avoiding stairs, and perhaps even access to a person's cherished garden or favourite view from their home. Identifying the team of people who wish to help with personal care and giving them a sense of what is involved helps to avoid undue stress, especially if the person has become much weaker since the previous time they were at home.

Unless it is anticipated that the person's time at home will be brief, carers need to consider their own responsibilities, needs and limitations, and include this in the care plan. Community-provided home-care packages involving paid carers up to a certain number of hours per week can be looked for. Depending on availability of these carers, as well as need or urgency, families may feel they can provide sufficient care themselves, or look into private care provision to fill in 'gaps' in the care plan. The Covid-19 pandemic has impacted the availability and methods in which community care at home is provided. However, every effort is made by community teams, as well as families and friends, to facilitate getting a person home for end-of-life care when safe and possible to do so, if this is their wish.

In addition to practical preparations, it is crucial to give psychological support to those preparing to take on what is usually a new experience amid dealing with a sense of loss. Special consideration needs to be given to those who are closest or most vulnerable, such as children of a parent affected by a terminal illness, or parents caring for a terminally ill child. It is remarkable to see the courage that parents and guardians display in this regard. There are resources to support communication with children in an age-appropriate way regarding a serious illness in a family. The care team involved may be able to guide people directly or advise where to access support. Local cancer support centres or online cancer support services can be a treasure trove of support and a way of accessing reliable information, some of which may be applied to other types of illness also.

Coping with Dying and Death
It leaves me without a sufficient response when people comment how difficult it must be to work in palliative care. It is even more difficult if this comment arises within a conversation where I have had the responsibility to break bad news, or describe the road ahead for a loved one, like the above description. I find the expression of such empathy amid personal sadness to be very moving. There is a sense of privilege in being involved in the care of a person at this final stage of their life. Like any healthcare professional or carer dealing with serious illnesses on a daily basis, we need to make space to reflect on the impact this has on us. While self-care is essential, there is also a potential to become more detached from suffering than we should be.

Describing the most likely physical changes of dying in words is one thing, but it feels inadequate to convey the experience, as anyone who has been on this journey with a loved one can attest. As someone commented to me, it is analogous to the difference between a written description of a beautiful artwork and experiencing the artwork itself. This is not to understate the importance of end-of-life care, but it has

2: An Approach to the Challenge of Dying and Death

helped me to consider how multifaceted the experience is. For all the focus on the material world, there is an undeniable reality that dying is a spiritual and psychological journey, at least as much as a physical one. No one with even a little awareness of our common humanity fails to be affected in the presence of death. As James Shirley's 'Death the Leveller' puts it with great eloquence:

> Early or late
> They stoop to fate,
> And must give up their murmuring breath
> When they, pale captives, creep to death.[10]

From my personal as well as professional experience of encountering death and bereavement, recognising our common humanity leads me to stress the importance of providing high-quality palliative care. This involves caring for body, mind and spirit. Acknowledging the intrinsic value of each life is crucial for maintaining human dignity for all. This is core to the palliative care approach. The *Catechism* describes 'palliative care [as] a special form of disinterested charity [and] as such it should be encouraged' (*CCC*, 2279). This is worth further reflection beyond the scope of this present essay. What is easier to recognise is the impact that providing this support for patients and their families can have. When the situation of dealing with incurable illness confronts us, I hope that consideration of some of the issues I have discussed may help to provide the beginning of a framework to start to deal with this most difficult of situations. A palliative care approach matters because each of us matters.

---

10   Poem 288 in Arthur T. Quiller-Couch (ed.), *The Oxford Book of English Verse* (Oxford: Clarendon, 1919).

Questions for Reflection and Discussion

1. In what ways might the language we use help, or create barriers, in dealing with serious illness, dying and death?
2. What perceptions do you have about palliative care at end of life? Do these perceptions make you more or less likely to be open to palliative care involvement? What sources inform these perceptions – for example, personal experience, stories relayed by others or media sources?
3. Palliative care focuses on improving quality of life for patients with advanced, life-limiting illnesses. What does quality of life mean to you?
4. What do you understand by the term 'disinterested charity' (*CCC*, 2279)? In what ways is 'palliative care a special form of disinterested charity'?
5. Do you feel comfortable having conversations with your loved ones about dying and death? Do you think making known your wishes for how you wish your end of life to look would cause or relieve worry?

3: The Power of Story in Accompanying People towards the End of Life

Anne Francis

I would love to live like a river flows, carried by the surprise of its own unfolding.

John O'Donohue[1]

My nurse colleague says, 'Anne is a member of our Pastoral Care Team. You can have a good chat with her.' Clare[2] eyes me, smiling. She has just arrived and is settling in. She introduces her daughter and her boyfriend. I ask where they are from and, after a friendly chat, withdraw, saying I'll be back in the next day or two. When I call to her room over the coming week or two she is tired; on the phone; preparing for physio; folding clothes. We arrange a convenient time. She changes her mind. Eventually she tells me, 'I don't want to go there. It will just upset me too much.' We understand each other. She has identified me as a threshold; a doorway to 'going there', and it's true, I am. I stand at one of many thresholds to the deep story. Actually, we all do.

---

1   John O'Donohue, 'Fluent,' in *Four Elements: Reflections on Nature* (London: Transworld Digital, 2011), xi.
2   Names and other details have been changed throughout, to protect anonymity.

In a multidisciplinary palliative care team it is recognised that a person will choose their own moments for sharing deeply. We acknowledge the mysteries of each person's life and how these find expression as life moves towards its end. Sometimes this involves words, and sometimes not. The healthcare workers, nurses and hospitality staff have daily and nightly interaction with patients; doctors are involved in momentous conversations with them; social workers address myriad areas of personal and family need; physiotherapists literally walk with them, and their story might unfold as they go. Spiritual matters are the realm of the everyday and everywhere. The deep story is always there and happening like a river. Engaging with it in a life-affirming way is a task for all the team, and especially those entrusted with psycho-spiritual care. Here I would like to explore the role of story for people nearing the end of life.

Why Story?

When we are asked about ourselves, we quite often respond with story: 'My mum came over'; 'The kids had chickenpox'; 'We got to the beach.' Stories are the way we human beings express ourselves. The small stories we tell about the car being serviced, or the queue at the shop may seem insignificant, but are part of the story of our lives. They also give us the opportunity to connect with one another. They form a reaching out and a deepening relationship between us. When stories are told, something is revealed to us about ourselves and the other person. In his Nobel Lecture in December 2017, literature laureate Kazuo Ishiguro offered:

> But in the end, stories are about one person saying to another: This is the way it feels for me. Can you understand what I'm saying? Does it also feel that way for you?[3]

---

3   Kazuo Ishiguro, Nobel Lecture, December 2017, https://www.nobelprize.org/uploads/2018/06/ishiguro-lecture_en-1.pdf, downloaded 2 January 2022.

Stories are never static. Once the story begins (before our first breath? before our mother's first breath?) it is dynamic and has momentum. It is a river that gathers and ebbs, moving around obstacles and changing constantly. This gives a quality of energy, and also a sense of something beyond our grasp. A story cannot be wrapped up and defined. We are always saying more than we are saying, and maybe more than we consciously know. Though our rational minds want to create order and interpretation, our stories allow us to express truths in incomplete and sometimes contradictory ways, with side-stories escaping from the main narrative like tributaries. We know and half-know things in the story's truth. We react, respond and accommodate many characters and contingencies, and the story keeps moving. It is enough for any day to glimpse the core of what is important.

We live in our interweaving stories. My story is not my story without your story, without the big stories of the nations, communities and cultures we live in. In Ireland, for example, our stories around dying and death are deeply embedded and embodied in our culture – here, what we do surely tells its own story. We sometimes make critical choices about how we relate to these cultural narratives with all their symbols and seasons, but mostly we just live and move within them.

Before we ever speak our story to another person, the story takes shape within ourselves, and we, in turn, inhabit our story. The way we do this includes layers of living. Story is a primary way in which people hold, interpret and evaluate their experience. Our *story about our story* is made up of the stories we tell ourselves, or that we hear from others throughout life about our realities. 'I never have any luck'; 'I am blessed'; 'I should never have married'; 'Cancer always gets our family in the end … '. These, themselves, play a deep part in meaning-making, adding to or alleviating our suffering.

When we tell our story, we do so in the faith that it has value, that we, in fact, have value. We are seeking a witness to our lives. It is an act of immense trust. Ruard Ganzevoort observes:

Intrinsic to the narrative challenge of finding and reaching out to an audience is the spiritual desire for recognition and love. In the end, we share our life story hoping for someone who will be willing and able to hear our entire story and still love us ...[4]

Often another person can help us unravel the story from the interpretations that thread through it. Listening is far from passive, but is a witnessing and a faithful accompaniment of the other person which includes recognition and love. The act of sharing story involves an encounter that is spiritual in nature, and that takes the teller and the listener to a new place.

Nearing the End of Life

The time of knowingly moving towards death is a very particular moment for story. Here people may have a perspective they have never had before. It can be a time to ask what it has all been about. Allan Kellehear focuses on memories and life review as tools for engaging with identity and relationships at this time:

For people dying from a serious illness, review and reminiscence appear to hold the promise of self-understanding and identity maintenance. A clear purpose is to establish, if it wasn't already, who and what they are as people and in relation to other people in their lives.[5]

This is not merely the recounting of facts from past experiences; it is the way these take their true place as part of our deep story. This may mean allowing them in retrospect to be as significant as they are *to us*.

---

4 Ruard Ganzevoort, 'Minding the Wisdom of Ages: Narrative Approaches in Pastoral Care for the Elderly', *Practical Theology* 3, no. 3 (2010), 331–40, at 335–36. See also Mark Newitt, 'The Role and Skills of a Hospital Chaplain: Reflections Based on a Case Study', *Practical Theology* 3, no. 2 (2010), 163–77.

5 Allan Kellehear, *The Inner Life of the Dying Person* (New York, NY: Columbia University Press, 2014), 156.

Ganzevoort explicitly links this with the spiritual journey in which people seek integration and a sense of completion:

> Intrinsic to this narrative challenge to develop a coherent story is a spiritual desire of wholeness.[6]

This cannot mean that things are resolved or wrapped up – we are human after all – but that the desire of the human spirit for wholeness itself opens up a field of possibility.

The terms 'spiritual distress', or 'total pain', used in palliative care, indicate distress that includes psychological or spiritual elements, and that contributes to the person's suffering, including physical symptoms of their illness.[7] The experience of being close to the end of life may itself cause spiritual distress. Of course, this is intrinsically storied. People may need some accompaniment as they discover aspects of their life, relationships or memories that are taking away their well-being, or which, if allowed, can greatly contribute to it. Sometimes there is physical pain that can *only* be reached by crossing spiritual thresholds.

Heather Walton rightly points out that theological attempts at theodicy (understanding the problem of evil) have sometimes hurried towards 'happy endings', offering answers to suffering without honouring the challenging realities of human experience.[8] She distinguishes story as (merely) narrative from poetics, and proposes that the metaphors and symbols in the latter can more properly assist us in living with suffering. She proposes that literature has the metaphorical or parabolic qualities that allow it to represent a depth of trauma and suffering.

---

6   Ganzevoort, op. cit., 333.
7   Cicely Saunders defined the concept of total pain as the suffering that encompasses all of a person's physical, psychological, social, spiritual and practical struggles. The breakthrough in her understanding came from a conversation with a patient who told the story of her pain. Cicely Saunders, 'The symptomatic treatment of incurable malignant disease', *Prescribers' Journal* 4, no. 4 (October 1964), 68–73.
8   Heather Walton, *Writing Methods in Theological Reflection* (London: SCM, 2014), 168.

> What is needed is not narrative but the other resources offered by poetics: images, symbols and metaphors that carry the pain of trauma without committing the blasphemy of trying to represent, comprehend or reconcile the horror in story form.[9]

These metaphors or symbols, present in story too, access spiritual realities that may not otherwise surface for healing. They do not require a coherent narrative but emerge for particular moments and can carry heavy burdens without the need for explanation.

Suffering itself can make spiritual wholeness difficult. A patient told me, 'I just want it to happen now, because I am not me any more.' Jennifer De Jong and Linda Clarke make the following claim:

> Suffering experienced by those who are living with dying ... may result in a loss of integrity of the person; story provides one possible avenue for reintegration of the self.[10]

This possibility of reintegration of the self or a journey to wholeness indicates a spiritual reality. One person, who spent a considerable time in hospice before his death, repeatedly told staff: 'This place has been the making of me – I have found joy.' Aspects of his life story came together, and he unexpectedly found a new sense of wholeness.

A woman told me she needed to talk to me about faith. The difficult challenges she and her family had faced had made her choose to disconnect from God. Her interpretation of what had happened had left her with an understanding of a God and a faith community who did not care about children or, indeed, their mothers. Spending time with this aspect of her story, and how it had connected with other

---

9   Ibid. I am including different manifestations of story here without wishing to define them so closely.
10 Jennifer D. De Jong and Linda E. Clarke, 'What Is a Good Death? Stories from Palliative Care', *Journal of Palliative Care* 25, no. 1 (spring 2009) 61–67, at 66.

stories, she became able to revisit her relationship with God, and, in her words, 'get to know the God I want to meet'.

A man kept the pastoral care team at a distance over several admissions. When he became more unwell, he asked a member of the team to light a candle and say a prayer for him. Although he did not subscribe to personal faith, the big story of faith in which he had been raised held resonance for him at an important time.

Ultimately our life story impacts the way we die. James Hillman uses the term 'healing fictions' for stories that help us find meaning in living and dying.[11] Joan Halifax offers case studies of the ways people's stories helped, hindered or betrayed them at the end of life. She discusses the story of a 'good death', which can put pressure on people, observing that

> the stories we tell ourselves – good death, death with dignity – can be unfortunate fabrications that we use to try to protect ourselves against the sometimes raw and sometimes wondrous truth of dying.

And she adds:

> Our stories can also be bridges to freedom …[12]

We have choices here, and these can be made in the light of how we want our story to close or transition to the time after death. This involves the style and substance of relationships, practical arrangements, legacy and inner peace. Kellehear addresses the question of the ending itself. He proposes that the story of our dying opens up the story of what is coming beyond death.

---

11 James Hillman, *Healing Fiction* (Dallas, TX: Spring Publications, 1994), cited in Joan Halifax, *Being with Dying: Cultivating Compassion and Fearlessness in the Presence of Death* (Boston, MA: Shambhala, 2008), 64.
12 Ibid., 66.

Our sense of an ending requires us to rise to the challenge of coherence and finish the tale of what *I* thought it meant to be me. For however poorly or partially realised, … our final story may yet be our most important companion – the best light we have to guide us into that dimly lit journey ahead.[13]

Pastoral Care with People Nearing the End of Life

When we meet people who are nearing the end of life we see only a tiny snapshot of their life: who they have been; their relationships and work; and what is important to them. One thing we can be sure of is that we don't know most of what they are about. Nevertheless, they may invite us into their deep story, and we may be present to them at that important threshold.

In the pastoral encounter, we are invited to pay attention to the person and the story. We are aware of the landscape, setting and emotion of the story as we listen. We notice the pace, the breath, the pauses, and the eyes that focus on us, close, fill or gaze into the distance. We see the river in the shallows: deepening; becoming lively as it negotiates stones and branches or is filled by the rain. Light may be dappling the water, or shadows may obscure the depths. There is life everywhere, and everything keeps moving and changing. We don't mistake the landscape for the heart of the story in this moment. We wait and watch and, particularly, enter the silences. To some extent we accept the invitation to let go of the critical evaluating part of our mind; trusting our intuition or our body as we move along with the storyteller. In this way we are present and attentive.

Sometimes there is a point at which we know that we who are travelling together will not emerge from the story as the same people. There will be a fork in the river, and it will choose a direction. Our own story inevitably connects with the story of the other. We choose the depths, not knowing whether there will be an eddy or pool to rest

13   Kellehear, op. cit., 217.

in later. We calculate the risks while experiencing the depths. This is spirituality. We will emerge altered. Experience tells us that these storied encounters hold the threshold to transformation. In daring to enter the mystery of their own stories, people may discover hidden truths and graces that bring comfort, clarity or even forms of redemption. Change can happen imperceptibly or with struggle and cost. There can be a letting go, a reframing or lifting of a lifelong burden.

While this often happens in words, there are times when verbal communication is not possible or is not chosen. A shared presence, holding a hand or simply bearing witness to someone's deep distress can also facilitate the threshold to the deep story. Some people contain and embody their story without ever divulging what is happening for them. The hospice context is designed to hold this wisely in its everyday living.

Palliative care acknowledges the presence of suffering in its various forms and puts every resource in service of relieving it. However, there are times when, for all sorts of reasons, we cannot alleviate the spiritual suffering of patients. Staying with story can help practitioners to draw back from being outcome-driven and to be present with people in their own reality on their own terms.

A colleague comments on the change he sees in a patient who had been feeling distressed. After a chat with me, she seems brighter, more willing to engage, and has been seen in the corridor with the physiotherapist. I tell him that, while this may not entirely be coincidence, this is not my work. I know that in our time together, we have gone deeply into her distress, not out of it. That, while she has talked a lot *about* her distress previously, in my recent encounter she spoke and wept *from and within* it. I do not think this will be a 'fix' for her tears, but her deeper engagement may be part of a healing process. In pastoral care we are not there for comfort only. Sometimes we are there so that patients and family members can 'go there' – to the most uncomfortable or painful places in their lives. Story, including poetics, can make this journey sustainable, and both deepen and brighten the encounter. Sometimes this happens in one meeting, but for others it might happen in a series of encounters, with engagement ebbing and flowing at different times.

When something important emerges, it is beautiful to offer short, meaningful rituals. These are powerful encounters which hold the experience and continue to accommodate paradox and suffering, as well as peace or resolution. Some of these may be the sacraments and others may be for letting go, forgiveness, healing or transformation. Although we often use words, the important elements in ritual do not need them. Metaphor and symbol, gesture as well as prayer, poetry or scripture hold the experience at a depth while a person is guided lightly with the practitioner at her side. Afterwards, these words and symbols may remain and continue as meaningful parts of the spiritual journey.

All experiences and relationships are potentially thresholds through which we can access the deep story of our lives. This journey is associated with core identity and spiritual wholeness – the meaning of our living and dying. We intentionally honour the humanity, value and mystery of our patients and their contribution to the world. The commitment we give is that we will show up, and will be open to being changed by the stories occupied by those we meet. Here we leave behind the possibility of controlling the encounter, or being comfortable.

This requires a steady nerve, which comes from honest and courageous travelling of the twists and turns of our own river; from the disciplines of spiritual practice, receiving support and supervision, and the experience of navigating these waters with others. We occupy a space of knowing and not-knowing, with a world of story, symbol, soul and silence to draw on. In the context of faith, this is the realm of the Holy Spirit, who does not recognise boundaries and who relentlessly gives life.

The deep story is always there but is not always told. The story has no beginning and no end and is never fully grasped or understood. It is not a rendition of facts, but an act of imagination which changes with each new morning, relationship, diagnosis. The story belies artificial separations of God, people and earth. Walton writes:

> In constructive forms of narrative theology it is in *the human capacity for storytelling itself* rather than in a pre-existing grand narrative, that redemptive power is located.[14]

The deep story, then, belongs to all of us, and our dying will become a part of it. As the end of life approaches, it may be possible to connect beyond ourselves to the great story in which we have participated and to which we will continue to belong.

Questions for Reflection and Discussion

1. What are the stories in your culture or faith about dying and death?
2. What do you find there which might help the journey towards death?
3. In these stories, is there anything you would change?
4. What elements of your own story help you live well?
5. If you were approaching your final weeks or days, how do you think your own story might enrich, guide, bring ease or unease to this time?
6. Are there elements of your story that call for some attention now, so that you can approach your death peacefully?

---

14 Walton, op. cit., 165.

4: Love in the Pastoral and Professional Care of the Dying

Chris Hayden

A particularly vivid memory from my seminary days is of a scenario presented at a pastoral workshop. I was one of a group of young deacons, just a few months away from priestly ordination. We were taking part in a workshop on ministering to the seriously ill and dying, and the workshop facilitator had outlined a pastoral situation he wanted us to consider:

> You are visiting a patient in hospital. He has received a terminal diagnosis. He has no religious faith. He has no living relatives and no close friends to whom he can turn. How will you minister to him?

To say that this scenario challenged us would be an understatement. We wriggled on the hook for a long time. We broke into groups to discuss the matter in depth. We attempted to script how we might address the man. We despondently thumbed our bibles, in a search for what might be regarded as comforting verses, mindful that, as an unbeliever, the individual concerned would be unlikely to derive much comfort from a religious text. Eventually we reconvened, and a representative from each group shared its deliberations with the full gathering.

Unsurprisingly, none of our 'solutions' was a solution, and our attempts at pastoral adequacy were singularly inadequate. While we were convinced that we should, personally and out of our own faith conviction, pray for the man in his need, we did not seriously consider the possibility of a miraculous healing through our prayers; and while a small number of believers might fault us for that, it seemed clear to us that we should defer to the inevitability of death. Another thing we could not do was supply the want of friends or relatives: we were making a brief visit to a man whom we had never met before. As for the dying man's lack of faith, while we might assure him of our prayers, we certainly could not force him to believe. And might not the very assurance of our prayers serve only to heighten the poor man's sense of isolation? Might it not merely underline the great distance between ourselves and him, and in that way, drive him still further into the loneliness he might well be facing?

So, what could we do for the man? What was the answer to this pastoral conundrum? I will return to this difficult scenario in a moment, but first, an observation on the broader issue of illness and mortality. I think it is fair to say that within the past couple of decades, there has been a subtle change in the manner in which people speak of infirmity, ageing and dying. One commonly hears such phrases as 'old age is no fun', 'infirmity is a terrible thing' or 'terminal illness is a dreadful burden'. I am not suggesting that this kind of language is now universal, or that it was never to be heard a generation ago, but I believe there has been a subtle shift, a culturally sanctioned problematising of infirmity and dying. What was, in an earlier generation, more readily accepted as part of the cycle of life, is now perceived as an intruder, a problem.

In hindsight, I can see that the pastoral scenario presented to the group of young deacons was carefully crafted to confront us with the limits of expertise and experience. Insofar as it questioned us, it asked a leading question: it led us to consider the dying of a lonely man as a problem to be solved. Pedagogically, it was a clever set-up and we fell for it. We became so engrossed in trying to solve a problem that we no longer saw a person. We exhibited task-focused, solution-driven blindness to the reality of a potentially bewildered, lonely, dying man. Nobody suffered on account of our failure to address the reality. We were, after all, engaged in a simulated exercise; our deliberations took place around a flip chart, not around a hospital bed. Yet the scenario offered us a most insightful exercise. It exposed fault lines and invited us to ponder them in a way that would – and hopefully did – lead us to become more effective and sensitive pastors in due course.

Today, our culture as a whole has substantially fallen into the trap set for us, as a group of deacons in pastoral training. Our culture's tacit 'leading questions' centre on quality, productivity, efficiency, use of resources. Where we saw a problem waiting to be solved, contemporary culture tends to see a problem with no possible solution. We do well to be alert to this problematising: it is part of the broad cultural background to any pastoral engagement with the dying.

The cultural issue is not merely one of language. We would not fully address it simply by practising greater 'hygiene' in how we speak of infirmity and dying (though that would certainly be a good thing – we should indeed be hygienic in our speech, and guard against unwitting contamination by cultural toxins).

It would likewise be mistaken to suggest that as Christians, we should view the issues around dying only through the lens of explicit Christian faith. As believers, our faith in Christ deeply conditions our approach to life, dying and death. But our faith also insists that, precisely as believers, we have a contribution to make to the common good, and this is an instance of where faith can and should reach out to culture and society. What we think dying is, is very much a function of what we think death is. But the fact that contemporary culture does not necessarily share our understanding of death should not prevent us from seeking to offer and foster a compassionate and ultimately hopeful approach to dying.

If we seek to influence secular approaches to dying, to turn them, however slightly, toward Gospel values, even with no expectation that this might offer an opportunity for explicit Christian proclamation, we are being entirely true to our faith. In a 2005 letter, commenting on the requisites for professional caring relationships, Pope Benedict XVI writes: 'While professional competence is a primary, fundamental requirement, it is not of itself sufficient. We are dealing with human beings, and human beings always need something more than technically proper care. They need humanity. They need heartfelt concern.'[1]

These concerns are not the exclusive preserve of theological reflection. In professional social care, there is an ongoing conversation regarding the place of love. If those who are engaged in social care *love* those who are in their care, if they do not carefully monitor and work against feelings of affection towards those in their charge, are they being 'unprofessional'? Are they 'blurring boundaries' in a way that might lead to harm? It is worth engaging with this social care conversation, even though its questions arise from a different context. After all, the issue of love in relationships of social care transfers naturally to relationships involving care of the dying.

Irish social care academic John Byrne puts the question starkly in the title of his article, 'Love in social care: Necessary pre-requisite or blurring of boundaries?'[2] The article begins: 'Is there any place for "love" in the professional helping relationship? Or have we clinically sanitised care to the point where there can no longer be an emotional component to our relationships with our clients?' For Byrne, love is indeed a necessary facet of social care. He is critical of a certain rigid approach to professional boundaries, and writes of the need to hold the boundary between the giver and the receiver of care 'in a complex relationship that is based on emotion, not intellect, and which cannot be clinically sanitised by rules, boundaries or regulations'.

Byrne is certainly not cavalier about the issue of boundaries; he clearly acknowledges that standards in the past were often poor, and

1   Pope Benedict XVI, *Deus Caritas Est*, 31, https://www.vatican.va/content/benedict-xvi/en
    /encyclicals/documents/hf_ben-xvi_enc_20051225_deus-caritas-est.html.
2   *Scottish Journal of Residential Child Care* (2016), Vol. 15, No. 3. https://www.celcis.org
    /application/files/5116/2308/4011/2016_Vol_15_3_Byrne_J_Love_in_social_care_Necessary
    _pre-requisite_or_blurring_of_boundaries.pdf.

that reform was needed. At the same time, however, he argues that his profession has 'forgotten that we are not just professional thera-peutic social care workers with the rigid boundaries of a counsellor/psychotherapist'.[3]

Byrne, it is worth emphasising, writes as a secular commentator. He is not trying to import religious concepts or convictions into social care. Yet the parallels between his comments and those of Benedict XVI are clear: *'something more* than technically proper care' / *'not just* professional therapeutic social care'. In fact, Byrne quotes from Benedict's encyclical, finding support in its reasoning, without appealing to its theological conviction.

Following Byrne's secular lead, Christian commentators need not fear appealing directly to love in the care of the dying. A clarification may be necessary here. Christian commentators appeal to love all the time, do they not? Indeed. However, what is at issue here is not a principled appeal to the virtue of love, but love and compassion as *acknowledged and intentional* aspects of the pastoral and professional care of the dying.

This gives rise to a further necessary clarification. It would be absurd to suggest that those who care professionally for the dying currently do so in a purely clinical way, and that they need, going forward and in keeping with new insights, to be instructed to love those in their care. It is clear to any thoughtful observer that caring professionals are just that: caring. They show heartfelt care and kindness within the confines of their professional boundaries; they are not inured to the sadness and grief that attend dying and death. Undoubtedly, kindness and empathy are evidence of love, but what I have been suggesting is that in the care of the dying, there may be scope for viewing love more explicitly and more intentionally, as part and parcel of the caring relationship, and as an element of the conversations around that relationship.

The 'not just' and the 'something more' referred to above are present already. They may not be subject to direct observation or

3   Ibid.

assessment, but they are deeply human and powerfully therapeutic, and we need not be afraid of acknowledging them and of drawing them into our professional, pastoral and supervisory conversations. Love in care for the dying will certainly engage the emotions of professional carers, but this does not mean transgressing boundaries of privacy or sensitivity. The love of carers can, rather, be seen as a natural aspect of the engagement between the carer and the person being cared for.

Imagine a situation in which love and affection were prohibited, in which a dying person was being looked after with zero affection from carers and professionals! This simple thought experiment can remind us that affection is, in fact, normal. My point is not to argue – pointlessly – for the introduction of something that is already present, but to stress that love and compassion in the carer are to be welcomed, acknowledged and reflected on, rather than automatically suspected or merely tolerated as a concession to the carer's human frailty.

In a non-religious context, to emphasise the place of love in the care of the dying does not amount to importing or imposing a specifically Christian notion. In a letter subsequent to the one quoted above, Pope Benedict XVI, noting that the human person is 'redeemed by love', goes on to insist that 'this applies even in terms of this present world'.[4] For believers, the deepest underpinnings of love may well be theological, yet believers and non-believers alike share the conviction that love is a value, 'even in terms of this present world'.

There is not, or need not be, anything proselytising about love. When carers experience and show love towards the dying, they do not do so instrumentally, in view of another end or purpose: they are simply being person-centred, responding to the person they encounter. So far, in using the word 'love' to describe this person-centred stance, we have taken the meaning of the word for granted. But just what *is* love, this quality or stance whose place in the care of the vulnerable

---

4   Pope Benedict XVI, *Spe Salvi*, 26, https://www.vatican.va/content/benedict-xvi/en/encyclicals
/documents/hf_ben-xvi_enc_20071130_spe-salvi.html.

and dying we have been discussing? Some description, however tentative or general, is in order.

For Dietrich von Hildebrand, love is fundamentally a response to value.[5] Beneath Hildebrand's philosophical elaborations is the conviction that to love is to respond to a person's inherent value and dignity, rather than to see them through such lenses as usefulness, productivity or allocation of resources.[6] Obviously, there is much more to be said about love, yet the understanding of love as response to value is a good, indeed prophetic, foundation for conversations about the role of love in the caring relationship.

In a technical and technocratic culture, value tends to be associated with processes and outcomes, rather than being understood as something that is inherent in human beings. This tendency can be at odds with the impulse of affection, and we should have the confidence to allow the latter impulse to limit the former tendency, rather than vice versa. A 2020 Vatican document on the care of the dying notes that the basic bond of trust between doctor and patient can be adversely affected by the technical context in which that bond is lived: 'The organisational management and sophistication, as well as the complexity of contemporary healthcare delivery, can reduce to a purely technical and impersonal relationship the bond of trust between physician and patient.'[7] The same concern may be raised regarding caring relationships more generally, including care of the dying.

If love is a response to value, it is also, perhaps even more fundamentally, a generous acceptance of the existence of the other. As Joseph Ratzinger (later Pope Benedict XVI) puts it, 'it is the way of love to will the other's existence'.[8] At first blush, this might appear to set the

5 Dietrich von Hildebrand, *The Nature of Love* (trans. John F. Crosby) (South Bend, IN: St Augustine's Press, 2009), 58.
6 For a critical engagement with von Hildebrand's understanding of love as a response to value, see John F. Crosby, 'Is Love a Value-Response? Dietrich von Hildebrand in Dialogue with John Zizioulas', *International Philosophical Quarterly* 55:4 (2015), 457–70.
7 *Samaritanus Bonus: On the Care of Persons in the critical and terminal phases of life*, Introduction, https://www.vatican.va/roman_curia/congregations/cfaith/documents/rc_con_cfaith_doc_20200714_samaritanus-bonus_en.html.
8 Joseph Ratzinger, *Principles of Catholic Theology: Building Stones for a Fundamental Theology* (San Francisco, CA: Ignatius Press, 1987), 80.

bar rather low: there does not seem to be anything particularly meritorious in merely willing that a person should exist. The alternative, willing that they should not exist, is hardly to be countenanced. Yet it may be argued that such an alternative has been finding a foothold in our culture and in our attitudes. At the very least, the door has been opening to a more widespread attitude to the critically ill and the dying that is, in the Catholic understanding, far from a response to their inherent value, and far from positively willing their existence.[9]

Our attitudes surface in our affections. Carers who approach the critically ill and the dying with affection as well as technical and professional excellence are showing a deep and authentic response to the value of those approaching the end of life. Rather than seeing affection as a more or less superficial emotional response which needs above all to be monitored, we can see the response of affection and compassion as pointing to the deepest truth about the person being cared for.

The 2020 Vatican document quoted earlier states: 'Those who assist persons with chronic illness or in the terminal stages of life must be able ... to keep vigil, with those who suffer the anguish of death ... to be with them in their loneliness, to be an *abiding with* that can instil hope.'[10] The kind of care described here is not something that technical expertise alone can provide. Nor is it simply a matter of pastoral expertise or acumen. It is, finally, a matter of love.

To acknowledge this is to resist cultural forces that both instrumentalise human life, and problematise dying and death. It is also to encourage carers. There will always be a need for enlightened monitoring and self-criticism, but this does not mean that those who care for the dying should fear to bring the fullness of their humanity

---

9   In noting this I allude, of course, to the question of euthanasia, or assisted dying. What can be overlooked in the controversy surrounding euthanasia is that those who favour making it available may be seeking to 'respond to value' – as they perceive it – and motivated by the concern that the sick and dying be spared intolerable suffering. Radical and fundamental disagreement with the 'solution' they propose should not blind one to the fact that they may be motivated by love.
10   *Samaritanus Bonus*, op. cit., section V.1.

to their essential and sensitive task. To love the dying is to challenge any insidious calculus of the 'quality of life'. It is to alleviate a kind of suffering which adds, unnecessarily, to the burden experienced by the dying: 'the suffering caused when society equates their value as persons to their quality of life and makes them feel like a burden to others'.[11]

In conclusion, as we have noted, love for the dying is not 'instrumental': it does not serve an ulterior function, but responds to value, to the reality of the dying person. At the same time, such love speaks eloquently, underlining and defending the dignity and worth of some of the most vulnerable members of our society. Love, tenderness and compassion are as old as humanity. We need not mount a campaign for their incorporation in professional and pastoral care. What we may be able to develop, however, is a greater ease and intentionality in focusing on love as an aspect of the caring relationship.

Questions for Reflection and Discussion

1. Do you think that anything should be offered to the dying, above and beyond the best possible technical and physical care? If so, what might that be?
2. Regarding the possible role of love in the care of the dying, have you any concerns about emotional and behavioural 'boundaries'? If so, how might those concerns be addressed or assuaged?
3. How would you sum up the attitude of our contemporary culture to dying, death and the dying person?
4. 'Human beings always need something more than technically proper care' (Pope Benedict XVI). How would you describe this 'something more'?
5. How would you describe the kind of 'love' that those who care for the dying might appropriately feel and show?

11 Ibid.

5: Facing Life's End: The Transformative Power of Palliative Care

Sinéad Donnelly

I am a palliative medicine physician who has cared for people who are dying at home, in hospital and in specialist palliative care units. Over the past thirty years, I have worked in Ireland, Scotland, the US and now in Aotearoa, New Zealand. I come from a long line of doctors since 1905, comprising three generations and seven doctors. From my physician grandfather I learnt the art of attending in medicine. From my physician father I learnt the art of observing. I practise the art and science of palliative medicine.

The title of this book is *Facing Life's End* but, in my view, the book is equally about how we face life. I want to introduce you to core aspects of palliative care: non-abandonment; being present and the mystery of what happens; dying healed; dignity; caring and suffering. All these concepts are abundantly present in the area of palliative care.

I am not a theologian, nor do I think as a philosopher, but I am a lover of the wisdom that I find in the encounters with people who are dying. I do not profess to truly 'know' anything but, as a palliative care doctor, I seek to be present fully in the moment with the patient before me; in that moment, at some mysterious level, I know all I need to know.

What drew me towards palliative care? As a trainee doctor, I participated in a multidisciplinary course on holistic palliative care in the mid-1990s facilitated by Dr Michael Kearney, one of the first palliative medicine physicians in Ireland. I was inspired by what he and the hospice team presented to us on the concept of caring for the whole person, on the importance of listening with the whole of one's being, on the importance given to the patient's story and the family's story, on the caring team approach, and on the concept that one could die healed. And, finally, it was the quietness and softness of the flooring in the old Harold's Cross Hospice, Dublin. I thought: 'If these nurses and doctors think so much about the care of the person that they attend to quietening the sound of shoes, their care is infinite. Even if they do not achieve perfect care, the fact that they strive for such is inspiring. What happens here, in such a place as this, should happen everywhere we live and die. Caring for people who are dying in this holistic way actually teaches me about living.'

What is palliative care? Palliative care is a term coined by Balfour Mount, a Canadian surgeon, based in Montreal. The word palliative is derived from the Latin *pallium* – a shield, mantle or a cloak. We who work in palliative care are cloaking the person in care, shielding them from suffering, acknowledging that we cannot take away the reality of their dying, but we strive to care in a holistic way for their physical, psychological, emotional, social and spiritual needs.

Ireland has a rich tradition in understanding the mystery of dying, expressed through the Irish language and through traditional practice.[1] When the grave had been dug by the men, and the community had followed all the ancient tradition of funerals, in Ballyferriter, County Kerry, my friend Eibhlín Bean Uí Mhurchú told me that the people would say: '*Tá an méid sin déanta – Agus déanta go maith*'. I translate that phrase as 'That piece of our work has been done', to

---

1   See especially Salvador Ryan (ed.), *Death and the Irish: a Miscellany* (Dublin: Wordwell Press, 2016).

which the other replied: 'And has been done well'. That sums up my aim in practising palliative medicine, in every encounter.

'*Ag saothrú an bháis*' is a way of saying in Irish that someone is dying – a literal translation being 'earning death'. When someone has died, we say: *Tá sí imithe ar shlí na fírinne* – 'She has gone on the way of truth'. Another interesting word used to describe dying is '*claochlú*' – translated as 'transformation'. These words reflect a community's view and values around dying and death over many, many centuries. Why do these phrases or this language interest me as a doctor? They remind me that, long before all the 'advances' in palliative care, communities grappled with dying and the care of their dying people, and had a depth of wisdom and understanding born of daily community engagement with dying and death.

The death of a person is a community event. It affects us all. The Irish traditions of the wake and the big funeral were wise community events, recognising the need for support in the work of grieving, the need for us all to wrestle with our understanding of death, suffering and grieving. Indeed, we, and many other ancient rich cultural traditions, have much wisdom that we need to hold on to in the twenty-first century.

Into this world we bring the newer healthcare specialty of palliative care and, in this, Ireland was to the fore. In 1879, the Irish Religious Sisters of Charity founded Our Lady's Hospice in Harold's Cross, closely followed by St Joseph's Hospice in Hackney, London. These are both recognised as the first hospices focusing on care of the dying patient. In 2022 we have world-renowned hospices and a highly trained, experienced and skilled multidisciplinary workforce of doctors, nurses, occupational therapists, physiotherapists, chaplains, art and music therapists, social workers and bereavement therapists caring for patients who are facing death at home, in hospital, in nursing homes and in the hospice or palliative care unit. In my view the strongest foundation for this service is the recognition of our common humanity, our rich culture of care for each other, the importance of community, an ability to recognise suffering, and an ability to be with and to stay with people in the face of the ultimate existential experience, i.e. dying. With this foundation, born of centuries of community engagement with suffering, dying and grief, we now add excellence in professional training as palliative care workers.

It is a source of great sadness for me to see the complexity of care, the complexity of suffering, the extraordinary vulnerability of those facing death, and the centuries of understanding – all this being reduced to binary, black-and-white solutions to this multifaceted human experience. The answer often proposed in today's fast-paced society is 'What we need is euthanasia.' In my view, euthanasia is the antithesis of holistic, loving palliative care. In fact, euthanasia legislation puts a knife through the heart of the palliative care way of being and caring.

Perhaps it is useful here to recall the WHO definition of Palliative Care: 'Palliative Care is an approach that improves the quality of life of patients and their families facing the problems associated with life-threatening illness, through the prevention and relief of suffering by means of early identification and impeccable assessment and treatment of pain and other problems, physical, psychosocial and spiritual.'[2] The WHO goes on to note that palliative care provides 'relief from pain and other distressing symptoms, affirms life and regards dying as a normal process, intends neither to hasten or postpone death, integrates the psychological and spiritual aspects of patient care, offers a support system to help patients live as actively as possible until death, using a team approach helps the family cope during the patient's illness and in their own bereavement, enhances quality of life, and may also positively influence the course of illness'.

One particular phrase in this definition deserves our attention. The statement 'affirms life and regards dying as a normal process, intends neither to hasten or postpone death' puts palliative care workers and

2   World Health Organization, *National cancer control programmes: policies and managerial guidelines* (Geneva: World Health Organization, 2002), 84. See also World Health Organization, *WHO Definition of Palliative Care* (2013), online: http://www.who.int/cancer /palliative/definition/en.

their service into direct opposition to euthanasia and assisted suicide. Internationally, the majority of palliative medicine doctors are opposed to the legalisation of euthanasia. Their opposition is based on their experience of being with patients facing their death. Patients who have advanced illnesses and are facing the reality of dying, may indeed say to us, 'This is too hard. I wish it was all over.' Our response as doctors and as a multidisciplinary team to those words would be to lean in, and to listen even more carefully to what this person means when they express this distress. We are not saying that this process is easy, nor are we romanticising dying or glorifying palliative care, but again and again we witness the transformative power of being cared for, being heard, and not being abandoned physically or emotionally.

Let me share two stories exemplifying the holistic nature of palliative care, the healing power of the moment, the importance of dignity. Here is my first story. It is Christmas Eve on a surgical ward and one more palliative care referral seems a bit too much for me. Following this consultation I reflected as follows. She was ninety-eight. Being admitted to hospital at ninety-eight years – why? She is from Turkey with an irreducible hernia. Using fentanyl and midazolam intravenously, they tried to relieve it manually. She sits sideways across the bed, her swollen limbs dangling over the edge. Her curved body is propped up by many pillows, her white cotton scarf, turban-like, knotted at the front on her forehead. She is dozing. Her daughter translated in a beautiful accent as I asked about her pain and nausea; so plain a language in comparison.

A woman arrived in a rush of brown clothing and tension. I greeted her and the tall young man ahead of her: 'You need not greet him, my son is autistic, he will get upset' … She rubbed the tall man's back kindly and constantly as he looked away, his thumb in his mouth … I tried to explain palliative care again, to both daughters this time. 'The surgeons think operating would be unwise … '. 'Too old you mean, her age, of course … '. 'No, I'm not saying it is because of your mother's age … the anaesthetic … she might not survive … '. 'Well, you mean her quality of life … she has no quality of life … '. 'No, I am not commenting on the value of your mother's quality of life ... she just might not survive the procedure.'

As I was preparing to leave, I knelt down straight in front of this lady, held her hand, and caught her attention. She looked straight at me and smiled broadly. I complimented her on the turbaned scarf, knotted skilfully. 'When you compliment something, she will offer it to you,' her daughter explained. So I complimented her on her smile; the magnificent wrinkled ninety-eight years of life smile. She gave it again. The stressed daughter in brown with the tall autistic son in black softened, eagerly sitting close to her mother and translating. In one look, one smile, I was enriched. If I had not knelt before this woman, I would have missed those beautiful lifelong eyes. I would have missed my Christmas gift.

In palliative medicine much is written about dying with dignity, about treating someone with dignity; but what do we mean? Harvey Chochinov, who has studied this concept in relation to people who are dying, writes:[3]

> One of the most confounding challenges faced by end-of-life care providers is helping patients achieve or maintain a sense of dignity. Our prior studies of dignity and end-of-life care have shown a strong association between an undermining of dignity and depression, anxiety, desire for death, hopelessness, feeling of being a burden on others, and overall poorer quality of life.
>
> ... patients deem a sense of spiritual peace, relieving burden, and strengthening relationships with loved ones among the most important facets of end-of-life care. Several studies have linked these issues, including a loss of sense of dignity, loss of meaning, and a sense of being a burden on others, with heightened requests for a hastened

3 H. M. Chochinov, T. Hack, T. Hassard, L. J. Kristjanson, S. McClement, M. Harlos, 'Dignity Therapy: A Novel Psychotherapeutic Intervention for Patients Near the End of Life', *Journal of Clinical Oncology*, 23–24 (2005), 5520–25, at 5520 and 5521.

death. Clearly, palliative interventions must reach beyond the realm of pain and symptom management to be fully responsive to a broad and complex range of expressed needs.

I recognise dignity when I see it, yet I struggle to articulate what dignity might be. Is it a decision one makes? Is it what others do to you? Is it how you respond to others? How do you die without dignity? Is vomiting as you die an undignified death? Is being alone when you die an undignified death? How will I recognise dignity? Will I hear it? Will I smell it? Will I contribute to it? Will I detract from it? Can it exist in a hospital setting?

It is said that 'rather than viewing death with dignity as a separate construct, it might be viewed as an interactive process between the dying and their caretakers .... Terms such as pride, self-respect, quality of life, well-being, hope and self-esteem all overlap conceptually with the term dignity ... While most of these terms refer to internal states of mind, dignity is distinctive in that it also has an external component based on the perception of one's worthiness of honour and esteem from others.'[4]

So here is my second story of a palliative care encounter with a patient in hospital. It is not enough to relate facts, definitions and opinions about palliative care. I use these real stories to invite you, with your heart, mind and soul, into the world of palliative care.

Gold is the colour that comes to mind. Her little face without teeth was wrapped in a scarf of deep blue and gold. As we entered the hospital room we saw the hands that tucked the scarf around her face. She smiled with her eyes and her whole face. Her two daughters by her side, watchful, were totally engaged. The photograph of a handsome soldier leaning against an Italian stone building in sunshine many years ago rested on the shelf to her right. The photographed face of her great grandchild, a baby, was on the hospital wall opposite her

---

4   H.M. Chochinov, T. Hack, S. McClement, L. Kristjanson, & M. Harlos, 'Dignity in the terminally ill: a developing empirical model', *Social Science & Medicine* 54 (2002), 433–43, at 441.

bed. There were three vases of lilies – maroon, orange and white. This space embodied dignity. I just wanted to linger here, to be a part of this inspiring space. How was this created?

Two days earlier the night doctors said, at the handover to the morning shift, that this ninety-one-year-old lady was dying. She had collapsed at home the previous night and was unconscious. At this age and this presentation, clinically it was deemed highly likely that she had had a brain stem stroke. In view of the poor prognosis, nurses had thoughtfully placed the patient in a side room rather than a ward space. The lighting was low. There were three generations of family in the room. The daughter, a nurse, stood closest, leaning in attentively. The air was of concern in anticipation of her dying. When I saw Mrs B, felt her hand, asked for more detail from the family, I wondered whether her situation was irreversible. So, in the dim light, trying not to counter all that had been said by Emergency Department doctors, all that had alerted three generations to arrive in the early hours, I introduced the new idea that we will wait and see and that maybe she will wake up.

By that evening she was arousable. By the next day she could say a few words and smile, though she was a bit confused. We treated her kidney infection. She gradually sipped water and smiled more. There we had the resurrection of a lady attended with the infinite patience of a caring family. They loved their mother. They loved their grandmother. I hoped that the young doctors understood the mystery and power of what was going on in that room as we visited on our rounds each day – not the fact that she got physically better, but the honour and dignity that was in the air. We entered that space of dignity and breathed that same air. It did not belong to one person. It was co-created.

The essence of the therapeutic relationship is listening with particular attention. I have laboured to achieve that over many years as a doctor, honing my skills in several countries, adding to my experience to serve others. These two stories are about listening; in every interaction listening to oneself and to the other. It is said that listening in medicine is not to be perceived as an act of benevolence born out of compassion, but instead approached as an essential skill that is as much science as art. These stories remind me of the exquisite character of listening, how one listens with the whole of oneself. Listening is a form of touch and, viewed in that way, is central to how we treat others with dignity and respect.

By telling these stories I remind myself of what matters: By telling you these stories I bring you with me to T. S. Eliot's place, where we stand at 'the point of intersection of the timeless with time' and 'at the still point of the turning world'.[5] In these narratives the ordinary contains the extraordinary and with careful attention we can hear in the humdrum of human existence the divine heartbeat.

M. Therese Southgate, who was Deputy Editor of the *Journal of the American Medical Association*, described the practice of medicine in a manner that fits perfectly with the practice of palliative care. 'One looks first with the eyes of the body, next considers with the eye of the mind, and finally, if one has been attentive enough, one begins to see with the eye of the soul. If we remain in this vision, are patient enough and still enough, we begin to hear as well somewhere deep in the depths beyond where words are formed (…) It is in this same wordless language of the human spirit that the physician sees not just a disease nor even a patient but the person. It is in that moment that healing begins. Paradoxically, the healer is healed as well.'[6] This is the transformative power of palliative care.

Questions for Reflection and Discussion

1. Think about a time when you were truly listened to, when someone was fully present to you. How did it feel for you?

---

5 Dry Salvages V and Burnt Norton II, from T. S. Eliot, *Four Quartets* (New York, NY: Harcourt, Brace, 1943; London: Faber & Faber, 1944).

6 M. Therese Southgate, ed., *The Art of JAMA: One hundred covers and essays from The Journal of the American Medical Association* (St Louis, MO: Mosby, 1997) p. XII. Quoted in Robin Downie, 'Paying attention: Hippocratic and Asklepian approaches', *Advances in Psychiatric Treatment* 18/5 (2012), 363–68, at 367.

2. Think about a time when you were fully present to another. How did it feel for you?

3. Reflect on the paradoxical meaning of 'dying in a healed state'.

4. Reflect on the paradox that 'everything is important and yet nothing matters'.

5. Reflect on Irish traditions around dying and death. What communal wisdom lies behind these traditions?

6: The Art of Dying Well

Michael Shortall

With a poignant observation, Lucy Kalanithi takes up the story of her husband: 'Paul died on Monday, March 9, 2015, surrounded by his family, in a hospital bed roughly two hundred yards from the labor and delivery ward where our daughter, Cady, had entered the world eight months before.'[1]

Paul was thirty-six, and soon to complete his training as a neurosurgeon, when he was diagnosed with inoperable lung cancer. Suddenly, the doctor who wanted to treat the dying was the patient struggling to live. To help him make sense of what he was going through, he wrote a short memoir. *When Breath Becomes Air* (2016) became an international bestseller. It recounts the story of diagnosis, struggle and acceptance of his illness. Qualified in both literature and medicine, he was looking forward to a successful and purposeful life. He wrote that when terminal illness struck:

> I'd had no idea how hard it would be, how much terrain I would have to explore, map, settle … I hadn't expected the prospect of facing my own mortality to be so disorienting,

---

1   Paul Kalanithi, *When Breath Becomes Air* (London: Vintage, 2016), 201.

so dislocating … Looking into my own soul, I found the
tools too brittle, the fire too weak …[2]

Most share Paul's confusion when facing life's end. While everyone's
experience is unique, there are identifiable patterns in accepting
its reality. Perhaps the most recognisable model is the five stages of
Elisabeth Kübler-Ross:[3] loss, bargaining, anger, depression and
acceptance. Throughout this journey, people struggle with real questions: 'What am I to expect?' 'What am I to do?' For these anxieties,
the Catholic Church, in ministering to the dying, has built up a
wealth of experience. Traditionally, it is called 'the art of dying well', or,
in Latin, *Ars Moriendi*.

Ars Moriendi
It's an unusual phrase, implying that death is something that could be
'done well', and, more unusually, that dying is 'an art'. Few would dis-
agree with the desire for a good death for ourselves and for our loved
ones: to be at peace at the end, as comfortable as possible and
surrounded by loved ones. Yet to be gifted such an experience is not
automatic. In fact, it needs to be prepared, or created, which is why it
is called an art. It is then a type of work, undertaken by the dying
person, by those who care for her or him, and by the community.

On one level death renders someone radically vulnerable and
passive. But the dying person can face it in a way where it can also be
transformed into a passage imbued with meaning. Recently, David
Kessler, a collaborator with Kübler-Ross, identified 'meaning-making'
as a sixth stage in the process of facing death.[4] In other words, it is
possible for the person to reclaim agency or power in a most fundamental way in the face of death.

2   Ibid., 147.
3   Elisabeth Kübler-Ross, *On Death and Dying* (New York, NY: Macmillan, 1969).
4   David Kessler, *Finding Meaning: The Sixth Stage of Grief* (New York, NY: Scribner, 2020).

The *Ars Moriendi* is the name given to two Latin texts written in the 1400s.[5] Europe had just experienced the plague known as the Black Death. With such a traumatic experience, the texts offered guidance and reflection, for people and priests, on how to face death. They were widely translated and spread quickly. Many other works followed on the same theme, and the phrase *Ars Moriendi* became the name of the tradition that developed. It flourished at first but has faded in recent times with the professionalisation of medicine and the movement of the primary place of death from home to the hospital setting.

There are some parallels between then and now. We too have had our own global pandemic. As then, we are going through many social challenges such as economic woes, war and climate change, to name a few. However, while death was very present then, it is now often removed from the everyday experience of people and families. As a result, to help people prepare for dying and death, there has been a revival of interest in this tradition. In the medieval period, the books tended to focus on the deathbed. They provided tips on how the dying person could avoid losing faith or hope and how those at the bedside might support the dying.

How might the tradition be made relevant for today's world? This tradition faces challenges, in part because of the context of death in the contemporary world.

The Place of Dying and Death

Paul Kalanithi died in hospital, the place where he had intended to dedicate his life as a surgeon. Hospital is now the most common setting for dying. There are good reasons for this, such as supervising pain management, the acuteness of many illnesses and cost efficiencies. But where death occurs can affect how death is experienced. Many are worried that the technicalisation of medicine in hospitals is shaping the process in such a way to make the dying person more and

---

5   For an updated translation of the original texts, see Columba Thomas (trans.), *The Art of Dying* (Washington, DC: National Catholic Bioethics Center, 2021).

more passive. The patient can unwittingly become reduced to a body, on which the physician is 'battling' to stave off illness and its symptoms. Such a way of looking at medicine can easily reject any talk of dying and death because to do so would admit defeat. The consequence is that a person with a life-threatening or terminal illness is deprived of opportunities to ready herself or himself to face dying and death.

In Ireland, hospital is the most common setting for death to occur. The recent Irish experience was captured in a report commissioned by the Irish Hospice Foundation, in which Soraya Matthews and her co-authors surveyed data from the Central Statistics Office between the census of 2012 and 2018, and other sources.[6] The report opens by considering the locations in which people die: hospital, home, nursing homes (including other long-stay residential care facilities) and hospice. Over the six-year period, they observed little change in the proportion of deaths in each of these settings. While there was a small decrease in the proportion of deaths that occurred in hospitals (from 45% in 2013 to 44% in 2018), there was a small increase recorded in the proportion of deaths that occurred in long-stay residential settings (from 22% to 23%) and hospices (from 6% to 8%). Deaths at home remained constant in proportional terms (at 23% in both 2013 and 2018). While the percentage for death in hospital is a little lower than the average across Europe, it is still significantly greater than in the Netherlands and Norway. The report observes:

> The proportion of people in Ireland who die in hospital *remains far in excess of the proportion of people who state a preference for dying in a hospital.* Moreover, deaths in hospital often offer poor-value care: acute in-patient care costs are high, and often the needs of dying patients would be met more appropriately elsewhere ... The goal should be to

---

6   S. Matthews et al., *Dying and Death in Ireland: what do we routinely measure, how can we improve?* (Dublin: Irish Hospice Foundation, 2021).

reduce the in-hospital mortality rate without compromising the level or quality of care for a person at the end of their life.[7]

The dominant preference for dying in Ireland is at home. Home deaths comprised a consistent proportion of state deaths across the time period (23%), yet there were significant regional variations. While 17% of deaths in Dublin were at home, most other counties were above the national average. The report suggests that the lower rate in Dublin may be due to low home-care capacity and over-reliance on hospitals. Equally, the high rate of home deaths in rural areas may be due to improved accessibility to other services or high reliance on unpaid family carers. The urban-rural divide may also reveal other cultural factors, such as smaller family units in urban areas, employment pressures and small living environments, which are not conducive to families taking home a dying relative. In other words, the place of dying and death is not just a medical concern. It is affected by many cultural factors, which, taken together, can make facing dying and death even more difficult.

A Personal Experience

The report admits that 'while population-level indicators of home and hospital deaths may tell us something about how the overall system is performing, they tell us nothing about individual experiences, which will vary very widely'.[8] Leaving statistics aside, allow me to share the story of one person who I believe practised the art well.

Mrs Elizabeth Redmond was known to all as Betty. When I got to know her, she had an adult family and her husband had already passed away. She had been the sacristan for many years at the parish church in Saggart, County Dublin. Although hampered by advanced scoliosis, she lived life to the full. She was actively involved in parish,

7   Ibid., 24 (italics added).
8   Ibid., 93.

community and family, in their joys and sorrows, including visiting the homes of the recently bereaved. Every morning, she would gather with other parishioners for the Rosary and devotions before daily Mass. During her prayer, she would be sure to name those in need of prayer, especially those seriously ill and close to death. Among her daily devotions, she prayed for those whose memorial cards she kept in her prayer book; and for herself, a prayer for a happy death.

> Jesus, Mary and Joseph, I give you my heart and my soul. Jesus, Mary, and Joseph, assist me now and in my last agony. Jesus, Mary and Joseph, may I breathe forth my soul in peace with you. Amen.[9]

When diagnosed with a terminal illness, she continued to live life as fully as she could. In time, prayer for healing became prayer for acceptance.

Betty was able to have her preference to be at home. Her last days were surrounded by family, and neighbours respectfully keeping in touch by leaving in food and cards. It was above all a time of sharing: memories, goodbyes and expressions of love. She received the last rites and was held in prayer. On a lovely September afternoon, Betty died peacefully. A month later, her first granddaughter, named Isabel – a variation of Elizabeth – was born.

What could we learn from her witness? There are striking elements in the short account. Firstly, she knew in a deep way the reality of human finitude because of her struggles with health. While desiring to live and see her grandchildren, she accepted that an end would come. Secondly, she was embedded in networks of support: family, neighbours, community. In other words, she was accompanied in a personal and rich way on her final journey. Acceptance and accompaniment are not so easily attained at the end of one's life. They are best cultivated

---

9   See also Brendan McConvery, 'Praying for a happy death', in Salvador Ryan (ed.), *Death and the Irish: A Miscellany* (Dublin: Wordwell, 2016), 202–204.

throughout a person's lifetime by the set of liturgies, rituals, beliefs, virtues and practices that have shaped the person's life. Betty had experienced dying and death deeply, of course, in the loss of her husband and loved ones, but, importantly, it was also a part of her daily reflection in prayer and how she lived her life as a neighbour. She visited another bereaved family when her husband died – just as her own family, following her example, did in the days of her passing. The final lesson, then, that Betty can teach us is that the 'art of dying well' is 'the art of living – while facing life's end – well'.

It is important to acknowledge that it does not always end so. A good death, understood as peace at the end surrounded by loved ones, can be robbed from a person by tragedy, sudden death and circumstances. For instance, the necessary regulations put in place during the Covid-19 pandemic put many families and friends in a situation where they could not be by the side of the dying.

There are, then, three duties or requirements: awareness, acceptance and accompaniment. The Christian tradition has long provided ways in which these tasks, or works, can be undertaken.

Christian Meaning of Death

In the Old Testament, a long life was a sign of blessing from God (Deuteronomy 30:15). Yet death always remains a tragic part of life. In the words of the Psalmist: 'The days of our life are seventy years, or perhaps eighty, if we are strong; even then their span is only toil and trouble; they are soon gone, and we fly away' (Psalm 90:10). Death is not some supernatural force that sweeps in like the grim reaper dressed in a black hood holding a sickle. Rather it is a dreadful event that separates the person from God, the community and, of course, life itself. Existence beyond death is rarely considered in the Old Testament. Any reference to the resurrection is in the context of restoring the people of Israel. Take the prophet Ezekiel: 'Therefore prophesy, and say to them, Thus says the Lord God: I am going to open your graves, and bring you up from your graves, O my people; and I will bring you back to the land of Israel' (Ezekiel 37:12).

For Christians, death takes on a new meaning in the Gospels and the letters of St Paul. The central moment of God's revelation and salvation takes place in the death of one person: Jesus Christ. Christians believe that God defeated death through the life, death and resurrection of Jesus Christ. As St Paul concludes: 'The last enemy to be destroyed is death' (1 Corinthians 15:26). Death is not some neutral fact about life, but a tragic outcome of the fall of humanity. It causes real pain, physically, emotionally and personally. But the overcoming of death is not the elimination of death.[10] Recall that the resurrected Jesus was still marked by the wounds of his violent death (Luke 24:39; John 20:27). Our individual deaths remain but are set in a new context: hope for union with God beyond death, 'a new heaven and a new earth' (2 Peter 3:13). This new reality is both 'already-but-not-yet'. In other words, Christians both proclaim the loving mercy of God expressed in his victory over death, and, at the same time, mourn and wrestle with the tragedy of death. To return to the words of St Paul to the Church in Thessalonica:

> But we do not want you to be uninformed, brothers and sisters, about those who have died, so that you may not grieve as others do who have no hope. For since we believe that Jesus died and rose again, even so, through Jesus, God will bring with him those who have died. (1 Thessalonians 4:13–14)

The belief in the defeat of death counters prevalent approaches to death today. Firstly, it denies that death is just 'natural' or simply 'the way it is', without any personal consequence. Secondly, it resists the temptation to think that death can be eliminated or fended off endlessly by medicine and technology. What both approaches share is a denial of the fullest reality of dying and death.

---

10 Christopher Vogt, 'Death and Dying,' in Tobias Winright (ed.), *T&T Clark Handbook of Christian Ethics* (New York, NY: Bloomsbury, 2021), 319–28.

Ars Moriendi for Today

Awareness, acceptance and accompaniment are tasks. As such they empower the person and communities in facing death. The practices that foster these values for a person can counter the passivity, and hence the fear of dying, that contemporary medicine can unintentionally cultivate. The vulnerability and tragedy of death can be faced in a manner in which 'sense is made' of the experience.

The memoir of Paul Kalanithi was a task that aided his dying well. Through it, he recognised the importance of making sense of the experience:

> The physician's duty is not to stave off death or return patients to their old lives, but to take into our arms a patient and family whose lives have disintegrated and work until they can stand back up and face, and make sense of, their own existence.[11]

This making sense is 'the art'. Finding meaning in death does not lie in some inherent aspect of death itself, which always remains tragic. Neither is it inherent in the dying person, who is becoming more and more vulnerable. Rather, it happens in the willingness of the dying person to participate in the task(s) of dying well (acceptance), the resources offered by the community (awareness), and the commitment of others to paying attention in a caring way to what the dying person is experiencing (accompaniment).

Yet the medical system can struggle with thinking in this way. While there is a long-established practice in Ireland of 'waking' the dead at home, the percentage of those dying at home is not as high as the stated preference of people. The Irish Hospice Foundation rightly argues for more practitioners and greater training in specialised palliative care in acute hospitals and in support of families.[12] Facing life's

---

11   Kalanithi, op. cit., 166.
12   Matthews et al., op. cit., 93.

end well is a concern of us all and so provision of support services is a matter of social justice.

However, provision of support to face the end of life well cannot be left to the professional healthcare practitioners. Rather the system needs to facilitate rather than replace the personal and communal practices – including, and especially, religious practices – by which meaning is made. In turn, communities and churches need to develop new ways, or encourage old ways, in which death can be faced in a supportive and realistic way. For example, an especially attractive initiative was created by the English Roman Catholic Bishops, and is now hosted by St Mary's University, London. It is an online website called the artofdyingwell.org, which offers many accessible and insightful resources for those struggling with the questions for themselves or their loved ones.

Paul Kalanithi wrote: 'My highest ideal was not saving lives – everyone dies eventually – but guiding a patient or family to an understanding of death or illness … In these moments, I acted not, as I most often did, as death's enemy, but as its ambassador.'[13] But death does not have the final word. It has been 'swallowed up by victory' (1 Corinthians 15:54).

Questions for Reflection and Discussion

1. Can you identify spiritual and social practices that help us reflect on death and dying?
2. Recall someone you know who practised the art of dying well. What lessons do they teach?
3. Read 1 Corinthians 15:50–58, in which St Paul writes of Christ's victory over death. Spend time with it. What does it say to you?
4. Visit the website: www.artofdyingwell.org. Spend time with its videos, reading and questions. What strikes you?

13 Kalanithi, op. cit., 86.

Two: Facing Goodbye
7: Memento Mori: Reflecting on the Music of My Own Death

Salvador Ryan

It was September 2008 and I had just arrived in Grand Rapids, Michigan, to speak at an international conference. As the event was not due to begin until the following day, I took a stroll downtown to see the sights. Fourteen years on, I can't tell you much about what I saw downtown, but there's one particular memory that has stuck with me. You see, my stroll soon evolved into a 'church crawl' of sorts, as I found myself entering a number of church buildings of different Christian denominations along my route. Most were empty and, on each occasion, I would walk up the aisle, take a seat, and spend some moments in silence, absorbed in the wonder that comes with being in a new city with so much yet to explore. But the silence didn't last long. In many of the churches I visited that day, there were hymn books to be found in the pews. I picked one up, leafed through its index, and soon found some of my favourite titles. The first my eye fell on was 'Dear Lord and Father of Mankind' and, having quickly found the appropriate page, I spontaneously burst into song.

This might seem an odd memory with which to begin a reflection on my own mortality; nonetheless, I hope that the connection will become apparent. That afternoon, I sang all verses of 'Dear Lord and

Father of Mankind', my voice resounding through the cavernous structure in full-throated joy. Next was 'Come Down O Love Divine'. Once again, every single verse. Then, 'O Thou who at Thy Eucharist didst Pray'; again, in full. The church still empty. No one to hear me sing. Except myself, and, I trust, the divine subject of all those beautiful verses. It was glorious; uplifting; it raised my mind, my heart and my body, my whole self, onto another plane. I moved on to the next church. And the next hymnal. And, again, I began to sing. Sometimes the same hymns; at other times, different ones. And on the afternoon went. Only much later, while reflecting on this experience, would I come to realise the depth of meaning that certain pieces of hymnody can carry, and how, in a way, they can form the spiritual soundtrack to our lives. But not only to our lives. They also have something significant to say when we are brought before the sanctuary in death.

From my earliest years I have contemplated death. At first, it was the thought of my parents dying. I have a very strong memory of one of my earliest prayers which ran: 'Dear God, please make Mama and Dada live for a very long time ... '. But I also remember pausing after uttering those words and reassessing their meaning – what if *my* idea of a very long time was not *God's* idea of a very long time? And, so, at what must have been about four years of age, I inserted what I considered to be a crucial amendment: 'Dear God, please make Mama and Dada live for a very long time (to me).' The revision made, I could now rest assured that there was no ambiguity in my petition.[1]

Some years later, I became fascinated with the idea of heaven and the desirability of moving on to the next life as soon as possible (this may well have been fuelled by stories of the children of Fátima who, at a tender young age, similarly longed to be brought away by the 'beautiful lady' they claimed to have visited them in 1917). Indeed, I remember one particular day in primary school in my home village of

1 A petition which, incidentally, I consider to have been granted.

Moneygall, when we were discussing the figure of Colonel Gaddafi with our headmaster, Paddy Maher – it must have been mid-April 1986, during the US air strikes against Libya – I came out with a rather disturbing statement. It happened when we had moved on from the Libyan crisis, and were discussing more pleasant matters such as the question, 'If you had your choice of being anywhere in the world right now, where would it be?' Some of my classmates shouted out 'Disney World'; others, 'Spain'; others still, 'New York'. When it came to my turn, I declared that I would very much like to be positioned straight in front of one of Gaddafi's surface-to-air missiles. The poor headmaster, who was nearing retirement at the time, blinked, swallowed hard, and blinked again, just to be sure that this revelation had, in fact, just unfolded before his eyes. I can't quite remember what he said next, and maybe it's because I've partially wiped that recording from my mind. Were this to happen today, it might well precipitate a referral to a child psychologist. But I wasn't a bit fazed by my revelation. Surely there was a logic to it, wasn't there? This was a vale of tears, after all (I'd already been familiar with the phrase from the end of the Rosary, which so many of us said at home); who wouldn't want to move on to infinitely superior heavenly prospects? I was quite sure at the time that I had learnt how to die; however, the thing was, I hadn't quite learnt how to live.

As I write, the people of Ukraine are currently experiencing the horrifying reality of living under a hail of Russian missiles. It makes me feel ashamed that, growing up in the idyllic surrounds of a rural Irish village in peacetime, I could ever have entertained such thoughts. I did not fully appreciate then that, although Christian thoughts of our ultimate homeland in heaven can be comforting, they should not hinder us from living to the full this earthly life – also a gift from God.

My aforementioned headmaster, Paddy Maher, was not just our primary school principal; he was also the local choirmaster. This meant that, whenever a funeral would come to Moneygall Church, we fifth- and sixth-class boys and girls would file down to make up the choir, with Paddy at the helm.[2] It was on these occasions that I first came to learn the basics of Gregorian chant, and to sing the *Missa de Angelis*. There was, more or less, a set repertoire for funerals in Moneygall, all set out on badly photocopied sheets that were kept in a cardboard box of music at the foot of the organ in the side aisle. Those were the days when 'special requests' from families of the bereaved were few and far between, and people were largely content to leave it to the choirmaster to look after these things. What that meant was that there was continuity in our funeral liturgies; a repeated musical mantra, as it were; a veritable soundtrack to death in Moneygall.

The requiem Mass. To a small boy, even the word 'Requiem' was mysterious; but there was also something noble about it. When the bell would ring, and the sacristy door would open to allow the procession of priests and altar boys (and yes, it was only boys at that stage) to emerge into the sanctuary, the organ would invite Paddy to intone the words: 'Eternal rest grant unto him, O Lord / and let perpetual light shine upon him'. Joe O'Brien was the organist, a former pupil of Paddy's (sure weren't half the village?). Paddy often remarked that he'd started Joe as organist when he was around twelve or thirteen, and he'd been playing ever since. Continuity. Predictability. Sameness. And it was wonderful. We'd repeat the refrain: 'Eternal rest grant unto him, O Lord / and let perpetual light shine upon him'. And then Paddy would take up the verses, standing out in front of the side aisle, flanked by the organ, the flimsy sheet of music waving in his hand with each stress of the key phrases. 'To you our praise is due in Sion, O God / To you we pay our vows, you who hear our prayer'. And, again, the refrain, and a second verse: 'To you all flesh will come with its burden of sin; / too heavy for us our offences / but you wipe them away'. I can still hear the lightness with which Paddy sang the words 'but you wipe them away', contrasting with the preceding stress on the word 'heavy'; with this, the modulation of his voice effected what

---

2   I have written about this experience elsewhere. See 'Introduction', in Salvador Ryan (ed.), *Death and the Irish: a Miscellany* (Dublin: Wordwell Books, 2016), 1–7.

the words themselves suggested the Lord would one day do for each of us. When I heard these words sung, over and over again, at funeral after funeral, they burned themselves into my spiritual consciousness, to such an extent that I can bring the scene to mind as vividly today as when I experienced it as a child. That child has since grown up, and has come to think very differently about life and the world than he did when he sat in Paddy Maher's church choir. Yet, when I come to think of my own requiem Mass, which comes closer with each passing day, it is to my childhood days in Moneygall that I return; and to a soundtrack that is ever familiar, and deeply comforting.

I tend to get puzzled looks from people when I tell them that I have already decided on the music for my funeral liturgy. Some find the thought macabre; others slightly odd; and still more no doubt conclude that I must have little to think about if I can afford myself such luxuries of forethought. But, for me, this is not a luxury. It's my opportunity to make a last statement; to say something significant about who I am (or who I perceive myself to be); to communicate what has been important to me; to make sure that my funeral liturgy is true to my character; perhaps even to control the musical narrative. So, for instance, I have told anyone who cares to listen that I don't want anything mawkish or saccharine at my funeral; and certainly nothing that risks morphing into a superficial tear-jerker. I've explained that there are certain musical pieces (I will be charitable enough not to name them here) which, if played at my funeral, would be sufficient to goad me out of my state of coffined rest and send me howling in protest at the relevant offenders. And no one really wants that. So, I've made a list. And every piece has its own significance.

When I began thinking about this in a serious way some years ago, my first urge was for my funeral liturgy to establish a sense of rootedness and connection. So much of my faith life, and my love of church music, has its beginnings in my upbringing in Moneygall. Although I've since been involved in several choirs, and have been privileged enough to have been given a thorough grounding in liturgical music at Maynooth College, largely thanks to its Director of Sacred Music,

Dr John O'Keeffe, my musical awakening began in my home village. It's there that I first learned to live the rhythm of the funeral liturgy. And so, God willing, that's where my funeral Mass will commence.[3] It will begin with those words sung by Paddy Maher at every funeral, so many years ago: 'Eternal rest grant unto him, O Lord / and let perpetual light shine upon him'. This will be my way of joining the long procession of my fellow parishioners whose requiem Masses opened in precisely the same way. It will be my way of saying, 'I am one of you. I am part of this community. Now that *my* time has come, I am proud to join this parish procession of the dead, this human litany of praise, thanksgiving and petition to the God we worshipped together'. And that's why the responsorial psalm will also be that which we sang in Paddy Maher's choir: 'My soul is longing for your peace / near to you, my God'.

Peace. I didn't realise it then, but I certainly do now, how precious a commodity this is. And I don't mean just the absence of war. I mean genuine, heartfelt peace. Freedom from distress, worry, grief, regret and a whole host of other things; peace of mind. Strange as it may sound, it's something I'm looking forward to in death – the idea of the 'fever of life', as John Henry Newman put it, being over, and the descent of a deep stillness, however brief or long that may be, before we are geared up again for the next stage. I have many good friends who are atheists, and, in more recent years, I've come to a greater appreciation of how they, too, can take comfort in the idea of life's end. Whether it is the hope of a transformed existence from beyond the grave, or the quiet acceptance of the stilling of the difficulties of this life (even if that stilling means extinction), here is surely one thing that both believers and non-believers can potentially agree upon – that the prospect of peace at the end of a well-lived life is no bad thing. From the very day we are born, we are already journeying towards death. Somehow,

---

3   When I speak about how I envisage my funeral and burial unfolding, I do so fully conscious that, however meticulously we might like to orchestrate these things, there are no guarantees about where one will eventually be buried, or in what circumstances. Each aspiration should therefore be preceded by a silently voiced 'DV' (*Deo volente*).

it's how we live the time in between that matters. But I am also pain-fully aware of those who, for whatever reason, feel unable to continue to live with life's burdens, and see no other way out other than has-tening, or cutting short, this in-between time, and the devastating effects that this decision can have on their loved ones. And yet, so many who find themselves in this awful situation also simply long for peace.

The first verse of the psalm follows: 'Lord, you know that my heart is not proud / and my eyes are not lifted from the earth' (Psalm 131:1). This may, at first, seem like what is often called 'humble bragging' today, a form of faux humility. The apostle Paul may have indulged in this kind of rhetoric when he professed himself content to boast all the more gladly of his weaknesses so that the power of Christ might dwell in him (2 Corinthians 12:9). Yet I'd really like to take Paul at his word; precisely because I'd also like others to take me at my word. If I were given the choice to be chiefly remembered for my weaknesses or for my strengths, I would, without question, choose the former. It is my weaknesses that most clearly define me. It is in these that you will find me at my most authentic; unguarded, vulnerable, flawed and exposed. And it's in my own brokenness that I have most often found deep wells of compassion for others. It's also what has given me an inherent suspicion of the human tendency to place people on pedestals, which is often accompanied by naive declarations of an individual's sanctity. I've met quite a few 'saints' in my time, but they're not the ones who have left the deepest impression on me. Indeed, experience has taught me that the gentlest, kindest, most compassionate and, yes, the most holy of people, are oftentimes those who are the most broken. If I am ever to emulate these people, it will be my weaknesses that will carry me there, rather than my strengths. When my body lies before the altar, I'll want people to know that this kind of earthy goodness was, at least, my aspiration.

And so to the offertory hymn. (Trigger warning: if you are a pro-fessional liturgist, feel free to skip over the next few lines as they may send you into paroxysms of protest). For this I have chosen 'A Mhuire Mháthair, 'sé seo mo ghuí', a popular Marian hymn in the Irish language.[4] There are a number of reasons for this. First of all, the piece acknowledges my love of our native language, and recalls for me some of my happiest summers, which I spent teaching Irish on Gaeltacht courses, chiefly on Inis Oírr, the smallest of the Aran islands. Secondly, ever since I was a child, I've always had a devotion to Mary, and I still find the Rosary to be a very meaningful and calming prayer. The third verse of the hymn appropriately petitions Mary: '*go raibh tú taobh liom ar uair mo bháis*' ('may you be by my side at the hour of my death'). However, my main reason for selecting this piece is that I first learned it in the West Kerry Gaeltacht in the summer of 1994, just as I was falling in love. Every time I've heard this piece since, I've been immediately brought back to that time and place, and the exhilarating excitement of how it felt. Such associations are often seared into our consciousness for the rest of our days. This piece, then, will recall that during life I have loved, and have been loved, and that this tremendous gift of human love, perhaps more than any other, reveals to us who God is (1 John 4:16).

I have chosen two pieces to be sung during the distribution of Holy Communion. The first, 'O Thou who at Thy Eucharist didst Pray', is significant as it bridges my early life in Moneygall and my later student, and working, life in Maynooth. I remember Paddy Maher teaching us a version of this text, which we would always (and, as far as I remember, only) sing on Holy Thursday night for the Mass of the Lord's Supper.[5] When I later went to Maynooth as a student, I learned a different setting of the hymn, which was sufficiently reminiscent of the one I remembered from childhood. I've loved it ever since. I remember, in particular, being struck by the line: 'So, Lord, at length, when sacraments shall cease … ', and trying to puzzle this out as a child. How could even *sacraments* cease? What could that mean? It was only many years later that I discovered the answer. And then there

---

4 I am fully aware that this Marian text does not constitute the most appropriate of offertory pieces, but, to be honest, I have nowhere else to put it. And, while liturgists might balk at my decision, I don't think God will particularly mind.

5 The liturgies of Holy Week and, especially, the Easter Triduum, left a deep impression on me from a young age.

was that wonderful petition that we might be 'one with thy saints in one unbroken peace / one with thy saints in one unbounded love'. Unbroken peace. Unbounded love. What a prospect. I long for this still.

And then there's 'Dear Lord and Father of Mankind', another hymn I learned in Maynooth, and simply my favourite of all – both to sing and to play. Here, it is a real challenge to select passages worthy of mention, such is the beauty of the text as a whole. 'Reclothe us in our rightful mind / in purer lives thy service find / in deeper reverence praise / in deeper reverence praise'. This is a hymn that I could sing forever, without tiring, either of its words or its melody. So many of us live our lives at breakneck speed, frenetically trying to keep up with all that we have to do; acutely conscious that there are never enough hours in the day, and filled with the realisation that, even if we had the capacity to forgo sleep for days on end, we would still hardly succeed in catching up with our ever-increasing to-do lists. If this description resonates with you (it certainly does with me), then the following verse might just offer some consolation, even as you imagine what this might actually feel like:

> Drop thy still dews of quietness,
> Till all our strivings cease;
> Take from our souls the strain and stress,
> And let our ordered lives confess
> The beauty of thy peace.

By the time this is sung at my funeral, I will (presumably) be at rest, the dews of quietness having finally settled upon me.

I will be carried out to 'Hail Queen of Heaven'. It's what some might term a 'golden oldie', originally written by the English priest and historian, Fr John Lingard (1771–1851). But golden oldies also have their merits. In this, I return to my childhood days in Paddy Maher's church choir. This is how so many of those gone before me were carried out of Moneygall Church. I want to make myself one with that long procession of parishioners. My people. But it's not just that. The words of this hymn also resonate deeply with me. Mary is 'guide of the wanderer here below'. Moreover, I also know what it is like to have been 'thrown on life's surge'.

It will take two verses of the hymn to take me out of the church. The procession down the aisle will begin when the second verse starts. The last line those attending my funeral will hear before they depart the church will be the most significant of all: 'Pray for the sinner, pray for me'. And that's how it should be. I am Salvador. And I am a sinner.[6]

When I think of my funeral liturgy, and I consider the pieces of music that I have chosen, they bring me a sense of deep peace. They reach back into the earliest development of my faith life; they acknowledge those who had a hand in awakening a love of liturgical music in me, and those who significantly built upon this; and, finally, they situate me firmly in the midst of the generations of my people that have gone before me, helping me to fall in with a rhythm of life and death that is far larger and far greater than me. And, when I am brought to lie among my people in Dunkerrin cemetery, County Offaly, accompanied by the echoes of hymns that are ever old and ever new, I will know that, for this stage of the journey at least, I am home.

Questions for Reflection and Discussion

1. It's not always easy for people to speak about their own deaths. What are your immediate reactions to this chapter? How does it make you feel?

---

6   I am writing these words on the eve of St Patrick's Day. Ireland's national patron began his fifth-century work, the *Confession*, with the words 'I am Patrick, a sinner'. Again, as in the case of Paul, I'm not quite sure if Patrick was 'humble bragging', or if this simply constituted the use of a pious trope. What I can assure you is that, for my part, it is neither. Hence the significance of that last line of 'Hail Queen of Heaven'.

2. Have you ever given thought to your own funeral? If you have done so, what do you imagine it might be like? Who do you see there? Who is missing from the congregation? What is being said?
3. How important is it for you to ensure that particular scripture readings, or specific pieces of music, are included at your funeral liturgy?
4. If this is important for you, what pieces of music might you select, and why?
5. As a simple exercise, choose one of your favourite hymns (and one that you might consider for your funeral liturgy). Why is this hymn significant for you? Is it the melody or the text of the hymn (or both) that makes it a favourite?
6. Have you considered communicating your wishes for your funeral to a friend or family member, or pre-planning your funeral with an undertaker?

8: Tea, Scones and Stories – the Liturgy of an Irish Wake

Bairbre Cahill

Mary and I had met as toddlers looking through a garden gate and from then had been in and out of each other's homes constantly. However, when it came to my brother's wake, Mary couldn't get over the threshold. Paul had been ill for nearly two years with a brain tumour and Mary was paralysed with fear at the idea of seeing my once strong and handsome big brother in his coffin. And then Eithne appeared, my five-year-old sister, who stepped out and took Mary by the hand saying, 'It's OK, I'll bring you in.' This she duly did, leading Mary by the hand right over to beside Paul's coffin where Eithne stood up on her tiptoes and gently kissed him. This is the reality of a wake; it is a place of encounter. We encounter the reality of death, our fear of death and an awareness of our own mortality – and I for one wouldn't change that.

The concept of the wake has been part of Irish culture for hundreds of years. There are a few theories as to where the word 'wake' comes from. One idea is that there were illnesses that could render a person insensate to the point where they appeared to be dead. Family members would keep watch over the body for at least twenty-four hours lest the dead should awake. Another idea is simply that as a mark of respect the one who had died would not be left alone but would be accompanied by a few hardy souls through the hours of darkness for two nights until the funeral. It is a sign of deep love and respect. Indeed, the Irish word for wake is *'faire'*, which means to 'keep watch' – and it is something we saw ourselves at my brother's wake, where a few of the cousins who had felt helpless during Paul's illness stepped up now to wake him through those dark nights until the funeral.

There are traditional customs associated with a wake – some of which remain to this day. Clocks in the wake house would be stopped at the time of death. This conveyed a sense of respect for the one who has died. But the gesture is perhaps even more needed in our modern high-speed culture to indicate that, for these days, time is irrelevant – we step outside of the normal restrictions of clock time and inhabit a liminal space where priorities are different. Mirrors would often be turned to the wall or covered – the idea being that the departing soul should not be distracted by its own image in the mirror. Candles would be lit and placed near the coffin. Indeed, many families have a set of candlesticks particularly for this function and, if they do not, then the undertaker will generally provide them.

In Ireland there is still a distinctly religious feel to the wake, even in situations where the family may feel quite disconnected from 'Church'. It is common practice for the Rosary to be recited late in the evening on each night of the wake, by the local priest or by some-one within the family. People will stand and say a prayer beside the coffin, Mass cards abound, and it is not unusual for the bereaved to ask family and friends to pray for them in the time ahead that they may find the strength to live with their loss.

For many people who struggle with faith, or with their experience of Church, a funeral, particularly of a loved one, offers an opportunity of encounter with a foundational experience of faith, a raw, real, embodied sense. I was struck recently by a Facebook post from a friend whose father had died: 'Although he chose the traditional old school route for his funeral, it really was a beautiful send off! We couldn't have asked for a more fitting way to head to his final destination. To those who fed us, sorted traffic, the funeral itself, everything, we are truly grateful.' Indeed, from a pastoral perspective, the Church has much to learn from the community that gathers around a grieving family. Here is an experience of what Church is called to be, an experience of communion, of Paschal Mystery, of love incarnate.

When our father died, Eithne was now a woman, married with two children, living in England but home for these last days. Her husband Dave was daunted by the prospect of travelling over to Ireland. He was already aware that the Irish Catholic approach to death and grieving was rather different from the secular English context in which he grew up. Dave knew that he would join us, but what of their children, Ciarán, seven, and Hannah, five – surely they were too young to be exposed to such an experience? As a family we were very clear that Hannah and Ciarán's place was here in the midst of us – and so they came.

It is customary in Ireland to bury the deceased on the third day after they have died. The speed of this mesmerises some who are used to a delay of weeks between death and burial. In such circumstances people have little option other than to return to some level of normality. Jobs need to be done, life must go on – despite the reality of an often deep and life-changing upheaval. To expect so much of people strikes me as absurd to the point of being cruel. Such a delay forces people to suppress their grief and to behave as if the world continues as it always has done.

With the Irish wake there is an acknowledgment that life has 'changed, changed utterly', to use William Butler Yeats's phrase.[1] My father had died at home with us but his remains had been removed by the undertakers and were returned now to us on that first day of the wake. His coffin took up residence where my brother's had been over thirty years previously. He had not been afraid to die and now, in death, he looked peaceful. There was a brief lull, a time for us as a family to be with him before the front door opened to welcome

---

1   William Butler Yeats, 'Easter 1916', in *Easter 1916 and Other Poems* (Mineola, NY: Dover Publications, 2000), 53–55, at 55.

neighbours, friends, extended family and the extensive network of our own friends and work colleagues who wanted to come and pay their respects.

By inviting us into a synodal process, Pope Francis has asked us to be open to encountering each other, listening to each other. It strikes me that a model for that is the wake. There is a particular liturgy of encounter – and I use that word *liturgy* deliberately. There is often a ministry of welcome, formal or informal. It may be the people standing around outside the wake house who will greet you, with a word or a nod of the head, sometimes with a direction given: 'Ah, he's in there in the front room.' On other occasions the local community will mobilise to offer very practical and much-needed help. I remember going to the wake of a little boy, just two years old, who had died suddenly. When I arrived at the road leading to the house, I was met by an army of volunteers directing traffic and organising parking in a local farmer's field. From there another group of volunteers directed people to the house.

Then there is the meeting with those who have been bereaved. There is a phrase in Irish, '*Is oth liom do bhris*' which can be translated as 'I'm sorry for your loss', but *bris* also means 'break', and there is a real sense at a wake that we are encountering brokenness, vulnerability. In so many ways, modern society and culture seek to distance us from the reality of death – and indeed the reality of ageing, illness and infirmity; basically anything that suggests we are mortal. At a wake we encounter the reality of death and the brokenness and vulnerability left behind.

At the wake of that little boy, many of us wondered how we could cross the threshold into that house. What could be said or done to give any glimmer of comfort? He was lying not in a coffin but in his cot. Hung on the walls around him were photos of himself with his sisters and his parents. Here were images of a smiling, mischievous, playful boy, so full of life – so stark a contrast to the little boy who lay in front of us. And within the brokenness and vulnerability of his mother and father there was the most powerful strength. We were amazed by them, in awe at the grace given to them to talk about their beautiful boy, to smile at shared memories, to reach out and hug those who came into this wake house and were overwhelmed with grief. I watched two heartbroken parents transcend their own devastation in order to comfort others.

The liturgy of the wake continues with rich Eucharistic resonances. There is a Word, broken and shared among us, and it is the Word of this person's life. I heard stories about my father at his wake and learned details about his life that were utterly new to me. He had always been a man deeply committed to his community and to doing everything in his power to make life better for people in that community but, in reality, I had only known the half of it. At his wake there was what I can only call a sacred remembering, where a tapestry of people flowed through our home, all with their own insights into my father. Together their memories wove a bright and splendid burial garment, a true celebration of his life.

Then there is the cup of tea, the mountain of sandwiches, the homemade scones. Liturgy is about work done for and on behalf of the community.[2] We think of particular liturgical actions, language, space and elements. The liturgical powerhouse for the wake is the kitchen. Here something almost beyond belief takes place and it resonates with gospel stories of the feeding of the five thousand. There is that moment before a wake begins where the family wonder how they are going to cope with so many people coming – and then, without fail, the community takes over. Additional chairs, cups, saucers, plates, kettles and teapots appear. Food seems to multiply, with many of those who arrive at the wake house bringing with them a loaf of sandwiches, a batch of home baking or a box of biscuits. Indeed, those particularly close to the family may arrive with pots of soup or casseroles to keep the family fed during these important but exhausting days. To gather and share food – this is not incidental. This is at the core of who we are, and the importance of food in the

---

2   Liturgy: http://www.dioceseofshrewsbury.org/catholic-faith/liturgy/what-is-liturgy.

context of a wake is not to be underestimated. Here is love made real. Here is incarnation. Those endless trays of tea and sandwiches carried out from kitchens are what create the space and opportunity for people to stop awhile, to talk, to remember, to add their thread to the weave.

At their grandfather's funeral Ciarán and Hannah – having initially been a little wary about the wake – soon took on the important roles of ferrying milk, sugar and plates of scones from the kitchen into the sitting room where their grandfather lay in his coffin. Reflecting on it later, Dave was amazed by how at ease they were, pausing every so often on their rounds to look at Grandad or to answer a question from one of the myriad visitors. Dave realised that the way he had been protected from death as a child and young adult (although well meant) was probably not as healthy as allowing Ciarán and Hannah to be involved. The children were able to begin to process their grief. Grandad did not look frightening. People were sad but the children did not feel threatened by those emotions. The wake creates that space in which loss can be held and lived and, perhaps reluctantly, be accepted as part of our lives going forward. My own children, aged at that time from their late teens into their early twenties, have spoken since of how being with their Grandad in his last days and throughout the wake has helped them to deal with their grief and to live well with their loss.

Good liturgy directs us forward in hope, with a glimpse of the transcendent. My experience has been that a wake can serve in a similar way. I remember at my brother Paul's wake we had an oversupply of egg sandwiches and had frozen some. On the second day of the wake we had taken them out of the freezer but only realised after the plate of sandwiches had done two circuits of the 'front room' that the egg ones were not sufficiently defrosted. My memory is of a group of us standing in the kitchen trying to figure out how we were to surreptitiously remove semi-frozen egg sandwiches from people's plates before we gave them all food poisoning! And I remember the laughter. In the midst of the absolute devastation of Paul's death, we found laughter, and it somehow gave me that glimmer of confidence that we would survive this terrible trauma, that death did not have the last word. It has occurred to me since that laughter is the music of the resurrection.

At my father's wake I found myself back in that same front room, aware of the somewhat surreal scene, – my father in his coffin, the room full of neighbours, friends and family, a gentle buzz of conversation, when a word popped into my mind. The word persisted through the day, hovering in the air around me, nudging me for attention, sparking my curiosity. That evening, when the house had stilled, I looked up the word – *pleroma* – and found that essentially it means fullness of being.[3] My father had been depleted by cancer. Here now, in the context of this wake, with that bright and splendid burial shroud woven with the love and goodness, the memories and stories of family and friends, my father was restored to the best of himself, to fullness of being.

In early 2020, just as the country locked down because of the global Covid-19 pandemic, a member of our extended family died. He was only in his early forties and, although he had a number of health issues when he collapsed and died, a swab was taken which revealed that he was Covid positive. The implications were clear – there could be no post-mortem, no opportunity for his loved ones to see him one last time. That was probably the most stark and lonely funeral I have ever been at. The coffin was brought from Dublin straight to the graveyard. There was no wake. Churches were shut, so there was no funeral Mass. His father and brothers had gone to Dublin as soon as news of the death broke, so now they stood, together with his young widow, at a distance from all other members of the family, isolated in an isolation in which they would have to continue for another ten days. It was a heartbreaking experience. It felt as if our usual means of supporting and nurturing each other at times like this had been stripped away and we were left forlorn in a cold graveyard.

3   Pleroma: https://www.collinsdictionary.com/dictionary/english/pleroma.

Just over a year later we gathered again, this time in the garden of his father's home. Together we would celebrate the Mass that could not happen for the funeral. Readings were well chosen, the music was beautiful, the priest spoke well, the grieving father spoke even better – grace, strength, faith and hope broke through the sadness. But we were not complete. Due to ongoing restrictions and anxieties about Covid we could not have the cup of tea, and this was a family home where the cup of tea was always offered with persistent generosity. And so the decision is made; we will gather again next year when, hopefully, all restrictions and fears about Covid will have lifted and we will come together as a Eucharistic community in the Mass and also in the cup of tea – or something stronger – that will follow it. There is a real sense that because there was no wake we now need to step back into that space, to gather, to talk, to drink tea, and to remember and celebrate the life of this young man. Until we can do that, there is unfinished business which stalls the process of grieving.

I am convinced that our grieving does not happen in straight lines. Some years ago, having spoken to people bereaved in a variety of circumstances, I wrote the book *Living with Grief – Walking the Spiral*.[4] Rather than proceeding through stages of grief in a linear fashion, I believe that we, time and again, touch back into that experience of grief, whether that is sparked by an anniversary, another bereavement, a memory of a place, a song or shared experience. That movement to the centre of our loss and back out again allows for ongoing healing of the multiple and sometimes unrecognised facets of our grief. One mother told me how she found herself grieving the loss of her daughter all over again when, years later, her son and his wife announced they were expecting their first baby.

The experience of a wake gives us our first tentative steps into that healing spiral, enfolded in love incarnated in the simple, practical and essential acts of those around us. We find ourselves touching back into

---

4   Bairbre Cahill, *Living with Grief – Walking the Spiral* (Chawton, Hampshire: Redemptorist Publications, 2015).

the circumstances of the death. We encounter the reality of our loss again with each person who comes through our door, each echoed conversation. And in that there can be healing. The wake, that sacred space, can teach us not only how to begin to grieve but also how to live.

Questions for Reflection and Discussion

1. 'Then there is the cup of tea, the mountain of sandwiches, the homemade scones … Here is love made real. Here is incarnation.' Incarnation can seem like a heavy theological word. How might your experience shift if you begin to think of incarnation as love made real in the bits and pieces of everyday life?

2. 'In the midst of the absolute devastation of Paul's death, we found laughter, and it somehow gave me that glimmer of confidence that we would survive this terrible trauma, that death did not have the last word. It has occurred to me since that laughter is the music of the resurrection.' What experiences have nurtured in you a hope and confidence that you will survive the experience of being bereaved?

3. 'Rather than proceeding through stages of grief in a linear fashion I believe that we, time and again, touch back into that experience of grief … That movement to the centre of our loss and back out again allows for ongoing healing of the multiple and sometimes unrecognised facets of our grief.' How does this understanding of grief connect with your own experience?

4. 'Here is an experience of what Church is called to be, an experience of communion, of Paschal Mystery, of love incarnate.' How best can we as Church respond?

9: What Happens when We Die?
Reflections on the *Order of Christian Funerals*

Liam M. Tracey OSM

Much of my time over the last years was devoted to forming and sustaining parish funeral teams. These groups came together in parishes to assist families in preparing and celebrating the funerals of loved ones. They also organised annual services in the month of November to remember those who had died. From these beginnings, some groups or individual members assisted the priest with the prayers as family members gathered in the family home or funeral parlour, at the reception of the body at the Church, and at the burial. As the years went by, and priests became fewer, team members in turn led the prayers at these various moments. The task of the team was to be of practical assistance in the organising of a funeral to those who lost a loved one and to be a resource group to the wider parish community in its practice of the ministry of consolation, as it is put in the General Introduction to the *Order of Christian Funerals* (*OCF*).[5]

---

5   All references to the *Order of Christian Funerals* are to the second edition, approved for use in the dioceses of Ireland (Dublin: Veritas Publications, 1991). See H. Richard Rutherford, *The Death of a Christian: The Order of Christian Funerals* (2nd ed.) (Collegeville, MN: Liturgical Press, 1990).

The ministry of consolation is a multifaceted one, and the funeral team is only one manifestation of it, with its particular concern for ritual and prayer. In fact, the General Introduction to the *OCF* 8 notes: 'The Church calls each member of Christ's Body – priest, deacon, or layperson – to participate in the ministry of consolation: to care for the dying, to pray for the dead, to comfort those who mourn.' According to *OCF* 9, 'The responsibility for the ministry of consolation rests with the believing community, which heeds the words and example of the Lord Jesus: "Blessed are they who mourn; they shall be consoled" (Matthew 5:3). Each Christian shares in this ministry according to the various gifts and offices in the Church. With the ministry of consolation, ritual and prayer are the principal ways a Christian community assists those who have lost a loved one.'

The ministry of the funeral team runs alongside that of the excellent accompaniment provided by 'Bethany groups' to those who mourn. Indeed, in many parishes there is an overlap of members in these groups, though their tasks are very different. Funeral teams function around the time of a funeral, whereas Bethany groups walk the journey of grief in the time after a funeral, and can do so for an extended period. Over the years of my involvement with funeral teams, we organised many parish and diocesan events, exploring the rites, learning how to lead these moments of prayer, attending to the formation and ongoing running of the groups, and taking many opportunities for further training from different agencies.

Despite these activities, one thing that struck me was the absence of the question: What happens when we die; or, to put it more formally in a theological fashion: What do we believe as Christians about death and beyond death? In preparing the liturgy, members of both groups and, indeed, family members, sometimes spoke of the death of a loved one as if the person had slipped into the next room or that their suffering was now over. Often at the death, especially of a young person, the enormous loss was felt, or was described, as a huge gaping hole. However, rarely did the discussion move beyond these general assumptions. Perhaps this was not the appropriate place or time for such a conversation. However, I remain convinced that it is a conversation that needs to take place as part of the formative process for a funeral team. What we hope for beyond death surely impacts on how we minister at the time of death and its aftermath.

In this chapter I would like to look at the question in light of the *OCF*, the ritual book that gathers the various funeral rites from the prayers at the time of death till the person is buried or cremated. It is important to recall that in this second edition of the book (1991) some very definite decisions were made that may influence our study and understanding of the text. The decision to use the term 'body' rather than the cold term 'remains' reminds us that the person who has died is total and whole, thus marking a return to the biblical sense of person.[6] This understanding is affirmed in the General Introduction to *OCF* 19: 'Since in baptism the body was marked with the seal of the Trinity and became the temple of the Holy Spirit, Christians respect and honour the bodies of the dead and the places where they rest. Any customs associated with the preparation of the body of the deceased should always be marked with dignity and reverence and never with the despair of those who have no hope.'

The very clear relationship between the funeral rites and those of baptism is underlined especially in the use of the pall and placing the body near the baptismal area with the use of the Paschal candle. Indeed the rites mirror each other – just as many of us were carried to the church by our parents for our baptism, so we are carried by others to the church for the last time.

While it is useful to reflect on the texts of the liturgical celebrations, I am acutely aware that this is a limited approach in understanding the rites. People don't study these texts, they live them. Indeed, how worshippers experience these rites and what they see and hear in the funeral liturgies are profoundly formative in shaping belief. How these experiences can be accessed and reflected has not found any agreement amongst liturgists despite unanimity that it is an essential part

---

6   The use of the pall is also presented as a sign of the Christian dignity of the person (*OCF* 38)

of understanding liturgical celebrations. This aspect is acknowledged in the General Introduction to the *OCF* itself, where numbers 40–43 are grouped under the title Ritual Gestures and Movement. Drawing from the history of the celebration of Christian funerals, especially in the city of Rome, emphasis is given to the stational nature of the funeral journey with processions linking the various 'stations' where the prayer texts are prayed, the readings are read and the songs are sung. These processions are a mirror of the journey of life itself as we move towards the heavenly city of Jerusalem. We may also mention the importance of music in the funeral rites, as *OCF* 84 recalls: 'In the difficult circumstances following death, well-chosen music can touch the mourners and others present at levels of human need that words alone often fail to reach.' Indeed, number 21 of the General Introduction notes: 'Since liturgical celebration involves the whole person, it requires attentiveness to all that affects the senses.'

The funeral rites are ecclesial events, and central to the celebration is the baptised community with its faith in the life, death and resurrection of Christ, and its ongoing presence in the celebration of the Paschal Mystery. The Word of God, the community, and belief in the death and resurrection of Christ are central to every liturgy. But funeral rites are also about the unique and personal spiritual journey of the person who has died, and the circumstances and time of their death. Some people die at the end of a long and happy life, but others die in tragic circumstances or before their time. Every death is a unique event for those who mourn the passing of a loved one, and all this takes time to process. A funeral is not just one celebration but a ritual process over and over in time.

What happens when I die, or where do I go when my life ends? These are questions about the meaning and, indeed, value, of my life. Does everything end when I die, or does what I have lived continue to be or exist in some way? Funerals are ritual occasions with many different purposes and moments. For many cultures, including religious ones, they are about praying for the one who has died and entrusting them to God, so that they may move on to the next stage of their journey and may continue to enjoy life, albeit in a very different way. The rites also offer consolation and comfort for those who mourn, providing a ritual and supportive path through the difficult task of grief. Like all rituals, they remember and recall beginnings, those of the individual and of the group, and they enable participants to face endings, in this case the ending of a life. In the celebration of ritual a congregation or group profess once more what they believe in and hold dear. There is some communication about the group's origins and destiny, its sacred texts are proclaimed and, in the case of the death of a loved one, faith in the future is once more affirmed.

The General Introduction to the *OCF* notes that in the face of death, the Church proclaims with confidence that each person has been created for eternal life, and Jesus in his death and resurrection has broken the chains of sin and death that bound humanity (*OCF* 1 and 2). The Introduction continues by reaffirming the centrality of the Paschal Mystery of Christ, his passage from death to life, in every liturgical celebration (*OCF* 3). Now, on the death of a Christian whose life of faith began, the Introduction recalls, in the waters of baptism and was strengthened by regular participation in the celebration of the Eucharist, the Church community intercedes for the deceased because death is not the end, nor does it break the bonds that have been forged along life's journey. The life of the dead person is returned to God, the author of all life.

In an important affirmation, the General Introduction goes on to recall that we are united: the communion of saints unites heaven and earth. While the living and the dead are now physically separated, we are one body of Christ and, one day in the new heaven and the new earth, we will be reunited where death is no more. It is within this context that all ministry and, indeed, participation in the funeral rites takes place. All are called to care for the dying, to pray for the dead and comfort those who mourn. It is the faith of the Christian community in the resurrection of the dead that is nourished by the leaders of the community, as they in turn offer support and strength to those who have lost a loved one.

The centrality of the Paschal Mystery of Christ is stressed many times in the General Introduction. It is this mystery of Christ's passing from death to life that is the promise that those who have died will one day be gathered into the reign of God, and is a comfort for those who mourn as they continue their path of Christian discipleship. Other images of eternal life, the journey to the city of the heavenly Jerusalem, and participation in the victory of Christ over the powers of death, are presented as part of the Paschal Mystery.

Prayer Texts of the Funeral Rite

When we move to consider some of the prayer texts of the *OCF*, it is interesting to note whether this same emphasis holds. Within the Concluding Prayer in the Rites of Prayers after Death (*OCF* 58), the minister prays:

> Holy Lord, almighty and eternal God,
> hear our prayers for your servant N.,
> whom you have *summoned out of this world.*
> Forgive his/her sins and failings
> and grant him/her *a place of refreshment, light and peace.*
> Let him/her *pass unharmed through the gates of death*
> *to dwell with the blessed in light,*
> as you promised to Abraham and his children for ever.
> Accept N. into *your safekeeping*
> and on the great day of judgment
> *raise him/her up with all the saints*
> to inherit your eternal kingdom.
> We ask this through Christ our Lord. Amen.

The ritual book observes that if this rite is used at the occurrence of death, or shortly afterwards, it can be a quiet and prayerful response to the death of a loved one. Death is seen as a calling out of this world to a place of peace and light – a reference to the first Eucharistic Prayer, and perhaps one of the oldest liturgical references to beyond death.

But this also requires a transition of passing through the gates of death. Being raised up with the saints will occur after the great day of judgment which will happen at some time in the future.

While the central funeral liturgy is the funeral Mass or a celebration of the Word, both are held before the rites of committal. The *OCF* does provide for a celebration of a vigil for the deceased, which is seen as the principal rite celebrated by the Christian community before the funeral liturgy, or, indeed, in place of it in some parts of the world. This celebration may take the form of a wake and be led by a lay minister. The vigil can be celebrated in a church or indeed in any suitable place, including the home of the person who has died. This liturgy is one of keeping watch with those who mourn and is focused on the Word of God as a source of comfort. It can include the reception of the body, either at the church building or elsewhere, and the vigil liturgy can be celebrated more than once if the main liturgy is not to be celebrated for a number of days. It is addressed to the mourners and prays that they may be comforted in this moment of grief. This vigil liturgy is used as the main funeral liturgy in many parts of the Church where there is a shortage of ordained priests, and this could occur in the future here in Ireland where it may not always be possible to celebrate a funeral Mass.

The movement of the body of the deceased to the Church has great significance for the *OCF*. It is seen as the movement of the one who has died now coming to the community where the dead person has been seen as one of their own, as one whose journey began in the waters of baptism and who was a member of this assembly of Christians. That assembly is the one who gathers in this building and throughout the world but is also joined with the assembly that celebrates the heavenly liturgy. There is a sense of the journey that began in baptism and now reaches its conclusion in death that gives way to a new life. The reception of the body finds its mirror image in the final commendation of the funeral Mass where the community offers a farewell to one of their members and entrusts them to the mercy of God. According to *OCF* 164: 'The final commendation is a final farewell by the members of the community, an act of respect for one of their members, whom they entrust to the tender and merciful embrace of God. This act of last farewell also acknowledges the reality of separation and affirms that the community and the deceased, baptised into the one Body, share the same destiny, resurrection on the last day. On that day the one Shepherd will call each by name and gather the faithful together in the new and eternal Jerusalem.'

The final commendation is perhaps one of the most poignant moments of the whole funeral liturgy where the loss and grief of the mourners is once more acknowledged, and the mystery of Christian hope is once more proclaimed. The invitation to prayer (*OCF* 180) expresses this hope: 'Before we go our separate ways, let us take leave of our brother/sister. May our farewell express our affection for him/her; may it ease our sadness and strengthen our hope. One day we shall joyfully greet him/her again when the love of Christ, which conquers all things, destroys even death itself.'

One might expect that in the rite of committal a clear affirmation of what happens to the dead person might be clearly stated. The prayers of this rite again affirm that the one who has died sleeps here in peace awaiting the call of God. The prayer over the place of committal prays: 'Grant that our brother/sister may sleep here in peace, until you awaken him/her to glory, for you are the resurrection and the life. Then he/she will see you face to face and in your light will see light and know the splendour of God.'[7] Once again this rite is about the person who has died and those who are left behind. The act of committal is a stark moment in the funeral rite as the separation brought about by death is clear to all. As the person is now laid to rest, one kind of relationship comes to an end, in the hope that a new one can begin, based on 'prayerful remembrance, gratitude and the hope of resurrection and reunion' (*OCF* 216).

---

7   This seems to be at odds with the introduction to this rite at *OCF* 215: 'The rite of committal is an expression of the communion that exists between the Church on earth and the Church in heaven: the deceased passes with the farewell prayers of the community of believers into the welcoming company of those who need faith no longer but see God face to face.' The question concerns how soon the deceased enters the full presence of God.

In conclusion, the *OCF* affirms that those who have died will rise again on the last day, and that their death finds meaning and purpose in the Paschal Mystery of Christ. It affirms that the Christian community will one day be gathered into the heavenly assembly that celebrates the heavenly liturgy in the new Jerusalem. Beyond that, the rites and prayers do not speculate what, or indeed where, that risen life will be.

Questions for Reflection and Discussion

1. The General Introduction to the *OCF* notes: 'The Church calls each member of Christ's Body – priest, deacon, or layperson – to participate in the ministry of consolation: to care for the dying, to pray for the dead, to comfort those who mourn.' How have you seen this ministry of consolation at work, and is there more that could be done in your parish community?
2. Reflect on what a parish funeral team can offer for the bereaved at the time of a funeral, and what service of accompaniment can be provided by 'Bethany groups' for those who mourn in the months after the death of a loved one.
3. Do you agree that what we hope for beyond death impacts how we minister at the time of death and in the months after? Explain your response.
4. Are the links between the rites of baptism and those of the *OCF* understood and can they be enhanced?
5. How might a community celebrate the *OCF* when an ordained priest or deacon is not available to preside?

10: Children and Death

John-Paul Sheridan

Many years ago, and not long after I was ordained, I was called to a man who had collapsed on the street. By the time I got there, he had died. At this stage he was in the back of an ambulance and the paramedics let me in to say some prayers. As I approached the man, I could hear the doors slam behind me and I was left there alone with the deceased. Not having had much experience with the dead up till then, I was more than a little uneasy. However, I did what I had to, left, and the ambulance departed. Later, I gathered with the man's family in the morgue of the local hospital to pray with them. What I remember in particular about that evening was one of the man's grandchildren. For some strange reason, the man's arm kept slipping away from his chest where it lay, so the child took his late grandfather's hand and put it in his grandfather's jacket pocket, where it remained.

I've never forgotten the incident, the ease with which the child was able to approach the death of his grandfather, and the way this young child was able to normalise the situation about which I had been so uneasy earlier in the day. It is an example of what Rebecca Nye says when she suggests that adults 'be prepared to learn from children'.[1]

---

1   Quoted in Tony Eaude, 'Creating hospitable space to nurture children's spirituality – possibilities and dilemmas associated with power', *International Journal of Children's Spirituality* 19:3–4 (2014), 243.

In the many years of ministry since, I have often been struck by the way children have been present in the days that follow a death in the family and during the time of mourning and funerals. This comes from both personal and ministerial experience.

As adults it is easy for us to infantilise the child and suggest that this is no place for little ones. While this might be true in places like hospitals, where all the machinery might be a little scary and over-powering, it is certainly not true of a wake house, funeral home or church when the life of a loved one is being remembered and cherished by family and friends. It is right and proper that children should be present to remember and also to cherish. Researchers on children's participation in rituals after the loss of a parent or sibling found that all children interviewed were pleased that they had participated in the rituals, even the children who initially did not want to attend the wake. Furthermore, based on their own experiences, all of them recommended other children to take part in rituals when they came to lose someone close to them.[2]

The literature on children and death is vast. Much of it focuses on the psychology of children and the assistance needed in respect of death and the attendant trauma. However, here I want to focus on the spirituality of the child and where this might assist the child, using the writings of Robert Coles and others. Coles's work links the psychological and spiritual dimensions of childhood in the way children cope with the existential issues of their lives: sickness, death and loss.

This essay does not offer solutions to the challenges surrounding how children experience the death of a loved one, but I hope it will show parents and educators that, despite our reluctance to speak of the topic or to present children with the reality of death, like the young grandson at the beginning of this introduction, children can often have a more wholesome approach to death than we are prepared to give them credit for.

---

2   Gunn Helen Søfting, Atle Dyregrov and Kari Dyregrov, 'Because I'm also part of the family. Children's participation in rituals after the loss of a parent or sibling: a qualitative study from the children's perspective', *OMEGA – Journal of Death and Dying*, 73:2 (2016), 150.

Relationship and Children's Spirituality

The experience of death for any of us is a 'hard and bitter agony', to quote T. S. Eliot ('Journey of the Magi'), and it must be more so for children who may lack the ability to face death in a 'mature' way. Yet children's voices are often missing from debates around death as a taboo subject.[3] However, when faced with death, children are not always able to articulate their feelings. Sally Paul says that,

> What we know about children and death is mostly concerned with how children comprehend death and their experience of death when someone important dies. It is suggested that between the ages of 5 and 8, most children will have developed a mature understanding of death that includes grasping its irreversibility, non-functionality (i.e. the body is no longer operational) and causality (i.e. how people die) (Smith and Hunter, 2008). How children master these areas of knowledge is mostly informed by developmental psychology.[4]

The basis on which death might be a meaningful experience is relationship. 'Interpersonal relationships consequently play an important role in the development of the child's spirituality,' wrote Champagne,[5] and the work of Rebecca Nye bears this out. Within *relational consciousness* 'seems to lie the rudimentary core of children's spirituality, out of which can arise meaningful aesthetic experience, religious experience, personal and traditional responses to mystery and being,

---

3   Sally Paul, 'Is Death Taboo for Children? Developing Death Ambivalence as a Theoretical Framework to Understand Children's Relationship with Death, Dying and Bereavement', *Children and Society*, 33 (2019), 556–71.
4   Ibid., 557. Also D. E. Smith and S. B. Hunter, 'Predictors of children's understandings of death: age, cognitive ability, death experience and maternal communicative competence', *OMEGA-Journal of Death and Dying*, 57:2 (2008), 143–62.
5   Elaine Champagne, *Reconnaître la spiritualité des tout-petits [Recognizing the Spirituality of Toddlers]* (Ottawa: Novalis, 2005), 167.

and mystical and moral insight.'[6] Here I would add the experience of death.

Nye proposed six conditions that nurture relational consciousness in programmes of spiritual formation for children:

* space
* process
* imagination
* relationship
* intimacy
* trust.[7]

Space might be considered in terms of physical, emotional and auditory space. Process is favoured over end result, in that the journey the child takes is just as significant as the eventual destination. Nye says that imagination and creativity need to be encouraged in children in order for them to go deeper. Relationship is a condition because anything that an adult tries to teach a child is always coloured by the quality of the relationship between them. Intimacy is a condition because the exploration of the spiritual can bring both parent and child to some deep places. Finally, there is trust. As with intimacy, the bond that grows between the adult and the child can be such that words are shared that need never be repeated. For this to happen the child has to know that the adult is trustworthy.

Lytje and Dyregrov mention the inclusion of a child in discussion about a cancer diagnosis with parents: 'When we started to realise that now she needed treatment, we opened up about it. We told the children that mum has a disease called cancer. They should not hear that from someone else. We were aware that any information the children

6   Rebecca Nye, 'Identifying the Core of Children's Spirituality', in David Hay with Rebecca Nye, *The Spirit of the Child* (London: Jessica Kingsley, Revised Edition 2006), 109.
7   Rebecca Nye, *Children's Spirituality – What it is and why it matters* (London: Church House Publishing, 2009), 41ff.

received needed to come from us.'[8] This is an excellent indication of the importance of relationship and the trust that lies at the heart of it. The parent felt that it was crucial that the child heard the difficult news from their parent, from the person that they could trust. The parent would be there for them possibly to answer future questions, to be open and to be honest, rather than asking this of a minister of religion or a healthcare professional.

All of these six elements require a level of relationship for this nurturing to be successful. While Nye mentions relationship as one of the conditions, each of the other five is predicated on relationship. When that conversation is focused on the topic of death and a child's articulation of their thoughts and feelings, a trusting relationship is key. Conversely, when adults try to protect children from death, this can foster confusion, ignorance and a lack of trust.[9]

The insights of children can often be deeply spiritual and can take adults unawares. Without the language to express, the intimacy to share, and space to encounter, a child may lose the ability, so evident in early age, to connect with that which is spiritual within them.

Experience and Children's Spirituality
In his monumental *The Spiritual Life of Children*, psychiatrist and teacher Robert Coles tells how a chance encounter would lead to a lifetime's researching and writing about the lives of children.[10] Coles had intended to enter the world of psychoanalytic child psychology, until he witnessed the events surrounding the admission of Ruby Bridges to the Frantz School.[11] In 1954, the US Supreme Court ordered the end of 'separate but equal' education of African-Americans. On 14 November 1960, Ruby Bridges was the first African-American

8 Martin Lytje and Atle Dyregrov, 'When young children grieve: supporting daycare children following bereavement–a parent's perspective', *OMEGA – Journal of Death and Dying* (2021), 7. Epub ahead of print, https://doi.org/10.1177/0030222821997702.
9 Smith and Hunter, 'Predictors of children's understandings of death', 149, cited in Paul, 'Is Death Taboo for Children?', op. cit., 558.
10 Robert Coles, *The Spiritual Life of Children* (Boston, MA: Houghton Mifflin, 1990), xi.
11 Ruby Bridges, *Through My Eyes* (New York, NY: Scholastic Press, 1999).

child to be enrolled as part of the desegregation of the school system in Louisiana, when she attended the William Frantz Public School in New Orleans. Coles was passing the school one day and noticed Ruby being brought into the school under a hail of savage racial abuse. He offered his help as a psychiatrist to the NAACP (the National Association for the Advancement of Colored People) and began to interview Ruby and other children in similar circumstances.

Through his research, Coles began to be aware of the religious and spiritual aspect of things that children were saying and doing: a remark, a drawing or painting, a dream or nightmare. He had to address his assumptions about religion as a psychological phenomenon and as a social and historical force, and how religious practices and beliefs should be regarded.[12]

Coles interviewed children with a specific religious tradition and the children of atheists and agnostics about the following topics: God; the supernatural; the ultimate meaning of life; and the sacred side of things. His aim was to investigate the ways that children sift and sort spiritual matters. 'Children try to understand not only what is happening to them, but why; and in doing that, they call upon the religious life they have experienced, the spiritual values they have received, as well as other sources of potential explanation.'[13] Coles was unimpressed with the type of pieties taught to his children at Sunday school:

> There's religion and there's the spirit ... St. Paul talked about 'the letter and the spirit,' ... the teacher said you can go to church all the time and obey every [church] law, and you're not really right in what you do, you're not spiritual.' We asked him how we could know if we were being

---

12 Coles states that this is a subject that is posed provocatively in Sigmund Freud's *The Future of Illusion,* translated by W. D. Robson-Scott (Garden City, NY: Doubleday 1964).
13 Coles, op. cit., 100.

spiritual, not just religious, and he promptly said, 'It's up to God to decide, not us.'[14]

The focus of *The Spiritual Life of Children* was 'not so much on children as students or practitioners of this or that religion, but on children as soulful in ways they themselves reveal: young human beings profane as they can be one minute, but the next spiritual.'[15] Concerning his research, Coles states, 'it is a project that, finally, helped me see children as seekers, as young pilgrims well aware that life is a finite journey and as anxious to make sense of it as those of us who are farther along in the time allotted to us.'[16]

According to Machteld Reynaert, 'Children's spirituality is seen as the capacity children initially possess to search for meaning in their lives. Children's spirituality is embedded in everyday life, has influence over the life of the child, and shapes the child's way of being. But it is also important that this spirituality, possessed by the child, be nurtured and stimulated.'[17] This is a spirituality that can be seen through the lens of a particular religious affiliation or not, depending on the child's background. In answer to the quotation from Karl Rahner, 'It is possible to talk about God without being spiritual',[18] Hay suggests that 'it is also possible to be spiritual without talking about God …. It is important not to get caught in the assumption that spirituality can only be recognized by the use of a specialized religious language.'[19]

This spirituality is the child's capacity to search, and children will do this with enquiring minds. 'The understanding of children as innate spiritual beings is further solidified when children are thought of as active participants in their own spirituality, instead of passive

---

14 Ibid., xvii.
15 Ibid., xviii.
16 Ibid., xvi.
17 Machteld Reynaert, 'Pastoral Power in Nurturing the Spiritual Life of the Child', *International Journal of Children's Spirituality* 19:3–4 (2014), 179.
18 Karl Rahner, 'The experience of God today', *Theological Investigations XI*, trans. David Bourke (London: Darton, Longman & Todd, 1974), 149.
19 Hay with Nye, *The Spirit of the Child*, op. cit., 63.

recipients of knowledge about God.'[20] They are constantly seeking to understand the world around them and the experiences that they encounter. As their personal history unfolds, they come to realise who they are. 'Experience is that dimension in religion without which no other dimensions would have existed. The scarlet thread through the whole of the history of the church is nothing but a continuous process of experience and a continuous process of storytelling – a continuous narrative of a person's experience with God.'[21] Marthaler states that 'experience undergirds understanding. To define water in terms of its chemical components as H_2O does not give one an understanding of its importance to life. One appreciates water only when one drinks it, bathes, and watches a garden wither because of drought ... If there is no experience of church, of sacramental practice, of catechism, mere talk about them remains empty and distant.'[22] This would imply that for children to be able to talk about death and to form an understanding of it as a part of life, they should not be removed from it.

Coles's research shows that through conversation and reflection on their experience, children are capable of knowing a great deal and, in processing this information, can take a great deal of meaning from it. Any question concerning the religious or spiritual nature of the child came from the child's reflecting on, and asking questions about the meaning of life, the nature of death, and the world around them. The perspective and meaning-making of the child in one area leads to an understanding in another area. Goldman states that 'religious precepts and concepts are not based upon direct sensory data, but are formed from other perceptions and conceptions of experience ... there are no definite religious sensations and perceptions, separate from the child's other sensations and perceptions. Religious thinking is the process of generalizing from various experiences, previous perceptions and already

20 Heather Nicole Ingersoll, 'Making Room: A Place for Children's Spirituality in the Christian Church', *International Journal of Children's Spirituality* 19:3–4 (2014), 166.
21 Trond Enger, 'Religious Education between Psychology and Theology', *Religious Education* 87:3 (summer 1992), 435.
22 Berard Marthaler, 'Catechesis as Conversation', *The Living Light* 27/4 (summer 1991), 312.

held concepts to an interpretative concept of the activity and nature of the divine.'[23]

A shift in thinking may be needed on the part of parents and educators to value the conversations of children around death and other existential issues. Adults need to both trust and value the conversations of children. Reynaert states that adults 'are willing to listen to the experience of children, but they do not attach value to the experience of the children, or they do not examine the experience further because they do not know how they have to react to what the children tell. Adults are often afraid of a free exploration of children in the area of faith and therefore choose to keep everything under their control.'[24] Coles's wife had suggested that a good way to initiate research was 'to sit down with children … and then hope that they will become colleagues, instructors, guides'.[25] Anna Freud had told him, 'Let the children help you with their ideas on the subject.'[26] This method worked very well for Coles, and the proof is in the moving accounts of children's experiences in all his writings. One of the easiest ways to approach the topic of death with children is simply to sit and listen and let the child speak. We may not always agree with their ideas or their opinions, and we may seek to correct them, in the misguided understanding that we have all the 'correct' answers. As adults, we should restrain ourselves and let their voices be heard.

Since death is part of the reality of life, Chadwick suggests that we explain this reality. 'Fantasy is far more frightening than reality and a child who is told that he cannot see his dead relative or would find the funeral too upsetting will find his mind running wild, off into the realm of horror films. While it is not easy to take a child to see a

---

23   Ronald Goldman, *Religious Thinking from Childhood to Adolescence* (New York, NY: Seabury, 1968), 14.
24   Reynaert, 'Pastoral Power in Nurturing the Spiritual Life of the Child', art. cit., 181.
25   Robert Coles, *The Spiritual Life of Children* (Boston, MA: Houghton Mifflin, 1990), 35.
26   Ibid., xvi.

deceased relative or loved one before they are buried or cremated, it can be a valuable reassurance that death has occurred.'[27]

Speaking about death as a general topic with children might be a profound experience, but this might be difficult when speaking about death in the context of one's mortality. Here our relationship with death has at its heart the conflict between moving forward in life and moving towards death. It is difficult to contemplate children in situations where the end of their lives might be imminent. Inasmuch as we face this with others by our side, ultimately we face death as individuals. 'Fear of life arises when we move forward and become more individuated, but individuation arouses the threat of having to face life as an isolated being. This in turn arouses the threat of extinction and the loss of individuality by being dissolved again into the whole. It is this oscillation that causes the anxiety, as flipping the light on and off stirs anxiety on a more surface level.'[28] Coles spent a great deal of time with children who had come face to face with their own mortality, and this brought a profound level of response from the children. Most of us don't like the idea of children dealing with their death, but it is a reality that parents, doctors and nurses, and clinicians know only too well.

Jerome Berryman suggests that children do not fear death, and are more likely to fear things like animals, ghosts or darkness.[29] Carole Klein says that where uncertainty exists, fear exists. Furthermore, she says that 'the sense of physical and intellectual inadequacy that comes from being so small in a world that looms so large makes a child hostage to a host of fears – that all in some way relate to his overriding worry about becoming separated from the protective clasp of his

---

27 Ann Chadwick, *Talking About Death and Bereavement in School* (London: Jessica Kingsley, 2012), 48.
28 Jerome Berryman, 'Teaching as Presence and the Existential Curriculum', *Religious Education* 85/4 (fall 1990), 520.
29 Ibid., 519. Berryman refers to the work of Jersild in the 1930s. None of the 200 children under the age of nine, and only six out of the 200 between nine and twelve were afraid of getting ill or dying. A. Jersild and F. Holmes, *Children's Fears* (New York, NY: Teachers College, Columbia University, 1935).

parents'.[30] Klein tells the story of a girl who goes into hospital for an operation. After the operation, and while she is in recovery, she begins to take toys from the other children in the ward, during the night. The surgeon gets to the bottom of the problem, and he tells the little girl of a patient the previous week who thought that while she was in hospital her brothers and sisters would take her toys. 'I told her that lots of times children in hospitals worry about such things. They're even afraid that when they go home or back to school, people will have forgotten them altogether. I told her that this was just a kind of hospital worry, and that people would never forget who she was.'[31] The story is remarkable because the surgeon was able to articulate for the child what she couldn't articulate for herself. Notably, the child seemed not to be worried about illness or the surgery, but whether her siblings would take her 'stuff'.

Closing Thoughts
In speaking to children about death or helping them to speak about it in pastoral or educational spheres, relationships are of vital importance, and the need for the child to speak from their experience is the key to helping children negotiate and understand one of the hardest things in their young lives.

One of the children Coles interviewed said to him, 'We'll never know about God, until we die.'[32] It's a profound statement, coming from a limited knowledge, but not from a limited imagination. The child has the ability to handle only a certain amount of mystery but will embrace that mystery, seeking to find meaning and to comprehend something of the God who loves them. It is also true of death, and the mystery that lies therein. 'For children, even those quite healthy and never before seriously sick, death has a powerful and continuing meaning. They hear what their elders hear in sermons and stories, in

---

30 Carole Klein, *The Myth of the Happy Child* (New York, NY: 1975), 38.
31 Ibid., 33.
32 Coles, *The Spiritual Life of Children*, op. cit., 313.

songs, in scriptural warnings.'[33] Adults need to put aside their own fears and ambiguities around the subject of death and assist children in ways that will help them during the grieving time, and to have a healthy and natural attitude to the reality and regularity of death.

While in Ireland we are usually very good at including children in the rituals around death and dying, we are perhaps not always easy or comfortable articulating our own thoughts or responding to the questions and thoughts of children. Chadwick suggests that death and grief are not subjects that 'children are encouraged to address until it hits them, and when it does families want things tidied away as quickly as possible. I suggest that we put the subject on the curriculum, teaching it alongside the facts of life!'[34] This is where the work in the primary religious education programme can assist. In the primary school religious education programme for Catholic schools (*Grow in Love*), the children are introduced to the topic in First and Second Class in the context of the month of November, the traditional time of the year to remember those who have died. It affords an ideal place to talk about death in a manner that does not have the immediacy of a bereavement in the family or community. It also gives the children the ability to respond to death in prayer, and to remember all who have died from families, the school, the community and even the wider world. Communal prayer for the dead in the school community helps children to realise that they are not alone in the grief they feel for a loved one who has died. It helps them to reflect and respond in a prayerful way, while knowing about and appreciating the support of all their classmates. It helps them to realise that grief does not go away by forgetting about it or suppressing it, but that it will never be overwhelming when we express it. Most importantly, it validates their tears.[35] This type of work in school can only assist parents in what is a most difficult task. If the child has some experience around

---

33 Ibid., 109.
34 Chadwick, *Talking About Death and Bereavement in School*, op. cit., 15.
35 Ibid., 13.

the language of death – words, rituals, symbols etc., then it cannot but assist parents in including children at times of death.

Questions for Reflection and Discussion

1. What are your earliest memories of death and dying?
2. From a ministerial or familial point of view, what have been your experiences of children at the various stages of dying, death and ritual?
3. How would you begin to speak to children about dying and death?
4. How might you include children in the rituals around death?

Three: Facing Challenging Questions
11: Scriptural Perspectives on Our Mortality

Jeremy Corley

As I write this chapter in November, the leaves are falling from the trees. The weather this year has been mild, and so the autumn colours on the foliage have stayed for a long time. There have been some glorious days, with golden leaves remaining on the trees till they are now falling. In other years, when the weather is harsh, the leaves can sometimes fall almost overnight, with no great show of glory. Similarly, for human beings, some lives reach their end in a long and glorious old age, while others are suddenly cut short. The falling of the leaves in November reminds us of our human mortality, as nature prepares for the dead of winter, when everything seems lifeless and still. Perhaps it is no coincidence that the Church traditionally meditates on death and the dead in the month of November.

Thoughts of mortality, based on the falling of the leaves in autumn, go back at least as far as Homer, the father of Greek poetry, around the eighth century BC. In the *Iliad* (6:146–49), Glaucus declares: 'Like the generations of leaves, such are those of human beings. As for the leaves, the wind scatters some upon the earth, but the forest, as it burgeons, puts forth others when the season of spring has come. Even so, one generation of human beings springs up, and another passes away.'[1] Around 200 BC, the Book of Sirach makes a similar comparison of the human life cycle to the repeated sequence of leaves forming on trees and later falling from them: 'Like abundant leaves on a spreading tree, that sheds some and puts forth others, so are the generations of flesh and blood: one dies, and another is born' (Sirach 14:18).

Such imagery finds vivid expression in 'Spring and Fall', a poem composed in 1880 by a Jesuit writer, Gerard Manley Hopkins – himself buried in Dublin's Glasnevin Cemetery in 1889. The poem addresses a young girl named Margaret, who is feeling melancholy at the sight of golden leaves falling from the trees in autumn. In fact, she is being confronted with decay and, ultimately, death, represented by the falling foliage. As Hopkins realises, the girl is unconsciously mourning the gradual passing of her own life, which will end in mortality. Even though she is in the springtime of her life, she has some realisation that her life will eventually reach its own fall or autumn.

> Margaret, are you grieving,
> Over Goldengrove unleaving?
> Leaves, like the things of man, you
> With your fresh thoughts care for, can you?
> Ah! as the heart grows older
> It will come to such sights colder
> By and by, nor spare a sigh
> Though worlds of wanwood leafmeal lie;
> And yet you will weep and know why.
> Now no matter, child, the name:
> Sorrow's springs are the same.
> Nor mouth had, no nor mind, expressed
> What heart heard of, ghost guessed:

---

1   Adapted from A. T. Murray, *Homer: The Iliad*, vol. 1 (London: Heinemann, 1924), 273.
    Scripture quotations in this chapter are from the New Revised Standard Version (NRSV).

It is the blight man was born for,
It is Margaret you mourn for.[2]

The poem begins with Margaret grieving over the sight of golden trees losing their leaves as winter approaches. In her youth, she feels the melancholy with a fresh sharpness, but in subsequent autumns she will see whole forests losing their foliage without feeling the same sympathy. Nevertheless, loss is a universal human experience, and later griefs will have the same basic origin as her childish sadness, because in an intuitive way she is already grieving over her own mortality. Even though at her young age she cannot express the deep reason for her grief, nor even understand it, she has an instinctive feeling about it. In some profound way, she senses that all mourning ultimately refers to a person's own suffering of losses, which will culminate in death. Thus, this poignant poem depicts a young girl beginning to face up to the eventual end of her own life.

As we move from youth towards old age, there comes a time when we can no longer easily deny our mortality. For many people, old age brings a gradual decline in physical and mental capacities. After my father retired and was living alone, as he grew older, he would often refer to an Old Testament reading from Sirach, which is read at Mass on the Feast of the Holy Family just after Christmas. After reflecting on the commandment to honour one's parents, Sirach speaks of a parent's mental decline and senile dementia – a condition that my father feared might eventually happen to him. For Sirach, honouring parents includes taking care of them when they become frail (Sirach 3:12–14).

My child, help your father in his old age,
and do not grieve him as long as he lives.
Even if his mind fails, be patient with him;

---

2   W. H. Gardner (ed.), *Gerard Manley Hopkins: A Selection of his Poems and Prose* (Harmondsworth: Penguin, 1963), 50.

because you have all your faculties, do not despise him.
For kindness to a father will not be forgotten,
and will be credited to you against your sins.

As things turned out, in his very advanced old age, my father did indeed suffer from some memory loss and the beginnings of dementia. While my sister and brother and I tried to heed Sirach's admonition, the main care was provided by a well-run residential home where he spent the last few years of his life.

Death is the common fate of humanity, as Sirach notes: 'All living beings become old like a garment, for the decree from of old is: You will die!' (Sirach 14:17). From a scriptural perspective, the description of death as the 'decree from of old' alludes to God's warning to Adam and Eve that death will follow if they eat the forbidden fruit (Genesis 2:17; 3:19). Sirach warns readers to be ready for death and even be reconciled to it: 'Do not fear death's decree for you; remember those who went before you and those who will come after. This is the Lord's decree for all flesh; why then should you reject the will of the Most High?' (Sirach 41:3–4). Whereas a healthy person does not welcome death, someone suffering a severe illness may even long for it (Sirach 41:1–2). Paradoxically, the evil of death can appear good to a person with a poor quality of life.

The Book of Job offers poetry of unrivalled resonance and depth, even as it directly faces the question of human suffering and death. A recent document from the Pontifical Biblical Commission (*What is Man?*) surveys the book's poetic depictions of humanity as perishable and ephemeral: 'The life of the human being is like a breath (Job 7:7, 16), a flower of brief duration (Job 14:1–2), a fleeting shadow (Job 8:9; 14:2). A creature formed of clay and destined for the dust (Job 10:9), the human being goes towards death like a cloud that vanishes (Job 7:9).'[3] The document adds that 'suffering, the

---

3   Pontifical Biblical Commission, *What Is Man? A Journey Through Biblical Anthropology* (London: Darton, Longman & Todd, 2021), 38.

anticipation of death, forces one to confront one's own precariousness and, removing every illusion, places each one before a destiny essentially marked by the end'.[4]

As human beings, we know that our lives are marked by mortality. Indeed, the philosopher Martin Heidegger calls us 'beings towards death'.[5] Even when speaking of God's creation of humanity, Sirach mentions human mortality in the same breath: 'The Lord created human beings out of earth and makes them return to it again' (Sirach 17:1). The sage recalls God's sentence on sinful Adam in the Garden of Eden – a phrase often heard on Ash Wednesday: 'You are dust, and to dust you shall return' (Genesis 3:19). Human beings share mortality with other creatures, because 'all that is of earth returns to earth' (Sirach 40:11). Sirach is not afraid to speak bluntly of what happens after death: 'When one is dead, one inherits maggots and vermin and worms' (Sirach 10:11). In fact, many Old Testament books offer no clear hope of an individual afterlife but instead look forward to a shadowy kind of future existence in the underworld after death (Job 3:13–19).[6]

By way of contrast, the hope of human immortality appears in the Book of Wisdom, which was the last part of the Old Testament to be composed. Initially, Wisdom 2:1–3 presents the view of the unbeliever, who denies life after death: 'Short and sorrowful is our life, and there is no remedy when a life comes to its end, and no one has been known to return from Hades. For we were born by mere chance, and hereafter we shall be as though we had never been, for the breath in our nostrils is smoke, and reason is a spark kindled by the beating of our hearts. When it is extinguished, the body will turn to ashes, and the spirit will dissolve like empty air.'

Despite these common sentiments, sometimes found today, the Book of Wisdom promises immortal life to the faithful members of the people of Israel. Although the victims of suffering experienced

---

4   Ibid., 39.
5   Martin Heidegger, *Being and Time* (San Francisco, CA: Harper & Row, 1962), 260.
6   Jeremy Corley, 'Afterlife Hope Before the New Testament: A Descriptive Survey,' *Proceedings of the Irish Biblical Association* 41–42 (2018/2019), 1–22, at 3.

pains in this present life, 'their hope is full of immortality' (Wisdom 3:4). Rather than expecting merely a shadowy future existence, the author speaks of the hope of a glorious future life with God. While recognising that earthly life can be unjust and cruel, the Book of Wisdom expresses faith that the God of justice will reward the virtuous in the afterlife: 'Having been disciplined a little, they will receive great good, because God tested them and found them worthy of himself. Like gold in the furnace he tried them, and like a sacrificial burnt-offering he accepted them' (Wisdom 3:5–6). This passage can be consoling at the funeral of someone who suffered a difficult or painful death, because it expresses the hope that the suffering previously undergone is now overturned, when the deceased receives an eternal reward.

The hope of a happy afterlife, strongly affirmed in the New Testament, comes from Jesus' resurrection, even though the way to heaven can be difficult and challenging. John's Gospel offers us especially helpful wisdom on facing life's end. Indeed, some features of this gospel suggest that the author was writing from a perspective of old age. Valuable insights are given in the lives of both John the Baptist and Peter, as well as Jesus himself.

Near the beginning of the gospel, we read how John the Baptist prepared the way for Jesus' coming. Once Jesus has begun his ministry, John the Baptist realises that his role is complete, stating: 'He must increase, but I must decrease' (John 3:30). Although John the Baptist presents himself as the bridegroom's friend (John 3:29), bringing Jesus to his 'bride' – the faithful ones in Israel – we can reapply his statement to the changeover from an older to a younger generation. Grandparents looking at their children and grandchildren can recognise that the younger generation will take over positions of responsibility, while the grandparents themselves will retire from the limelight. In the order of nature, there is a time for a person to grow and increase, but there is also a time to diminish and decrease when one's role in life moves towards completion. The grandchildren will increase, while the grandparents will decrease. John the Baptist's readiness to relinquish his position can offer us a role model in being willing to let go at the appropriate time.

If we turn to the conclusion of John's Gospel, we see Simon Peter being warned of the need to let go at the end of his life. In fact, beside the Sea of Galilee, the risen Jesus prepares Simon Peter for his eventual death as a martyr: 'Very truly, I tell you, when you were younger, you used to fasten your own belt and to go wherever you wished. But when you grow old, you will stretch out your hands, and someone else will fasten a belt around you and take you where you do not wish to go' (John 21:18). These words point to Nero's persecution in Rome, when, according to tradition, the apostle was taken away to be executed. But we can find a lesser parallel in the way that many elderly persons also undergo the experience of being taken off somewhere unfamiliar and even unwelcome. As their health declines, they may have the experience of someone else putting a coat or blanket around them and taking them where they do not wish to go – perhaps to a care home or a hospital. Hence Peter's courageous acceptance of his fate can potentially serve as a model for us.

Most dramatically, we find wisdom for facing life's end in the pattern of Jesus' life and death. John's Gospel suggests that Jesus traces a pattern of *exitus* and *reditus* – going out from the Father and then returning to him. St Thomas Aquinas often employs this overarching pattern of *exitus* and *reditus*.[7] While this double movement is evident in all creation, it can particularly be seen in Christ within his earthly incarnation and heavenly return, and thereafter in the lives of each one of us. The first half of John's Gospel (the Book of Signs) depicts the incarnate Christ's outward journey into the world, while the second half (the Book of Glory) describes his return to the Father who sent him.[8] At the end of the Last Supper discourse, Jesus explains both these movements to his disciples: 'I came from the Father and

---

7   M. D. Chenu, 'The Plan of St. Thomas' Summa Theologiae', *CrossCurrents* 2:2 (1952), 67–79, at 70–72; Gaven Kerr, *Aquinas and the Metaphysics of Creation* (Oxford: Oxford University Press, 2019), 224.

8   Raymond E. Brown, *The Gospel according to John I–XII* (London: Chapman, 1966), cxxxviii.

have come into the world. Now I am leaving the world and am going to the Father' (John 16:28). The two movements – going forth from God and then returning to God – shape the pattern of our own lives also, and hence we are invited to walk this path with Jesus.

The Book of Glory (the second half of John's Gospel) begins with the Last Supper, which marks the closing stage in Jesus' mission: 'Now before the festival of the Passover, Jesus knew that his hour had come to depart from this world and go to the Father' (John 13:1). We can learn clear-sighted courage from the way Jesus squarely faced the end of his earthly life. Rather than clinging to his own life, he looks ahead positively to the future for his disciples without his physical presence. He tells them that after he has gone, they will do great things, precisely because he is going to the Father (John 14:12). Naturally, Jesus' concern is that those he leaves behind will continue to love each other, just as a dying person today will be concerned that when he or she is gone, the family members will not fall out but will remain united in harmony. Hence, at the conclusion of the Johannine farewell discourse, Jesus prays for the unity of his disciples.

Building on John's Gospel, Pope John Paul II taught that Christ united himself in some way to each human being as a pilgrim, journeying with us in our personal life story. In a Palm Sunday homily, he quoted Jesus' words about coming from the Father and returning to the Father (John 16:28), before suggesting that every human being is called to make the same pilgrimage in union with Christ.[9] Pope John Paul echoed the Second Vatican Council document *Gaudium et Spes* (22), which tells us that by suffering for us, Christ 'not only provided us with an example for our imitation, but he also blazed a trail, and if we follow it, life and death are made holy and take on a new meaning'.[10] The document adds: 'Through Christ and in Christ, the riddles

9   Pope John Paul II, *Palm Sunday Homily for the Diocesan Celebration of the 10th World Youth Day*, 9 April 1995, St Peter's Square, Vatican City, https://www.vatican.va/content/john-paul-ii /it/homilies/1995/documents/hf_jp-ii_hom_19950409_domenica-palme.html.
10   Second Vatican Council, *Gaudium et Spes* (1965), is available online, https://www.vatican.va /archive/hist_councils/ii_vatican_council/documents/vat-ii_const_19651207_gaudium-et-spes _en.html.

of sorrow and death grow meaningful. Apart from his Gospel, they overwhelm us. But Christ has risen, destroying death by his death, and he has lavished life upon us.'

For those who believe, the great hope when facing death comes in the promise of the resurrection. A rich expression of resurrection faith appears in a late poem by Gerard Manley Hopkins, 'That Nature is a Heraclitean Fire and of the Comfort of the Resurrection'. Composed in 1888, the year before the poet's death, this complex work reflects on human mortality in the context of the decaying beauty of the natural world.

Just as the biblical Ecclesiastes declares that 'all is vanity' because everything changes (Ecclesiastes 1:2), so Hopkins begins his poem by contemplating the clouds that are constantly changing shape. Similarly, the Greek philosopher Heraclitus emphasises that everything is in flux (Plato, *Theaetetus*, 182c). According to another work of Plato, Socrates recalls the view of Heraclitus that 'all things move, and nothing remains still, and he likens the universe to the current of a river, saying that you cannot step twice into the same stream' (Plato, *Cratylus*, 402a).[11] Such reflections can lead us to think that in the grand scheme of the universe's history, nothing is permanent, and hence an individual person's lifespan may have little importance. With such thoughts, Hopkins becomes dejected from contemplating change at work in natural processes.

> Million-fuelèd, | nature's bonfire burns on.
> But quench her bonniest, dearest | to her,
> her clearest-selvèd spark
> Man, how fast his firedint, | his mark on mind, is gone!
> Both are in an unfathomable, all is in an enormous dark
> Drowned. O pity and indig- | nation! Manshape,
> that shone

---

11   Harold N. Fowler, *Plato, vol. 4: Cratylus, Parmenides, Greater Hippias, Lesser Hippias* (London: Heinemann, 1921), 67.

Sheer off, disseveral, a star, | death blots
black out; nor mark
Is any of him at all so stark
But vastness blurs, and time | beats level.[12]

The poet sees that the human lifespan is insignificant, because we, like other earthly creatures, are destined to be 'drowned' in darkness. A person who once shone as brightly as a star will be quenched, like a candle being extinguished. Yet, while musing in the depths of his dejection, the poet is suddenly lifted up by the hope of the resurrection. With this realisation, Hopkins can now accept the mortal destruction of his body, because he knows that, through rising again, he will become what Christ is. Whereas an ordinary human being is destined to become dust and ashes, in the resurrection a person is 'immortal diamond' – eternally solid and impervious to change and decay.

Enough! the Resurrection,
A heart's-clarion! Away grief's gasping, |
joyless days, dejection.
Across my foundering deck shone
A beacon, an eternal beam. | Flesh fade, and mortal trash
Fall to the residuary worm; | world's wildfire,
leave but ash:
In a flash, at a trumpet crash,
I am all at once what Christ is, |
since he was what I am, and
This Jack, joke, poor potsherd, | patch,
matchwood, immortal diamond,
Is immortal diamond.[13]

---

12 Gardner, op. cit., 66.
13 Ibid.

Questions for Reflection and Discussion

1. To what extent does Hopkins' poem 'Spring and Fall' resonate with you?

2. Reflect on your experience if you have had to care for a relative or friend suffering mental decline or senile dementia.

3. The Book of Job compares our human life to a fleeting shadow (Job 8:9; 14:2). Does this comparison offer us any insight for how we live out our days on earth?

4. Realising that his role is complete, John the Baptist says of Christ: 'He must increase, but I must decrease' (John 3:30). How far are we able to let go of our own position and status when the time comes for us to do so?

5. By suffering for us, Christ 'not only provided us with an example for our imitation, but he also blazed a trail, and if we follow it, life and death are made holy and take on a new meaning' (*Gaudium et Spes*, 22). How far do we receive encouragement from Christ's sharing of our human journey through life to death (and beyond)?

6. To what extent does the hope of the resurrection offer inspiration to you personally?

12: Perinatal Death: Complex and Nuanced Life, Love and Loss

Daniel Nuzum

Pregnancy, by its very nature, is a journey of new life, new hope and a future. Happily, for the vast majority of parents pregnancy is a joyful experience, where a new baby is awaited with anticipation. As pregnancy comes to a close, the focus turns to the imminent birth of this new member of a family and a new journey begins. During the gestation of pregnancy a new life is nurtured within, as a baby develops and matures incrementally in preparation for birth. It is fair to say that most parents become 'parents' long before the birth of their baby and, likewise, most parents can describe a sense of relationship and of knowing their baby long before he or she is born. This parental-foetal bond is an extraordinarily visceral reality and holds within it something that is truly mystical and physical, intangible and tangible at the same time. The bonds of attachment are laid down from the earliest moments of pregnancy for both parents. In addition to the known physical influences on a baby *in utero* that can impact their future lives, the bonds of attachment weave an intricate web of connectedness between a parent and baby at each stage of pregnancy and remain long into the future.

No parent anticipates having to have a conversation about uncertainty or death when they embark on the journey of pregnancy. It is a sad reality, despite considerable advances in recent decades in modern obstetric medicine, midwifery care and scientific techniques, that some babies will not survive pregnancy. There is a number of reasons why this is so, and modern diagnostic techniques can identify many conditions long before a baby is born. Access to anomaly ultrasound screening is almost universal in the developed world and is in many ways one of the milestones of pregnancy. The diagnosis of a foetal anomaly presents parents and clinicians with complex challenges touching on the very essence of life and death. The use of a phrase such as 'foetal anomaly' fails to capture the depth of the human reality of bewildering loss accompanied by the burden of decision-making for all involved. Foetal anomaly carries within it a blend of uncertainty and certainty in terms of the breadth and complexity of prognosis and lethality that brings a family into an unstable reality concerning the future of their baby.

The bonds of attachment, accompanied by the investment of love and hope for this new baby, grow incrementally through pregnancy, as parents prepare for the time of birth when their hoped-for baby will emerge from the security of the maternal *in utero* home. Anticipatory preparation is realised as parents plan for the introduction of this new baby into their lives and family structure. A 'life map' is sketched out into the future where this new baby will take her or his place. It is into this scene of attachment and anticipation that a diagnosis of life-limiting uncertainty or a stillbirth intrude as the most unwelcome of guests. The high emotion of love and anticipation is ruptured by this devastating news and supplanted by the painfully low emotion of pain, devastation and uncertainty. Hope is replaced by grief, and love is enveloped by loss.

Birth and death are two of life's most significant events. Each on its own carries significant emotional and physical impact. However, in perinatal death, these two hugely significant life events collide, with long-lasting impact for all concerned. The lived experience of parents as they come to terms with the loss of hope, life and dreams brings grief and attachment theory into a painful reality. There remains a silence around pregnancy and reproductive loss in wider society and still today there remains a social awkwardness in finding quite the right language to describe, much less to empathise. This is part of a much longer narrative to which we shall briefly turn.

There has been a well-documented and distressing history of silence and isolation in our Irish history when it comes to pregnancy and infant loss. For too long the experiences of parents were silent, as were their stories of grief and pain. This silence and lack of acknowledgement was reinforced in civil and religious structures and resulted in a paternalistic and dismissive approach to the sheer enormity of perinatal death. There are well-documented stories of parents burying their baby in the darkness of night and outside consecrated ground. The existence of so many burial sites (*cillíní*) for infants who died before birth is an expansive map of grief and memory on our Irish cultural and religious landscape and cartography, where we were otherwise lauded for our healthy and community approach to death and grief. The supportive processes, traditions and rituals that we were well known for were markedly absent when it came to the loss of a pregnancy or the death of a baby. The existence of these burial places and the efforts to create and mark them highlights the importance that parents placed on this loss, and the natural and instinctual desire to 'do the right thing' in the honour and care of a baby who had died. These *cillíní* are testament to enduring love and the importance of life.

The lack of public or societal recognition of pregnancy and infant loss created a *de facto* invisibility of these short lives. This was manifest in the lack of civil registration, and thereby legal recognition, and also the denial of religious ceremony in many cases. Despite recent developments in civil legislation with the introduction in 1994 of the Stillbirths Registration Act,[1] and religious acknowledgement by the main churches, the experiences of many older parents continues to cast a long shadow where words like 'limbo' – although no longer used in

---

1   Office of the Attorney General, Oireachtas na hÉireann, *Stillbirths Registration Act 1994* (Dublin: Government Stationery Office, 1994).

religious association – continue to bear emotional and spiritual weight. The work and campaigning of bereaved parents and support organisations has in no small part influenced public thinking in this area to assist us as a society in acknowledging the importance of perinatal loss. As up to one-in-four pregnancies will result in loss, this is something that affects all communities and society at large. Pregnancy loss remains the most common adverse outcome in all pregnancies.

Despite the high incidence of pregnancy loss, nonetheless it remains a relatively silent area in public discourse. This contributes to the experience that many parents describe as a 'silent grief'. When parents receive the unwelcome news of a miscarriage or stillbirth, it is not uncommon for them to say: 'We never knew this could happen.' Often, it is only then that parents become aware of just how prevalent the experience of pregnancy loss is. This lack of discourse shrouds pregnancy loss in a way that can limit opportunities to seek or to offer support. Bereaved parents have in many cases not disclosed that they are pregnant and then endure their loss in silence and isolation in families, communities and the workplace. This is a disenfranchised loss on many levels. A further dimension of silence and isolation exists when the nature of the pregnancy or a diagnosis that poses challenging ethical decisions becomes apparent to parents. It is into this difficult ethical landscape we now venture.

The diagnosis of a life-limiting foetal anomaly brings with it considerable ethical burden for both parents and clinicians. This unwelcome news brings with it a dimension of crisis, where decisions of care can be heavily burdened. These situations are further compounded by the pressure of timing for all concerned. Terminology is laden with conflicting meaning, and phrases such as 'fatal foetal anomaly' or 'life-limiting condition' are understood in differing ways by parents as they come to terms with the reality of the impending loss of their pregnancy or the death of their baby during pregnancy or shortly after birth. For the purposes of this chapter the terms are used interchangeably.

The most challenging reality for parents, and those who care for them and their baby, is having to make decisions following a diagnosis that a baby is unlikely to survive. These decisions are challenging and complex personally, professionally and ethically; they require a robust engagement alongside emotional distress.[2] The ethical reality is that while the interests of a mother and her baby are intertwined and interdependent, as pregnancy progresses towards the point of viability outside the womb the life of a baby takes on an increasing ethical independence. The point of viability is now widely accepted as being from twenty-two weeks – although the legal point of viability implicit in Irish legislation is at twenty-four weeks and/or five hundred grammes weight.[3]

The right to life and value of life is the predominant ethical value in these situations. All care provided in these situations should be informed by the ethical principles of beneficence and non-maleficence, focused on the primacy of the value of life and the highest standard of comfort and care for a baby and the baby's family. Parents may well be presented with difficult choices if the diagnosis for their baby comes within the legislated and permitted provision of termination of pregnancy.[4] For others, the legislation will not provide this option should there be a level of uncertainty concerning lethality of a particular diagnosis. In both situations parents are faced with one of the most difficult choices they will ever make. Some parents see the termination of a much-wanted pregnancy as the most loving and compassionate care for their baby, because it minimises inevitable suffering alongside inevitable death. In their perspective this seems the ethically appropriate decision. Others will decide to continue with a pregnancy as the only appropriate ethical decision for them to honour their baby's life. As is perhaps becoming clear, these are rarely black-and-white decisions but are, rather, more nuanced and heart-wrenching, and distressing shades of grey. The role of healthcare

---

2   O. O'Connell, S. Meaney and K. O'Donoghue, 'Anencephaly: the maternal experience of continuing with the pregnancy. Incompatible with life but not with love', *Midwifery* 71 (2019), 12–18, https://www.ncbi.nlm.nih.gov/pubmed/30640134.

3   Stillbirths Registration Act 1994.

4   Keelin O'Donoghue, *Pathway for management of fatal fetal anomalies and/or life-limiting conditions diagnosed during pregnancy* (Dublin: Health Service Executive, 2019).

professionals is to provide open and non-directive information and support for parents as they consider very difficult options.

Ethically some clinicians and designated healthcare professionals (in accordance with professional codes of practice and conscientious objection procedures) may choose not to be actively involved in the active termination procedure in such situations. However, following the procedure, healthcare professionals must always continue to care for a baby and the baby's parents regardless of the circumstances of the loss. Pastorally, sensitivity and compassion are key dimensions of the care and approach where existential questions are explored by parents. The autonomy of parental decision-making should be respected in a judgement-aware way by staff.

In all cases a perinatal palliative care approach needs to be adopted. Perinatal palliative care is 'an active and total approach to care, from the point of diagnosis or recognition, throughout the child's life, death, and beyond', which 'embraces physical, emotional, social and spiritual elements' and includes 'care through death and bereavement'.[5]

The perinatal palliative care approach seeks to honour the life of the baby and the baby's family and to care for them in a way that provides the highest standards of care from all healthcare professionals. Every baby deserves the highest level of compassionate and professional care, and this applies whether a parent makes the difficult decision to expedite birth or to continue a pregnancy. A compassionate and professional approach from the pastoral care team is also needed towards a parent who takes the difficult decision to terminate a pregnancy.[6] In Ireland we have developed a comprehensive approach and skills set in providing care for babies and parents over many decades when continuing a pregnancy was the only available option except when a mother's life was in immediate danger. The principles

5   Áine Ni Laoire, Daniel Nuzum, Maeve O'Reilly, Marie Twomey, Keelin O'Donoghue and Mary Devins, 'Perinatal palliative care', in Richard Hain, Ann Goldman, Adam Rapoport, Michelle Meiring (eds), *Oxford Textbook of Palliative Care for Children* (3rd ed.), (Oxford: Oxford University Press, 2021), 325–31.
6   See O'Donoghue, *Pathway*, op. cit., as well as the Guidelines from the Institute of Obstetricians and Gynaecologists of the Royal College of Physicians of Ireland.

of perinatal palliative care provide a comprehensive approach to care and allow parents and families to prepare for what is inevitable loss. This approach also allows for important and protective anticipatory grief work to begin from the moment of diagnosis. The creation of memories, opportunities to mark milestones, and to prepare for birth and death are well recognised in the published literature to help families to adjust to the reality of this loss. This is prospective grieving that will most likely continue with parents for the rest of their lives.

A greater awareness of the complexity of the decisions faced by parents and clinicians in this very difficult area will help society at large to approach this particular loss with increased compassion and sensitivity. This requires a greater attention to language, alongside a more robust ethical and moral engagement with the clinical and human reality of what is commonly misunderstood as 'choice'. There is more to be done in this area for ethicists, healthcare professionals and religious communities to engage with the ethical nuances of perinatal loss while remaining faithful to unnegotiable ethical values concerning the right to life and the dignity of the human person. The contested complexities of this are acknowledged here.

In addition to the obvious impact on parents and families, perinatal death also impacts on healthcare professionals who provide care in these challenging situations.[7] Healthcare professionals working in the maternity services are faced with the challenges associated with the diagnosis and breaking of devastating news to expectant parents when a loss occurs. The presence of staff in large numbers at services of remembrance alongside bereaved parents and families is but one expression of the depth of compassion and shared grief experienced

---

7   K. McNamara, S. Meaney, O. O'Connell, M. McCarthy, R. A. Greene and K. O'Donoghue, 'Healthcare professionals' response to intrapartum death: a cross-sectional study', *Archives of Gynecology and Obstetrics* 295/4 (2017), 845–52, https://www.ncbi.nlm.nih.gov/pubmed /28210863; D. Nuzum, S. Meaney, K. O'Donoghue and H. Morris, 'The Spiritual and Theological Issues Raised by Stillbirth for Healthcare Chaplains', *Journal of Pastoral Care & Counseling* 69/3 (2015), 163–70, http://pcc.sagepub.com/content/69/3/163; D. Nuzum, S. Meaney and K. O'Donoghue, 'The impact of stillbirth on consultant obstetrician gynaecologists: a qualitative study', *BJOG: An International Journal of Obstetrics & Gynaecology* 121/8 (2014): 1020–28, http://www.ncbi.nlm.nih.gov/pubmed/24589177.

by healthcare professionals. These professionals have often accompanied parents for a number of years through pregnancies. The published literature, including a number of Irish studies, have documented the many dimensions of loss and burden, both personal and professional, for healthcare staff. In effect it is a grieving too. Much work has been done in recent years to acknowledge and respond to these burdens, but the reality remains that there is more to do to support our staff colleagues structurally and individually. The National Standards for Bereavement Care following Pregnancy Loss and Perinatal Death (2016) outline the importance of staff support and care in this challenging area.[8]

It is encouraging to see that pregnancy loss has been brought more into the foreground in recent years and many areas of quiet and compassionate care have thereby become recognised for their important role. The care of parents and their babies by bereavement and pregnancy loss teams – including midwives, obstetricians, pastoral carers/chaplains, social workers and pathology staff, to name but a few – has made a considerably positive impact on the grief and recovery of families. The provision of the first ever National Standards for Bereavement Care following Pregnancy Loss and Perinatal Death in 2016 arose from well-publicised and distressing reports of sub-optimal care in perinatal bereavement. These standards have been implemented in all nineteen maternity units in the Republic of Ireland and provide a major benchmark of care in this area. It is also important to recognise the influential and significant role of bereavement support and advocacy groups to raise the importance of perinatal death in wider society, in addition to their invaluable support to bereaved families.

The increased provision of pastoral resources and training for religious and philosophical communities and leaders has provided comfort and acknowledgement of this loss alongside a public recognition of the value of every life. This has included the regular provision of

---

8   Health Service Executive, *National Standards for Bereavement Care following Pregnancy Loss and Perinatal Death* (Dublin: HSE, 2016).

ceremonies of blessing and naming alongside some sensitive provision of appropriate liturgies and ritual to mark pregnancy and infant loss. From a bereavement perspective, these actions provide much-needed expression for families in their grieving process as well as honouring the lives of those who have died. For example, the provision of a blessing or naming certificate takes on a particular importance for babies who die before the legal point of viability according to the Stillbirths Registration Act. For these babies a blessing or naming certificate becomes de facto the only formal recognition of the existence and thereby the importance of this short but significant life. In this regard, the pastoral response of healthcare chaplains to recognise, celebrate and honour these babies born before twenty- four weeks' gestation is ahead of the legal provision and captures the reality of the significance of this loss. There is ongoing work still to be done in the review of legislation concerning late miscarriage and stillbirth definitions, and legal recognition of earlier loss.

Ireland has a recognised place in the global research arena into pregnancy loss scientifically, emotionally, spiritually and socially, and this is spearheaded in no small part by the Pregnancy Loss Research Group at University College Cork and Cork University Maternity Hospital, led by Professor Keelin O'Donoghue. This research team holds the care of babies and their families at the core of all work. Of significance is the integration of the multidimensional reality and understanding of pregnancy and infant loss where medical science, obstetrics, midwifery, spiritual care, emotional care, family care and policy development work together alongside global colleagues to reduce preventable pregnancy loss and improve experiences of care for all babies and families. The promotion of this work serves to provide evidence-based information for all healthcare professionals and members of the public through a website: www.pregnancyandinfantloss.ie.

In bringing this chapter to a close, it is fair to assume that the reader will know at least one and probably many more close family members/friends/colleagues who have experienced pregnancy or infant loss. Indeed, you may have experienced this loss yourself and may have carried this grief silently. The experience of a relative or friend may have been kept private and may not be known to others. Perhaps you were aware but felt unable or unwilling to mention it – usually for the kind reason of not wanting to make a difficult situation worse. Generally the worst has already happened, and so a kind word or gesture cannot make it worse. Initiating a conversation or gesture of support following pregnancy loss can make a difference to a grieving parent who may be struggling alone. In addition, the Pregnancy and Infant Loss website has a section offering information about support services: http://pregnancyand.wpengine.com/support-zone/.

It is hoped that this chapter has opened up some of the complexities of this loss and in so doing contributes to a more open conversation on matters so tender and personal, yet ethically complex. The aim is to help us to continue to provide the best possible care, to acknowledge this particular loss and to dispel some of the silence when words fail us.

Questions for Reflection and Discussion

1. Have any of these sensitive issues impacted you personally?
2. Have you any experience of assisting those who have suffered perinatal loss?
3. Pregnancy loss has often been called a 'silent grief'. In which contexts is it helpful to speak about stillbirth and pregnancy loss, and in which contexts is it better not to disturb people's grief?
4. Are there ways that friends or family members can sensitively offer support to a grieving parent who has experienced pregnancy loss?

Figure 1 www.pregnancyandinfantloss.ie

13: The Role of Prudential Judgements in End-of-Life Decision-Making

Pádraig Corkery

I n May 2021 the *Irish Times* carried a report on a High Court decision concerning the care of a young woman who was in a persistent vegetative state (PVS) for almost ten years. In particular, the order of the court was that the artificial life support, including artificial feeding/nutrition, be withdrawn so that she could die a natural death.[1] The decision of the court was tearfully welcomed by the young woman's mother and extended family. At the same time there was considerable discussion in the letter pages of the daily newspapers, the national airwaves and academic journals on the Dying with Dignity 2020 bill introduced in the Dáil by Mr Gino Kenny TD.[2]

Questions surrounding our obligation to sustain human life – both our own and those in our care – are not new. They have been raised and engaged with for centuries, both within the great religious traditions and civil society. The Roman Catholic tradition has a long and distinguished legacy of caring for the sick and dying. Catholic religious sisters, in particular, contributed generously to the establishment of

---

1 Mary Carolan, 'Court rules that life support can be withdrawn from woman', *Irish Times*, 10 May 2021.
2 See for example the summer 2021 issue of *Studies* ('Dying with Dignity: Ireland and Euthanasia'), and D. Vincent Twomey, 'Is Assisted Suicide the Compassionate Response?', *The Furrow* 72 (May 2021), 296–300.

quality healthcare across the globe. Accompanying this practical service to the sick and dying was a body of reflection and ethical guidelines that both set out the theological foundations of a Christian response to death and dying and also engaged with ethical dilemmas as they arose in hospitals, hospices and care homes.[3]

The Catholic tradition's approach to the care of the sick and dying is rooted in the example of Christ in the Gospel and a Christian anthropology. The example of Christ invites disciples 'to do likewise' (Luke 10:37); to comfort and care for all and, especially, those who are vulnerable or on the margins of society, either through age, poverty, persecution or sickness. A Christian anthropology reminds us of, amongst other things, our origin and destiny in God and our nature as daughters and sons of God created in the divine image. Though illness, suffering and death are part of who we are, they are experienced by the believer through the lens of resurrection hope – the ultimate triumph of life over death and light over darkness. A resurrection faith does not deny or downplay the significance of suffering, grief or death, but does enable the person of faith to experience them through the prism of Christian hope.

The case mentioned at the beginning of the article, and the debate in Ireland and across the globe on euthanasia, arise from the complexity of medical care and the ability of modern life-sustaining interventions to preserve life for many years. This has given rise to fears about the denial of a 'natural' death and the unwarranted prolongation of the dying process. It also raises, with renewed urgency, 'old' questions concerning the purpose of life and the meaning of suffering. How does the Catholic tradition approach these important pastoral and personal issues? Are we obliged to use *all* the interventions available to sustain life? Is the purpose of life to be measured in terms of longevity or in relational terms? This short chapter will highlight the theological

---

3   See the latest contribution from the Congregation for the Doctrine of the Faith to the corpus of Catholic teaching on life issues, *Samaritanus Bonus: On the Care of Persons in the critical and terminal phases of life*, https://www.vatican.va/roman_curia/congregations/cfaith/documents/rc _con_cfaith_doc_20200714_samaritanus-bonus_en.html.

framework and key criteria proposed by the Church in its teaching documents to approach such questions. It will also highlight the decisive role given in the tradition to the individual in making healthcare decisions about their own lives. Though the tradition provides a theological and ethical framework for healthcare decisions, the individual has to *apply* that framework and those criteria to the particularities of their life. This demands a prudential judgement on the part of the individual or, if the sick person lacks the capacity to decide, those responsible for their care.

Theological Tradition

The theological tradition has consistently argued that we are *not* obliged to go to extraordinary or disproportionate lengths to prolong our lives or the lives of those in our care. This is reflected in the lived philosophy and attitudes of countless believers as they engage with the reality of illness and mortality. In a recent publication, for example, Arturo Sosa SJ, Superior General of the Jesuits, stated that 'Jesuits often decide that they wish to die in peace without artificial life support', and that 'a clear distinction must be made between euthanasia and the unnecessary prolongation of life through artificial means.'[4] The Magisterium has argued in the *Catechism of the Catholic Church*, *Evangelium Vitae* and elsewhere that we are only obliged to avail of interventions that are ordinary or proportionate.[5] For instance, the Catechism says: 'Discontinuing medical procedures that are burdensome, dangerous, extraordinary or disproportionate to the expected outcome can be legitimate: it is the refusal of 'overzealous' treatment. Here one does not will to cause death: one's inability to impede it is merely accepted' (*CCC*, 2278). The refusal of 'overzealous' treatments is, furthermore, distinguished from suicide or neglect of one's well-being.[6] The foundation of this approach is to be found, firstly, in

---

4   Arturo Sosa, *Walking with Ignatius: In Conversation with Dario Menor* (Dublin: Messenger Publications, 2021), 137.
5   *Catechism of the Catholic Church*, 2278; *Evangelium Vitae*, 65.
6   See also *Samaritanus Bonus*, Section 5 [The Teaching of the Magisterium], paragraph 2, on the moral obligation to exclude aggressive medical treatment.

an acceptance of the 'naturalness' of death and, secondly, in a Christian hope that death is not annihilation but a return to God, who is our origin and destiny.

But *how* do we decide what is 'ordinary' treatment and hence morally obligatory? Or 'extraordinary' and 'disproportionate' and hence morally optional? And, as importantly, *who* decides – the individual, family, medical profession or courts? These are the questions that many individuals and societies have grappled with over the past few decades. Such questions lie at the centre of the human drama, mentioned in the opening paragraph, played out in the Irish courts and reported in the *Irish Times* and elsewhere.[7]

The How *Question*

The tradition used two criteria to aid in decision-making: *burden* and *benefit*. What is the anticipated benefit of a particular medical intervention and what are the burdens that may accompany the intervention? The theological tradition, books on medical ethics and the magisterium recognised, of course, that these terms are imprecise and need to be unpacked. The 1980 *Declaration on Euthanasia*, for example, having accepted the traditional moral framework of ordinary/extraordinary treatment, set out criteria to enable people to make a prudential judgement, such as 'studying the type of treatment to be used, its degree of complexity or risk, its cost and the possibilities of using it, and comparing these elements with the result that can be expected, taking into account the state of the sick person and his/her physical and moral resources.'[8]

There are *two* elements in this passage that are worthy of further reflection. Firstly, what they propose is a kind of benefit/burden calculus.

---

7   On the international stage there have been multiple cases where decisions regarding end-of-life care caused conflict and/or were resolved in the courts. See, for example, Arthur L. Caplan, James J. McCartney and Dominic A. Sisti, *The Case of Terri Schiavo: Ethics at the End of Life* (New York, NY: Prometheus Books, 2006).

8   Congregation for The Doctrine of the Faith, *Declaration on Euthanasia* (1980), Section 4, https://www.vatican.va/roman_curia/congregations/cfaith/documents/rc_con_cfaith_doc _19800505_euthanasia_en.html.

We try to understand the benefits of a proposed medical intervention and we compare that to the anticipated burdens that may accompany it. Most of the elements needed to make such a judgement – complexity, risk, expected results of a medical intervention – are dependent on the expertise and experience of the members of medical professions. To make medically responsible or prudent decisions we first need the knowledge and insights of professionals. It is worth noting that *cost* featured in the list of elements to be considered in the tradition. This may be less of a consideration today for some in developed countries, but it is still a significant consideration for other families, especially in developing countries with limited resources.

Secondly, the document recognises that people differ in their physical and moral resources. We all engage with illness and death in our own unique way, depending on those resources. The physical resource is easy to comprehend (age, strength, overall health), but the moral resource needs further elucidation. Moral resources include, I propose, our faith, our courage, our fear, our hope in the face of death. Some people are comfortable with the prospect of dying because they are at peace with God, self and others. For others the prospect of death is accompanied by fear, anxiety and, perhaps, the need to renew or repair relationships with God, self and loved ones. For such persons, the prolongation of treatment for a few more days or weeks may give them the time and space to approach their death with tranquillity, acceptance and hope.

This traditional framework – 'ordinary' medicine, 'benefit,' 'burden' – has served the Catholic faith community well over the centuries. It gives us a useful set of tools that need to be applied to a particular *person* and *context*. There are no ready-made answers or a 'one-size-fits-all' solution. This application demands a prudential judgement where, having taken into account all the information available to us, we reach a decision about what is to be done. In this regard the ethical framework of 'ordinary' and 'extraordinary' medicine, with its criteria of 'benefit' and 'burden', bears similarity to the 'just war' framework proposed for dealing with conflict. The latter framework also proposes criteria – last resort, proportionality, possibility of success – that need to be applied to a particular context by each moral agent through a prudential judgement.

The Who *Question*

The tradition is unambiguous in its insistence that decisions relating to healthcare in general, and end-of-life care in particular, should be made by the individual concerned whenever possible. Commenting on discontinuing medical procedures that are burdensome, the Catechism declares: 'The decision should be made by the patient if he is competent and able or, if not, by those legally entitled to act for the patient, whose reasonable will and legitimate interests must always be respected' (*CCC*, 2278). Having taken into account the advice of medical professionals on the benefits or otherwise of a proposed intervention, the person's prudential judgement should be honoured. If the person lacks capacity, those charged with her care should strive to respect the wishes or worldview of the dying person. In recent years in many jurisdictions, including Ireland, decision-making for those lacking capacity has benefitted from the introduction of advance care directives and the recognition of the right of persons to appoint a power of attorney. Though not without their own complications, these initiatives strive, on the one hand, to restore decision-making to the person and, on the other hand, to reduce the possibilities of conflict in families surrounding decisions about the care of a loved one.[9]

Challenges

Medical science has developed enormously over the past few decades and there is growing confidence that such progress will continue unabated. This has brought enormous benefit and comfort to the human family. Illnesses that once threatened life, or inflicted

---

9   For a brief reflection on the benefits and challenges of these developments, see The Consultative Group on Bioethics & the Council for Healthcare of the Irish Catholic Bishops' Conference, *Code of Ethical Standards for Healthcare* (Dublin: Veritas Publications, 2018), 42–43.

life-changing consequences, are now routinely overcome successfully. Because of these advances in medicine people, in general, live longer, healthier and more fulfilled lives. That is particularly true of people in the developed world. Sadly, access to quality healthcare is denied to millions worldwide. This reality is now receiving renewed attention in Catholic teaching and, especially, in the corpus of Catholic Social Doctrine.[10] The inequalities in the delivery of healthcare have been laid bare for all to see during the Covid-19 pandemic. Many citizens of developed countries were able to avail of a booster jab before the majority of citizens of the developing countries were inoculated.

The dramatic increase in the healing, generative and restorative power of modern medicine has also brought challenges. Significant ethical issues have arisen, for instance, in the area of reproductive medicine concerning the nature of human parenthood and the extent of human dominion in this area of life. Recently, questions have been asked about the ethics of surrogacy and the possible exploitative recruiting of women from less developed economies to act as surrogates for parents in the developed world.

Significant challenges, as noted already, have also arisen in the area of life-sustaining medical interventions. The provision of artificially administered nutrition and hydration to persons in a PVS has generated much debate worldwide amongst theologians, ethicists, medical and nursing organisations, civil society and the civil courts. Old questions concerning the exact content of the criteria of 'benefit' and 'burden' received new focus and urgency. Is there a 'benefit' in continuing to provide such care to a person who is in a vegetative state for ten years or more? Is continued existence a 'benefit'? Should the question of 'benefit' be measured against one's understanding of the purpose of life? In the Christian tradition, is that purpose ultimately viewed in relational terms rather than length of days?

---

10   For the growing conversation between bioethics and social justice see, for example, M. Therese Lysaught and Michael McCarthy (eds), *Catholic Bioethics & Social Justice* (Collegeville, MN: Liturgical Press, 2018), and Philip J. Landrigan and Andrea Vicini SJ, *Ethical Challenges in Global Public Health* (Eugene, OR: Pickwick, 2021).

The response of the Catholic moral tradition to the particular case of the PVS has undergone a process of development, refinement and clarification over the past few decades. This is quite a natural state of affairs, to be expected as the tradition grapples with new medical technologies and their consequences for persons and the dying process. Current teaching holds that 'nutrition and hydration whether delivered "naturally" or "artificially" should always be provided to patients unless they cannot be assimilated by a person's body, they do not sustain life, or their mode of delivery imposes grave burdens on the patient.'[11] The current stance of the Catholic moral tradition on this question is a result of several decades of theological reflection and debate.[12] This debate took place amongst theologians, Catholic healthcare professionals, individual bishops and episcopal conferences. In 2004, Pope John Paul II also made an important, though now seldom referenced, contribution to the content of the debate.[13]

From the beginning there was agreement amongst all contributors to the debate on several vital issues: the person in a PVS is a *living* person with rights and dignity; the central ethical issue is how *best* to respond to the person in our care in a way that respects their dignity; treatment cannot be withdrawn with the intention of *causing* death; treatment can, however, be withdrawn if it is deemed, after a prudential judgement, to be disproportionate, burdensome or futile. The language of 'vegetative' was deemed by all to be an inappropriate language when applied to persons – it could well give the impression that the person in a PVS is somehow less than a person and, as a result, less deserving of care and respect. In the intervention by Pope John Paul already noted, he acknowledged that the term 'vegetative' is now

---

11   The Consultative Group on Bioethics & the Council for Healthcare of the Irish Catholic Bishops' Conference, *Code of Ethical Standards for Healthcare*, 76–77. See also *Samaritanus Bonus*, 3 and 8.

12   See, for example, Ronald P. Hamel and James J. Walter (eds), *Artificial Nutrition and the Permanently Unconscious Patient: The Catholic Debate* (Washington, DC: Georgetown University Press, 2007), and Pádraig Corkery, *Bioethics and the Catholic Moral Tradition* (Dublin: Veritas Publications, 2010) Chapter 5.

13   Pope John Paul II, 'Life-Sustaining Treatment and the Vegetative State: Scientific Advances and Ethical Dilemmas', https://www.vatican.va/content/john-paul-ii/en/speeches/2004/march /documents/hf_jp-ii_spe_20040320_congress-fiamc.html.

'solidly established', but judged that the term is not 'the most felicitous when applied to human beings'.[14]

In the early debate there was also considerable and heated disagreement among theologians and Catholic healthcare officials on several questions. These included, but were not limited to, the following:

- Is artificially administered nutrition and hydration a basic first-order care that should be made available to all?
- Or is it a medical treatment that should be assessed using the traditional criteria of 'benefit' and 'burden'?
- What are the 'benefits' of the continued provision of artificial nutrition to persons in a PVS?
- By withdrawing artificially administered nutrition and hydration, are we causing the person's death or allowing the person to die from their underlying fatal pathology?
- Who should decide for persons in a PVS given that they lack capacity?

It is important to add that these questions caused discussion and division not only within the Catholic healthcare and theological traditions but also within medical, nursing and legal circles. This is reflected in the different stances adopted, for example, by the British, American and Irish Medical Associations to the care of persons in a PVS.

The current Catholic teaching, as reflected in *Samaritanus Bonus* and elsewhere, argues for a *presumption* in favour of providing artificially administered nutrition and hydration to persons in a vegetative state. However, this presumption yields if the continued treatment is deemed 'disproportionate' or 'ineffective', or if it creates an 'excessive burden'. As indicated earlier, it is not self-evident what these terms mean in a particular context. They have to be unpacked by looking at the particular circumstances of the person and their 'physical and moral

14   Ibid.

resources'. This requires a prudential judgement – weighing up the particulars of the case and, guided by the virtue of prudence, making a decision. This decision-making activity is at all times guided and shaped by the desire to respect the dignity and unique circumstances of the person. It is furthermore rooted in a vision of responsible stewardship that recognises God as the Lord of life and disavows attitudes and actions that bestow on humankind dominion over life and death. This vision also proclaims that human dignity is intrinsic to us as daughters and sons of God and is not diminished or erased by the 'quality' of our life in terms of health, capacity or well-being.

Though the Catholic Christian tradition identifies values, attitudes and dispositions that are absolute and non-negotiable, the *application* of those values to a complex world is a difficult task. It demands prayer, consultation, dialogue and reflection. This is evident in many areas of life, such as the application of 'just war' criteria to a particular conflict (e.g. the war in Iraq); the application of the principle of co-operation and scandal to a particular issue like voting or, indeed, the reception of a medical vaccine (for rubella or Covid-19) that may be remotely linked in its genesis to abortion; the applications of the principles of Catholic social doctrine to a particular economy or issue (e.g. the right to housing or access to healthcare).

Conclusion

This short article has highlighted the continuing role of *prudential judgements* in the Christian life. The role of prudential judgements has a long history in healthcare decisions. They will become even more important in the coming decades as medical care continues to expand its ability to combat serious illness and save many people from untimely deaths. The Gospel call to respect the gift of life and to care for those who are sick and vulnerable is at the heart of any Christian response to dilemmas in healthcare. However, the *application* of this Gospel vision to complex situations in contemporary medicine is not always easy or obvious. There will, for example, be occasions when the benefits of continued medical interventions will be uncertain, negligible or missing. In these circumstances prudential judgements will be required to determine a 'Gospel response'. In particular, they will be required to tease out, on the one hand, what is 'ordinary' care and hence morally obligatory and, on the other hand, what is 'extraordinary' care and hence morally optional. Decision-makers need to be guided in this conscientious task by the best medical advice available, the advice of their faith community, the wishes of the person at the centre of the human drama, and the Holy Spirit.

Questions for Reflection and Discussion

1. What is the theological foundation on which the Church's attitude to death and dying is built?
2. How useful is the language of 'ordinary'/'extraordinary' treatments when discussing the care of those who are ill?
3. What role does prayer have in making a conscientious decision in healthcare or, indeed, in any other sphere of life?
4. Pope Francis says: 'We have been called to form consciences, not to replace them' (*Amoris Laetitia*, 37). What role does Church teaching have in making a prudential judgement about the withdrawal of medical treatment from a loved one?

14: Death, Dying and Dignity: A Philosophical Perspective

Gaven Kerr

The question of human dignity is one that often comes up in the context of medical treatment, particularly end-of-life care. It is often felt that when an individual loses certain abilities, dignity has been affected or, in some cases, lost. Such individuals are commonly said to be without dignity, or to be lacking in the dignity that they once had. In this context, advocacy is sometimes made to end such medical treatment or indeed take measures to bring about the death of the patient.

This view is quite familiar in discussions of end-of-life care and the desire to die with dignity: if an individual no longer has the dignity that they once had, to allow them to choose when they will die would restore some dignity to an otherwise undignified situation. This is seen as a kind of compassion for the person whose dignity has been lost.

It is clear that on this view dignity is something that can be gained or lost, and that one has dignity because one has certain abilities. Hence, it is in the gaining or losing of certain abilities that one gains or loses dignity. So, one does not have dignity simply in virtue of being human; one has it based on what one can do. This view has affinities with a view of the person which maintains that to be a person is not simply to be human, but to be able to do certain things, often associated with thought, rationality and the ability to make choices. Indeed, it is often assumed that those abilities that make one a person are precisely the abilities that make one dignified. So, the loss of such abilities, such as the ability to make independent choices, signifies the loss of dignity.

I want to propose and defend a contrasting view of dignity. This view does not envisage dignity as a result of something that the individual can do, but sees it as a feature of what the individual is. Given that the individual is a being that is dignified, the individual has an intrinsic dignity regardless of what he or she can do. The individual that has dignity is a person, and on account of the dignity defended here, every human individual is a person whose dignity is not lost or gained at any point in that person's life. I shall begin by articulating my perspective on what a person is. Having done that, I shall demonstrate why it is the case that every person has dignity and why such intrinsic dignity cannot be lost or gained in the life of that person. I shall conclude with a salutary lesson on the treatment of such individuals at the end of life.

What Is a Person? A Philosophical Perspective
Views about the nature of the person and personal identity proliferate, and they generally tend to involve a commitment to the view that to be a person involves rationality in some way. Whilst these views are quite common, they trade on philosophical presuppositions that need to be brought to the fore and analysed. A general philosophical definition of personhood that captures much of our core commitments on personal identity is the following: a person is an individual substance of a rational nature.[1] There are two things to note about this definition of person: (i) a person is an individual substance, and (ii) a

---

1   Boethius, *De Persona et duabus naturis*, Cap. 3 in *Theological Tractates and the Consolation of Philosophy* (trans. H. F. Stewart, E. K. Rand, and S. J. Tester) (Cambridge, MA: Harvard University Press, 1918). For a discussion and defence of this view of person, see St Thomas Aquinas, *Summa Theologiae* (Turin: Marietti, 1926), Ia, qu. 29.

person is rational. This view captures what we typically take to be persons, since all the things that we take to be persons are individual substances that are rational. However, one worry is that, on this view, *only* rational things are persons, whereas there are some things that we understand to be persons that we do not typically take to be rational – including newborn infants, children prior to having reached the 'age of reason', and those who have (permanently or temporarily) lost the use of reason through intoxication or illness. Indeed, it would seem that, on this view, to be a person is to be able to do something (e.g. to think, desire or choose), all of which pertain to rationality; and surely that is precisely the view to which I am here opposed.

On the contrary, I wish to emphasise that a person is an individual substance of a rational *nature*. From a philosophical perspective, the rationality characterises the nature of the substance. The substance is a rational one, in which case it is a substance of a certain type. Substances are distinguished as the kinds of substances they are, not based on what they can do, but on the basis of what they are. Let us consider an example.

H_2O is a certain kind of substance – water. H_2O_2 is another kind of substance – hydrogen peroxide. Both substances are made out of the same kind of 'stuff', for both substances are made out of hydrogen and oxygen. What differentiates them as the substances they are is not the stuff out of which they are made, for they share that in common; rather, what differentiates them is how that stuff is put together or formed. Accordingly, the hydrogen and oxygen in water are proportioned in a way to make water as opposed to hydrogen peroxide, and vice versa. Thus, a molecule of water consists of two hydrogen atoms and one oxygen atom, whereas a molecule of hydrogen peroxide consists of two hydrogen atoms and two oxygen atoms.

Given the differences in what each of these substances are, they can do certain things. Thus, water can hydrate a human being and put out fire, whereas hydrogen peroxide can cause a human to be sick and make a fire more intense. Nevertheless, what distinguishes these substances is not what they can do, but how they are formed. On the basis of how they are formed, such substances have the abilities that they have, even when these abilities are not exercised; for example, water is still water, H_2O, even when it is not hydrating anyone or putting out any fires.

Returning, then, to the definition of the human person, a person is an individual substance of a rational nature. Accordingly, a person is a certain kind of thing, and so is not to be categorised as such solely on the basis of what he or she can do. Given what we have seen about how substances are constituted, a person is a kind of substance on the basis of being formed in a certain way. That being the case, a person comes to be when a certain kind of substance comes to be, and a person ceases to be when a certain kind of substance ceases to be. However, just as water doesn't cease to be water because it is not hydrating someone or putting out fires, so too a person does not cease to be a certain kind of substance just because he or she is not performing activities typical of being a person. A person is able to perform those activities from time to time given that he or she is a person, but being a person does not require the performance of those activities.

On this account, then, a person is not identified as such on the basis of what he or she can do, but on the basis of what he or she is. Hence, the entire life of the substance is the life of a person. So, from conception to death, a human person is a person, even though at times because of certain circumstances they cannot exercise certain abilities they have in virtue of being a person.

An interesting corollary follows from this to the effect that being a person is not the same as having a personality. A certain personality can often coincide with a person, and when that personality changes sometimes we say that the person changes. But in reality, the person remains the same person that they are, and what is striking is that whilst the person remains the same, he or she adopts some fundamental beliefs, outlooks or practices that heretofore we have not associated with that person. But because the person is identified not with their beliefs, outlooks or practices, but with what they are, such changes are not a change of person.

The foregoing view of persons has implications for dignity, to which we now turn.

Human Dignity

Dignity is often spoken about in a thoroughly intuitive manner, as if it is clear in what dignity consists. As noted in the introduction to this chapter, dignity tends to be attributed to a person on the basis of what they can do. Whenever a person cannot do things thought to be typical of a person, it is often said that the person has lost their dignity. But if we think about this in a little more depth, we can see there are some problems with this view. Dignity is a feature a person has in virtue of being a person; it is not something that is attributed to them independently of their personhood. Thus, a person doesn't have dignity simply because the state, the law or some other authority says so. Rather, the state, the law or some other authority recognises the dignity that a person has. It is something about being a person, then, that entails that a person has dignity, as opposed to not having dignity. Hence, dignity does not pertain to a person's abilities, but to the nature of personhood itself.

What Is It about Being a Person That Entails That a Person Has Dignity?

According to the philosophical definition, a person is a substance of a rational nature. In virtue of being such, a person is an individual subject of experience that does not merely exist, but lives a life. In living a life, a person, with growing maturity, comes to make their own choices and is able to intend ends for themselves. Even with infants, parents make decisions for their children because in their view these are good decisions to make, such as feeding, clothing and sheltering. Parental decisions made on behalf of infants are good because they are what the child *would* will for himself or herself (e.g. feeding), were he or she at a stage of maturity to do so. This is not to say that the child will grow up to make the same choices that we make for them, but that in our making such choices we are acting within the child's best interests. There is an implicit recognition, then, that in making choices for those too young to make them for themselves, even such choices are taken to be the choices that person would have made; hence they are made as if they were the person's choices. At no point are they taken to be choices that the infant would not have made were they at the appropriate stage of maturity. Accordingly, what is significant about a person overall is that it is their life to live.

Given that it is the person's life to live and not that of any other, the life of every person is to be treated as an end in itself and never used as a means for one's own ends.

How Do We Treat Things as Ends in Themselves?

There are certain ends that we seek, and they are valued for what they can give us. For example, money is something of value that everyone seeks; but not in itself. Rather, money is sought for certain things for which it can be exchanged. It is that for which we give the money that we value more than the money itself. Money, then, is not an end in itself; there is something that we value more than money. What this reveals is that to treat something as an end in itself is not to value anything greater than it, but to value it in itself. To be treated as an end in itself, a person has to be valued in themselves.

How Do We Value Things?

In order to value things, we love them as beings that are good in themselves. What is valued is a good, and in valuing what is good we love it. Given that every person is to be treated as an end, every person is to be valued as the good that he or she is. This then entails that every person is to be loved in themselves. The primary attitude that we must take with regard to any individual person is to love them. By contrast, to love the person only for what they can do would be to value something more than the person – it would be to value their abilities.

Hence, we do not treat persons as ends in themselves if we value them only for their abilities. Accordingly, we must love the person simply as the person that he or she is, regardless of what he or she can do.

It is in this that human dignity consists: every person is a subject of value and thus worthy of love. A person has dignity precisely because he or she is worthy of love. And just as a person does not cease being a person whilst he or she is still alive, so too a person does not cease being the subject of value that he or she is whilst alive. Nothing, then, that happens in the life of the person can alienate that person from their dignity; for they have such dignity and are worthy of love simply because they exist as a person.

Death, Dying and Dignity

The foregoing is quite a demanding account of personal dignity, for it holds that every human being is a subject of value worthy of love. This goes not only for the weakest but also the strongest; it goes for the most vulnerable, right the way through to the seemingly invulnerable. All are worthy of love as the beings that they are, regardless of what they can or cannot do, and regardless of what they have or have not done. In all our dealings with any other human, we are to treat them as the valuable goods that they are and not make use of them for our own ends. This is what generates the right to life that every human enjoys: one has such a right to life based on the fact that one is a good to be valued.

It follows from this that one cannot logically appeal to human dignity to end the life of an individual person. For this would be to value something more than the person (e.g. a prior state of health or comfort), as opposed to valuing them as an end in themselves. The latter can be contrasted with the case of applying anaesthesia to relieve pain, but not end the life; since in that case the life of the individual is valued and the anaesthesia enhances it, but in the euthanasia case, the life of the individual is not valued and enhanced by the administration of drugs, but is in fact terminated. When it comes to dying and dignity, then, one cannot appeal to a vague notion of dignity to justify ending human life; for dignity can only be used to affirm the value of the individual. It is right and just that a person receives appropriate medical care at the end of their life. But any medical care that seeks to end the life of the patient prematurely is inconsistent with valuing the individual as the good that he or she is. Such so-called care would be to value something more than the person – it would be to value or promote their death, and so is inconsistent with personal dignity.

Nevertheless, it is the case that there are certain features of human life that are consequent upon having dignity, and these features make life better, including robust health, sharpness of mind and community life. Whilst we cannot value these features of human life over the life itself that makes them possible, we can seek to preserve and promote them as best we can in whatever context the person is placed. So, whilst the loss of some of these features of human life does not justify losing the life itself, such a loss can justify a compassionate response from medical professionals to make better the final stages of human life, right up to natural death. Such palliative care reflects the natural consequence of human dignity – namely, that there is a human way to live that makes life better, and so there is a human way to die that, without seeking to hasten death, makes dying easier. Palliative care of the dying is a witness to the fact that because of human dignity, no matter the situation, the person's life matters and will be valued right up to the point of death.

Questions for Reflection and Discussion:

1. Try to think of those people whom you may find particularly hard to love. Now consider what transformation needs to occur in one's own thinking in order to value those whom we may find disagreeable.
2. Remaining with those we may find disagreeable, how would *their* lives be affected if we were truly to value them as the persons that they are?

3. Reflect on this account of human dignity and Christ's command to love your neighbour as yourself.

4. Consider how so much common thought on human dignity focuses on what we can do and so overlooks what we in fact are. Try to reflect on times when we value a person only for what they can do, or worse, for what they can do for us.

5. Reflect on the following: If we value nothing in itself, but only in its use for us, then nothing but death remains. For whatever is used is finally discarded, so if nothing is valuable in itself, everything eventually is discarded.

15: Being's Mystery: On Not Belonging to Ourselves

Philip John Paul Gonzales

Death, along with birth, is one of life's overwhelming mysteries. These mysteries are the bookends of human existence because in them are broached the questions of the before and after of human life. Death and birth are mysteries because they exist in a liminal or threshold space that provokes the question of what – if anything – is before and beyond human and earthly life. But here I will speak directly about death, understood as a fundamentally human and metaphysical question.

Death is an unavoidable question. It is a question that every child asks upon their first encounter with death, be it of an animal, friend or family member: 'What happens when you die, is there anything after … ?' Often, as we get older, the urgency of this childish question recedes, and the unavoidable fact of our death is muted in the living of a life that simulates immortality amidst the ever-increasing technological mastery of the planet and the dream of earthly eternity. But the impending reality of death is always there, regardless of how much we try to construct a life and society that seeks to screen out the urgency of this ultimate reality.

And when the question of death is front and centre, in the malaise of our late-Capitalist Western world, it is often there in a medicalised and politicised form of the question of euthanasia. In this view, each person has the 'right' to decide the manner and the hour of their death. We seek to master death and suffering, instead of receiving them as events that are beyond our control. Euthanasia is a metaphysical error in the most radical sense because it lives off the lie that we are autonomous beings and that we fully belong to ourselves.[1] But being's mystery is precisely that we do not belong to ourselves. Rather, we are tied inextricably and metaphysically to other humans, to creation as a whole, and to a divine source of being and freedom. We are radically relational and communal beings. If this is true, then death is not a 'right' that is mine to adjudicate. Rather, my death is a death that implies a life that is ever twined with others, lived in compassion – a suffering with and for others – beyond control or mastery. Death is a letting go and releasing of the self that understands that one is not a sovereign master over one's 'own' life. Death is a spilling forth and emptying of life to, and for, others.

In what follows I will offer a reflection on what it means to not belong to oneself. I suggest that if one is to die with dignity, this is only possible when death is received from something that is more than ourselves. Further, I argue that this acceptance of death only makes sense if what it means to be human is to belong to, and be gifted life and existence by, a divine source. In order to do this, I will turn to two prophetic counter-cultural voices in the Western tradition: Plato and St Paul. I will suggest that both this pagan sage and this Christian saint professed a wisdom of dispossession and a metaphysical humility that need to be heeded in our twenty-first-century world of possessive mastery and blinding pride. Both knew that what it means to be human is to understand that we do not belong to ourselves, and without this knowledge one cannot die with dignity. Death needs to be the dignified testament to the truth that we receive; and not something that constructs or controls what we are.

---

1 Similarly, abortion is the preventing and controlling of the mystery of birth, whereas euthanasia is the ending and controlling of the mystery of death. The logic is the same logic of controlling radical autonomy that refuses to see, and accept, life's great mysteries as gifts.

Plato's Pagan Wisdom – or on Belonging to the Gods
The *Phaedo* is Plato's deeply moving account of the final hours of the life of Socrates before his unjust death sentence was carried out. Socrates was falsely accused of impiety before the Olympian gods and of corrupting the youth. In this dialogue Socrates famously offers complex philosophical proofs for the eternal nature of the human soul. But beyond that, and, perhaps more importantly, it is an account of Socrates' love of, and commitment to, the philosophical life understood as a way of living. It is revealed that the whole of Socrates' life has been leading up to the moment of death. Indeed, Socrates defines the philosophical life as the practice or training for dying or death. One could say, in light of the theme of this present volume, that it is a dialogue on the dignity of death and dying.

Philosophy is seen as a virtuous, loving and desirous search for Wisdom. In the search for Wisdom, it was held that one must die to oneself by leaving behind our lower desires for wealth, fame, political power, obsession with sexual pleasure and so on. Plato is saying that philosophy is about an ordering of love and desire in which we must die to those aspects of ourselves that keep us from obtaining Wisdom. In this view, death is immanent to human life, and our end beyond earthly life is what is guiding and moving our way of living and actions here below.

Could death be that which gives human life meaning and purpose? This is the question that Plato was asking, through his dramatisation of the figure of Socrates. Could death be that reality that gives human life its drama and urgency? We are back to the question of the child: 'What happens when you die, is there anything after … ?' Plato's philosophical belief in eternal life was deeply religious in nature. Indeed, in the early part of the dialogue the question of suicide was broached. Socrates dismisses the ethical admissibility of suicide with a seemingly unphilosophical answer. He retorts that we are not allowed to do violence to ourselves for the simple reason that we do not belong to ourselves; rather, we are told, we are the possessions of the gods (*Phaedo* 62b). In response to this claim, one can react in many ways. One can laugh at such childish belief in things called 'gods'. One could say that Plato, as a rational philosopher, could not really have believed in 'gods' and that he was just speaking in the language or cultural idiom of his day. Or one could hear another truth that is *both* a metaphysical and a religious claim, namely, that what is deepest about our humanity is that we do not belong to ourselves, and that we find a meaning and purpose in a reality and force that is greater than the human.

For Plato, then, we belong to the divine, not to ourselves. But this belief hinges on the reality of eternal life where we live in communion with the gods and the divine, that is, Wisdom. Plato offers, as noted, many proofs for the eternity of the soul, but towards the end of the dialogue he acknowledges that what he is seeking to prove is itself a belief – and that one must 'risk' this belief because it is noble and good. Plato's philosophical arguments for the eternity of the soul are rigorous and powerful, but as 'proofs' there is always space for intellectual doubt or rebuttal.

To my mind, what is much harder to call into question is Plato's depiction of the passionately lived truth of Socrates' performance of philosophy as a practice of dying, and the dignified way he accepts his death. He accepts his death as a gift because of his risked belief that he – we – belong not to ourselves but are the possession of the gods or the divine. It is the Socrates of flesh and blood, his *being*-true to a life that is counter-cultural and out of step with his time and city, that is the most powerful 'proof' for the soul's eternal existence. Socrates lives and dramatically performs what he preaches to the point of death, a death which had been guiding – eschatologically – the whole of his existence since the moment he fell in love with philosophy as a young man.

Philosophy, for Plato and Socrates, was a spiritual practice that bespoke 'a beyond of this world'. Socrates was a martyr, in the etymological sense of the word, a witness to the truth. In our twenty-first-century world, which every day is losing more and more a sense of the religious and the transcendence of a beyond, models of witness that incarnate a counter-cultural desire are increasingly called for. True philosophy has always called into question the accepted norms of culture and the prevailing political systems. It has always been, in the words of Nietzsche, 'untimely' and subversive of the status quo. How much does our culture, which often prides itself on its sovereign control of the mysteries of birth and death, and a 'right' to die when and how we choose, need to be subverted?

Socrates offers, as in his own time, a model that testifies to a higher love and desire that needs to be heeded once again. Socrates died with dignity because he accepted his death as something that was beyond his own power, since he himself lived the truth that he belonged to the divine. He did not fearfully cling to his life, but nor would he ever wilfully take his own life. He received his death as a gift and released his self into the care of the divine with humble trust. His dying had a dignity that can only be given by a source that is beyond our power to construct. This is why he ended his life with a prayer, for I believe that prayer can only be uttered when we ourselves know that our very humanity has been received and we respond to this gift with radical thanksgiving.[2] But this truth of prayer is precisely the truth that is denied when our rights over life and death are absolute, because the only absolute is our own simulated autonomy.

Paul's Christian Wisdom – or on Belonging to Christ

Paul, like Socrates, was a witness to the truth of the divine order and that we belong not to ourselves. His life, too, was a continual spiritual practice of dying that manifests a truth that was (and is) counter-cultural (1 Corinthians 15:31). Further, this counter-cultural truth shook the foundation of the Roman Empire as Socrates' truth shook

---

2   Josef Pieper, *In Tune with the World: A Theory of Festivity* (New York, NY: Harcourt, Brace & World, 1965), 28–29.

the foundation of the Athenian city-state. But with Paul the divine was not the Olympian gods or an abstract divine of the platonic Good. This truth was the truth of the foolishness of the cross, of the incarnate God, Jesus Christ. His continual practice of dying to self was rooted in the free-flowing grace of baptism through which we participate in the death and resurrection of Christ, as opposed to the tremendous ascetic feats of Socrates' practice of philosophy. His shaking of the established order was rooted in a life whose strength comes from embracing weakness. Thus, if Paul boasted, he boasted of Christ; if he offered himself as a model of imitation, it is because he himself was humbly imitating and modelling himself on Christ, through the power of the Holy Spirit, without whom he could not profess Christ, let alone pray.

Like Plato and Socrates, Paul is making metaphysical claims that dovetail with the religious because the two cannot be separated. Paul is professing an eternal life that has been opened via Christ's sacrifice and the overcoming of death and sin. This is why the Christian is baptised into Christ's death and resurrection as members of the one body, and the one head. Through baptism we are claimed by Christ, renamed, made new. In this baptismal calling we come to see a twofold truth. First, that in the Christian God 'we live and move and have our being ... We are his offspring' (Acts 17:28). Plato understood this truth partially insofar as he knew that we do not belong to ourselves and that our being comes from a divine source. But Paul knew it more radically via the personal self-revelation of the divine source of our being. Paul also knew, through this same revelation, that theologically we are transformed into members of Christ's body through the power of the Holy Spirit. 'Or do you not know that your body is a temple of the Holy Spirit within you, which you have from God, and that you *are not your own?* For you were bought with a price; therefore, glorify God in your body' (1 Corinthians 6:19–20; italics mine).

Paul radicalises the truth of not belonging to ourselves in a double sense beyond the beautiful truth of Plato. First, metaphysically, the

God through whom we have our being is a personal and loving God that has created us from nothing (*ex nihilo*), out of love. Second, theologically, we are claimed by Christ and become temples of the Holy Spirit, and thus by being within Christ's body we are theologically not our own. The first truth says that as creatures we are created by God, and thus we do not belong to ourselves; our being is given and received. The second truth, theologically speaking, is that we have been ransomed, 'bought', and claimed by Christ's redeeming love that saves us from the death of sin. The result is a 'graced metaphysics' that sees the very being of the redeemed creature as a radical response to the twofold creative and redeeming love of the Christian God. We are, fundamentally, beings of radical response. It is the truth that all is gift: 'What do you have that you did not receive? And if you received it, why do you boast as if it were not a gift?' (1 Corinthians 4:7).

Conclusion

We belong not to ourselves. Thus, we need to live as models of testimony to a truth that is not of this world. Such truth is at war with the prince of this world that teaches this lie: that because we own and belong to ourselves, we have the right, as sovereign masters over life and death, to decide when and how we die. But if we do not accept the lie of radical and absolute autonomy, then our lives increasingly become a living testimony to a truth that is other. The mystery of being (i.e. human existence) rests on the radical truth of a dispossession of the self, claimed by others. Here we are claimed by the gift of our fellow humans, claimed by the gift of the whole creation, and most especially claimed by the double gift of the God who has both created and redeemed us. Only once this truth is accepted can we show what it means to die with dignity because we can proclaim with Paul: 'Where, O death, is your victory? Where, O death, is your sting? The sting of death is sin, and the power of sin is the law. But thanks be to God, who gives us the victory through our Lord Jesus Christ' (1 Corinthians 15:55–57).

Our twenty-first-century world is a 'throwaway culture' (Pope Francis) and a 'culture of death' (Pope John Paul II). In this world that no longer knows how to die – or worse, believes itself to be a master over death – we need radical models of counter-cultural desire. Hence my appeal to Plato and Paul, who sought to incarnate the Wisdom of death in their lives, thereby showing that there is hope beyond this life, this world. There is a source that *is Love*, and this source has breathed us forth into being and is calling us into a body of communion of love, beyond all imagining. Life, being, existence, is a communion of love.

But if Christians themselves have lost this truth of knowing and living the reality of not belonging to ourselves, how will others find the way …? Catholic philosophy and theology have perhaps never been in more need of a radical metaphysics of testimony that shows that life is lived most fully in accepting death as a gift. Life and being consist in laying down one's life in love and service for the other. This death is a spiritual way of life, fructifying life's journey towards its end, even in the messiness that can accompany that stage of the journey. Only then can one die with dignity – not one's own death – but a death lived in compassion and solidarity with others. With Paul, then, metaphysics needs to be a radical imitation of Christ's death; with Plato this means that our very lives must risk everything for this belief to the point of death, a death whose truth we have been meant to be incarnating in our daily lives all along.

Questions for Reflection and Discussion

1. Is it true that we do not belong to ourselves?
2. Are there more concrete ways in which we experience the truth that we do not belong to ourselves?
3. What in our culture most militates against the truth that we do not belong to ourselves?

4. How do we conceive the Christian faith, and is it really meant to be a counter-cultural reality that challenges societal and political norms? In other words, does it have a robust prophetic dimension and, if so, how is this to be carried out in today's world?

Four: Facing Suffering with Hope
16: Raising the Victim of the
Good Samaritan Parable:
A Scriptural Reflection

Luke Macnamara OSB

The parable of the Good Samaritan (Luke 10:25–37) is perhaps the best-known of all Jesus' parables.[1] The popular reaction to the parable is to focus very much on the hero rather than the many other characters, and especially the victim on the roadside. Indeed, the designation 'Good Samaritan' has entered popular discourse to indicate one who renders the disinterested and generous assistance of a stranger to someone in grave need. The image that springs to most minds is that of a gallant stranger coming to the rescue, with the victim fading into the background.

The parable has received much attention from Pope Francis,[2] especially in chapter two of the encyclical *Fratelli Tutti* on fraternity and social friendship, which quotes the entire parable and includes an

---

[1] Since frequent reference will be made to the Gospel of Luke, only chapter and verse numbers will normally be indicated.

[2] At the last count (27 December 2021), there were ten references to the Samaritan parable in discourses or writings of Francis, contrasting with only one mention at a papal audience for Benedict XVI.

extended interpretation.[3] The parable features prominently in the recent letter of the Congregation for the Doctrine of the Faith, *Samaritanus Bonus – on the care of persons in the critical and terminal phases of life*, which focuses on the Samaritan as a model for provision of care to the dying.[4] Finally, a recent joint publication by the Pontifical Council for Interreligious Dialogue and the World Council of Churches employs the parable to reflect on the Christian response to the Covid-19 pandemic.[5] Although these documents refer to the victim, the principal focus is on the Samaritan. Taking inspiration from Francis's interest in this parable and its current popularity in official Church documents, particularly *Samaritanus Bonus*, the parable is here examined from the point of view of both the victim and the Samaritan, developing both a Christological and theological reading to provide a wider theological framework for the dying and for carers.

The Forgotten Victim

Few consider the victim of the robbers in this parable. Stripped of clothes, his bruised and bloodied body lies exposed. Unable to get up and continue the journey, he must wonder about his prospects. The painful wounds are deepened by the absence of a comforter. Many with severe illness share this sense of vulnerability and isolation, while nearby their able-bodied neighbours are busy with everyday life.

Anybody passing by the victim of this story would likely recoil in horror as they drew close enough to see, much as the priest and Levite, who are quick to cross over to the other side of the road (10:31–32). The disfigurement of illness can make it difficult to recognise a fellow human being. For such a sufferer, there is little

---

3   See *Fratelli Tutti*, 56–85, http://www.vatican.va/content/francesco/en/encyclicals/documents/papa-francesco_20201003_enciclica-fratelli-tutti.html.

4   See especially chapter 3. Congregation for the Doctrine of the Faith, *Samaritanus Bonus*, 14 July 2020, https://www.vatican.va/roman_curia/congregations/cfaith/documents/rc_con_cfaith_doc_20200714_samaritanus-bonus_en.html.

5   *Serving a Wounded World in Interreligious Solidarity – A Christian Response to Reflection and Action During COVID-19 and Beyond*, Pontifical Council for Interreligious Dialogue/World Council of Churches, 2020, https://press.vatican.va/content/dam/salastampa/it/bollettino/documentazione-linkata/ServingWoundedWorld_.pdf.

quality of life, often a meagre prospect of recovery and no curative treatment. Some might rationalise that it is best to let nature take its course. For prospective helpers, the sight of the victim recalls uncomfortably the fragility of their own lives. The choice of so many readers of the parable to associate with the Samaritan may be as much about avoiding uncomfortable thoughts of personal vulnerability evoked by the victim, as about finding a model helper to imitate. Many readers may be unwittingly close to adopting the attitude of the priest and the Levite.

Seeing with the Victim

Located within a dialogue between Jesus and a lawyer, who comes to test him, the parable is Jesus' response to the lawyer's question: 'Who is my neighbour?' (10:29). In his later interpretation of the parable, Jesus inverts the question of the lawyer and asks instead: 'Which of the three was a neighbour to the man who fell among the brigands?' (10:36). Jesus pre-empts the avoidance strategy employed by the priest and Levite by asking the lawyer to take the vantage point of the half-dead man on the roadside. Few like to reflect on the fragility of human existence that accompanies every person, especially at either end of life, during the years of nurturing in infancy and those of necessary care in advanced old age. The lawyer is invited to judge the response of the three travellers from the perspective of the victim, and thereby assume his own personal vulnerability.

Jesus – Also a Traveller on This Road

The Good Samaritan is seen by Church Fathers through to contemporary scholars as prefiguring Jesus, who rescues us from death and brings us to life. However, it is worthwhile taking up Jesus' invitation to consider the point of view of the victim and to see whether the victim on the roadside might prefigure Jesus' own destiny. This requires an exploration of Jesus' story and how his story might be linked with that of the victim. Jesus recounts this parable on his journey from Galilee to Jerusalem, which spans eleven chapters in Luke's

Gospel (9:51–19:44), and during which Jesus makes frequent reference to his imminent suffering, death and resurrection in the city (9:22, 31, 44; 12:49–50; 13:31–34; 16:31; 17:25; 18:31–33: 19:14). This is not another of the many pilgrimage journeys that Jesus makes to Jerusalem (2:41–42): rather, this journey will form the climax of his ministry. Jesus will later journey to Jericho on his way to Jerusalem (18:35), and so he will take the same road that features in the parable. As a traveller on this road, Jesus might be associated with any of the four travellers, perhaps even the anonymous traveller, who is badly beaten and left half dead.

The association of Jesus with the victim might be taken as a source of comfort by all who find themselves, through serious illness, in a similar situation. Jesus freely chooses to go to Jerusalem with all the consequences that it will have for him, even extreme suffering and death. Jesus, thereby, willingly shares in the fate and destiny of the roadside victim and all who face serious illness and death. The isolation of the seriously ill person is now transformed by the presence of Jesus, who also participates in the suffering. Jesus is compassionate in the deeper sense of the term, one who shares in the suffering of another. When carers come to care for those who are ill, they also encounter Jesus, as noted in the Gospel of Matthew: 'I was sick, and you took care of me' (Matthew 25:36). The accompaniment of the seriously ill and dying provides privileged moments of encounter with Jesus.

Jesus – From Jericho to Jerusalem
This road has wider echoes for Jesus as it connects the beginning and end of his ministry. Jericho is the principal city in the Jordan valley and only a short distance from the river. The mention of the city evokes Jesus' baptism (3:21–23). Several elements of the baptism account point forward to the passion, death and resurrection. Firstly, baptism implies immersion in the river, a descent under the waters and then a re-emergence, foreshadowing the future descent of Jesus into the underworld and his later resurrection. Secondly, the words of the voice from heaven to Jesus, 'You are my beloved child' (3:22), evoke

the outcome for many beloved children in the Scriptures, from the threatened sacrifice of Isaac, son of Abraham (Genesis 22), to the accomplished sacrifice of the daughter of Jephthah (Judges 11). The words of the Father from heaven already point to the cross. Finally, the Spirit that descends on Jesus points to the future gift of the Spirit to the disciples at Pentecost (Acts 2) after the resurrection.

Jerusalem, the destination, is most closely associated with the passion, death and resurrection (Luke 19–24), which Jesus describes as his second baptism (12:50). Jesus might have spoken of any Judean road for the purposes of the parable. This road carries strong connotations for readers of the gospel. Indeed, when he speaks this parable, Jesus is on his final journey to Jerusalem. The echoes of his baptism, celebrated ritually in the Jordan and accomplished through his second baptism in Jerusalem, invite a reading of this parable in the light of the central Paschal Mystery of Jesus, that of his death and resurrection.

Jesus is already a marked man on his journey to Jerusalem, shadowed by the spectre of death, when he recounts the parable. While many associate Jesus with the merciful Samaritan, the first association of Jesus is more directly with the half-dead man on the roadside. As the man was stripped, so too is Jesus stripped of his clothing (23:34). As the man is beaten, so too Pilate offers to have Jesus beaten (23:16), but this is not enough for the crowd, who insist repeatedly that he be killed (23:18, 31, 23). While the victim is abandoned, as good as dead, on the roadside, Jesus dies abandoned on the cross (23:46). To be sure, death is not the final word for Jesus. The women in the open tomb hear two men in dazzling white clothes proclaim Jesus' resurrection (24:4–8). As hope springs from the seemingly hopeless image of Jesus' lifeless body on the cross, so there is hope for the victim on the roadside.

The purpose of Jesus' journey to Jerusalem is clear. It does not end with death but with resurrection and new life. The victim's close association with Jesus is full of promise. St Paul puts it succinctly: 'If we have been united with him in a death like his, we will certainly be united with him in a resurrection like his' (Romans 6:5). The similar description of Jesus' and the victim's sufferings point to a sharing not only in suffering and death but also in the new life to come. The compassionate Jesus suffers alongside patients facing life's end and his suffering is part of the Paschal Mystery that leads to new life. No matter how invalided, patients can choose to contribute to Jesus's salvific work through sharing their suffering with Jesus. Again, St Paul points the way: 'I want to know Christ and the power of his resurrection and the sharing of his sufferings by becoming like him in his death, if somehow I might attain the resurrection from the dead' (Philippians 3:10–11). The horizon of suffering and death is transformed by the power of the resurrection into one of hope and new life.

The Samaritan's Roadside Liturgy

The first three travellers on the road, the victim, priest and Levite, are on their way down from Jerusalem, where it is likely that the three would have visited the Temple, especially the priest and Levite, who have specific duties in the sacrificial cult. There is no indication as to where the fourth traveller on the road is journeying from. As a Samaritan, he is allowed to access only the outer court of the Temple, and is thereby excluded from the sacrificial cult. While the priest and Levite see the wounded man and pass swiftly onwards, the Samaritan also sees him but is moved to compassion. The movement of the Temple officials away from the victim contrasts with the movement of the Samaritan towards him. The Samaritan tends to a man who is probably Jewish, given that the road is in Judea. His love extends beyond his kinship group to a member of a hostile people, who had destroyed the Samaritan temple (110 BC) and killed many of his people in regular skirmishes. In this context of ethnic hatred, his compassion is extraordinary.

The Samaritan binds his wounds and pours oil and wine on them (10:34). While the pouring of oil and wine on wounds is recognised as part of standard medical care for both Jews (Isaiah 1:6; Jeremiah 51:8) and Gentiles (Hippocrates and Theophrastus), the action has strong echoes with the Jewish liturgy and sacrificial cult. The fruits of the olive and vine are among the most valued harvest fruits of Israel and are understood as gifts of the Lord to his people. They are used widely in the liturgy. Each day the sacrifice of a one-year-old lamb morning and evening is accompanied by a grain offering (mixed with olive oil) and a drink offering of wine in the Temple (Exodus 29:38–42). While the priest and Levite during their time in Jerusalem would have offered sacrifices of oil and wine in the Temple, the Samaritan pours these out liberally on the gaping wounds of the maimed victim. The Samaritan, who is excluded from the Temple, celebrates the liturgy on the roadside in his paramedical ministry to the victim. God is worshipped in and through the care extended to the wounded man.

St Paul asks his hearers 'to present your bodies as a living sacrifice, holy and acceptable to God, which is your spiritual worship' (Romans 12:1). One way in which this command might be actualised is in the provision of care to the dying. The caregiver expends time and energy on someone who will shortly be gone. Objectively, it might be perceived as a waste of time. However, this offering of the carer's self is a living sacrifice, holy and acceptable to God. The Samaritan in this parable and Jesus in the wider Gospel both embody such a gratuitous offering. By caring for the dying, carers join with Jesus in the offering of his own body to God, a joint offering that takes place at every Eucharist. The dying can also participate in this liturgy by offering up the sufferings of illness as a sacrifice to God. The care of the dying is thereby is transformed into a liturgical celebration of the Paschal Mystery involving both patients and carers, pointing to the new life that awaits all.

The Victim, the Samaritan and the Innkeeper
The Samaritan lifts the victim onto his animal and brings him to an inn. The innkeeper welcomes an unlikely pair, a half-dead Jew and a Samaritan who rescued and now cares for him. Following the description of the close and tender attention on the roadside, readers know what this care entails. The Samaritan might have rested from his journey, but

instead gives priority to tending to the victim. The extraordinary care shown by the Samaritan is witnessed by the innkeeper.

The following morning the Samaritan must continue on his journey. He entrusts the man to the innkeeper's care, leaving two denarii to cover expenses and promising to make good any further expense when he returns. The innkeeper is now called upon to imitate the care modelled by the Samaritan. A denarius is the daily wage of a manual labourer, enough to cater for daily sustenance. There is a suggestion in the mention of two denarii that the Samaritan has provided enough for two days, and that he will return on the third day. For readers of the gospel, this hints at the resurrection of Jesus who returns on the third day. This confirms the promise of new life for the half-dead victim.

Care for suffering family members or friends can last many years. A point may be reached where carers must seek help and sometimes hand over to others. A move to a long-term care facility can be a heart wrench for both patient and carer. The Samaritan is a model for carers at this point. The handing over of care to the innkeeper is not an abandonment. The Samaritan, who has modelled the care to be given to the patient, now entrusts the patient to the innkeeper and provides funds. His support is not temporary but sustained, and he also promises to return. The Samaritan maintains his relationship both with the patient and with the new caregiver, the innkeeper. The celebration of the Paschal Mystery in the care of the patient at the roadside is now celebrated at the inn involving a new caregiver and, potentially, others. With the promised return there is a shift in emphasis from the suffering and death to the resurrection on the third day. Prolonged care can be daunting for both patients and caregivers but through such care the Paschal Mystery unfolds. An approaching death is already outshone by the rising dawn of the resurrection.

Love of God and of Neighbour
As already noted, the immediate context of the parable is a short dialogue between a lawyer and Jesus. The lawyer seeks eternal life and

when Jesus asks him what it says in the Law, the lawyer gives a summary of the whole Law: 'You shall love the Lord your God with all your heart, and with all your soul, and with all your strength, and with all your mind; and your neighbour as yourself' (10:27). This is a combination of two scriptural texts uniting the command to love God (Deuteronomy 6:5) and one's neighbour (Leviticus 19:18). Jesus commends the answer and invites the lawyer to do this, but the lawyer asks a further question: 'Who is my neighbour?' (10:29). This question implies another: 'Who is not my neighbour?' The lawyer perhaps seeks to limit the requirement to fulfil the law of love of neighbour. He asks no question regarding the love of God.

There is a dialogue in the Gospel of Matthew (22:35–40) which parallels the dialogue preceding the parable in Luke. In Matthew, however, Jesus quotes the twin commandment and concludes by saying that 'on these two commandments *hang* all the law and the prophets' (22:40). The choice of verb ('hang') is unusual both in English and in the original Greek. The term evokes death and is used later in Luke to describe the crucifixion of the criminals alongside Jesus (23:39), and retrospectively in Acts to describe Jesus' own crucifixion (Acts 5:30; 10:39). By this term Matthew suggests that fulfilment of the twin commandments to love God and neighbour comes at a cost. What Matthew intimates with a single verb, Luke suggests by situating the parable on the road between Jericho and Jerusalem, the destination of Jesus' final journey and location of his passion, death and resurrection. The dialogue and parable point to Jesus' motivation for taking this road, to love God and neighbour to the end.

A Christological and Theological Reading of Victim and Samaritan
In the wider context of the Gospel, Jesus conducts a ministry of release from sin and death. The goal of the journey to Jerusalem is to complete this mission through his own suffering, death and resurrection. If identified with the Samaritan, Jesus turns aside on the most important journey of his entire ministry to care for the wounded

man. No missionary imperative distracts him from caring for the victim before him. The goal of his ministry to bring life is exemplified by his care to the victim. In doing so, Jesus exposes himself to the risk of being attacked, a destiny he freely accepts. Jesus the traveller rescues the victim but ultimately switches places with the victim in Jerusalem. Through the figure of the Samaritan Jesus fulfils the role of a priest who offers sacrifice to God, while through the figure of the injured man he becomes the victim to be offered.

The Letter to the Hebrews speaks of this double role of Jesus as both priest and victim: 'But when Christ came as a high priest of the good things that have come, then through the greater and perfect tent (not made with hands, that is, not of this creation), he entered once for all into the Holy Place, not with the blood of goats and calves, but with his own blood, thus obtaining eternal redemption' (Hebrews 9:11–12). Through his passion and death Jesus as priest offers his own self as a perpetual sacrifice to God. Through this sacrifice he wins salvation for humanity, redeeming those condemned to sin and death. The prospects of the victim on the roadside are transformed. The new heavenly banquet, initiated through Jesus' Paschal Mystery, celebrates restored communion between humanity and God.

Conclusion

The parable focuses on several characters but principally the Samaritan and the victim. In the context of Luke's Gospel, the parable gives an overview of Jesus' ministry. Jesus is also a traveller on this road, from his first baptism in the Jordan near Jericho to his second baptism, namely his death and resurrection in Jerusalem. Jesus' healing ministry is reflected by the Samaritan, and his suffering and death is reflected by the victim, recalling in turn a paragraph on the anointing of the sick in the *Catechism of the Catholic Church*:

> By his passion and death on the cross Christ has given a new meaning to suffering: it can henceforth configure us

to him and unite us with his redemptive Passion. (*CCC*, 1505)

Jesus willingly takes on the suffering of the victim. Most interpretations encourage us to hope that the victim survives, but the parable is left open. There is no report of the man's recovery. However, the victim shares many traits with Jesus and is closely united to him in his suffering, which culminates in his death and resurrection. Viewed in this light, the victim's suffering and possible death are now eclipsed by the hope of new life. Furthermore, the current suffering is reinterpreted as participation in the salvific suffering of Jesus and so has meaning and value. In such difficult and yet privileged moments, patients and carers may observe the unfolding of salvation in their midst.

Questions for Reflection and Discussion

1. How might you answer Jesus' question: 'Who is my neighbour?'
2. In what ways might you negotiate personal fragility when caring for the dying?
3. How might carer and patient recognise the presence of Jesus in sickness and approaching death?
4. In what ways might dying patients understand their suffering as having redemptive value through their participation in the salvific suffering of Christ?
5. How might carers' participation at the Mass link with service of the sick and dying?

17: The Sacrament of the Sick and Its Role in a Christian's Sickness

Neil Xavier O'Donoghue

We might be living in an age that emphasises mercy and the modern in religion, but there is still something to be learned from the Church councils of earlier centuries. The Council of Trent informs us, with true sixteenth-century theatricality: 'If anyone says that these seven sacraments are so equal to each other that one is not for any reason more excellent than the others, let him be anathema.'[1]

Put in more modern terms, Trent is saying that sacraments are not equal and that some are 'more excellent' than others. Most Catholics would agree that the Eucharist is the 'Blessed Sacrament' and the summit of the Church's sacramental treasury. But while the 'least excellent' sacrament has not been defined, the Sacrament of the Anointing of the Sick may be a good contender for the distinction. Coming in seventh of seven does not relegate it to the also-ran category. It is still a precious gift that helps Christians to face sickness and suffering with the hope of Christ.

As a sacrament it has one of the clearest biblical foundations. St James instructs his listeners:

---

1 Council of Trent, Session 7, 'Second Canon on the Sacraments in General, 3 March, 1547', H. J. Schroeder (ed.), *The Canons and Decrees of the Council of Trent* (New York, NY: Herder, 1941; reprint Rockville, IL: Tan, 1978), 52.

Are any among you sick? They should call for the elders of
the church and have them pray over them, anointing them
with oil in the name of the Lord. The prayer of faith will
save the sick, and the Lord will raise them up; and anyone
who has committed sins will be forgiven. (James 5:14–15)[2]

The Gospel of Mark also tells us that the Twelve 'anointed with oil
many that were sick and healed them' (Mark 6:13). There has always
been a curative aspect to the Sacrament of the Sick – it continues Jesus'
healing ministry in the Church, and the sacrament still on occasion
serves to help people recover from their sicknesses.[3] More importantly,
as the *Catechism of the Catholic Church* explains, this sacrament is
'especially intended to strengthen those who are being tried by illness'.[4]

Unfortunately, this sacrament has been misunderstood throughout much of Christian history. In the Middle Ages it became associated exclusively with terminal illness and was usually restricted to the
dying. The famous Dundalk historian, Eamon Duffy, explains:

> It was widely and erroneously believed that the solemn
> anointing of all the senses involved in the reception of
> Extreme Unction was a sort of ordination or consecration,
> cutting the recipient off from the normal activities of life,
> even should they recover. They would have to live thereaf-
> ter as a sort of animated corpse, as it was widely thought
> that 'stinking Lazarus' had done after Jesus had raised him
> from the tomb.[5]

---

2   Scripture quotations in this article are from the Catholic Edition of the New Revised Standard
     Version (NRSVCE).
3   For more on Jesus' commission to his disciples to heal the sick, see Mark 6:7–13; Matthew
     10:1–15; Luke 9:1–6; 9:10; 10:1–20; 10:34.
4   *Catechism of the Catholic Church* (2nd ed.) (Vatican City: Libreria Editrice Vaticana, 1997),
     378, 1511.
5   Eamon Duffy, *The Stripping of the Altars: Traditional Religion in England 1400–1580*
     (2nd ed.) (New Haven, CT: Yale University Press, 2005), 313.

While there is no problem in administering this sacrament to those who are terminally ill, the Church has always given priority to administering the Eucharist to the dying in the form of Viaticum – a special manner of receiving the Eucharist before dying. The Second Vatican Council suggested that the Sacrament of the Sick is a more correct name than Extreme Unction for this sacrament of anointing. Additionally, it specified that anyone facing serious sickness or old age is eligible to receive this sacrament.[6]

Unfortunately many Irish people still consider this to be an 'extreme' sacrament. It is good to call a priest when someone is dying. However, it would be better to request this sacrament at the onset of illness, and, indeed, of the debilitating effects of old age. We live in an age that tries to avoid sickness. While we might joke that the elderly are only happy when they are talking about their ailments, medications and treatments, sickness is all too often excluded from polite conversation. Rather than being a part of the community, the sick and the infirm are frequently placed in 'homes', where they are all too often forgotten about. By this I do not mean to say that nursing homes are bad, nor do I deny that on many occasions they are the best place for a particular individual person to stay. Unfortunately, however, these institutions can often be places of extreme loneliness. This is one of the greatest injustices in our society, and unlike many other injustices it is well within our capability to help solve it. All of us could visit the sick and the elderly more often. Indeed, our society would be much more humane and caring if today's Christians recovered the traditional corporal works of mercy – including, but not limited to, the visiting of the sick.

No matter how we try to avoid it, sickness is a part of life. In spite of all our modern medical advances, sickness catches up on us. Today people take any number of tablets and supplements, and many do their utmost to remain at peak physical health. Many of us carry

6   Vatican II, *Constitution on the Sacred Liturgy: Sacrosanctum Concilium*, 73, https://www.vatican.va/archive/hist_councils/ii_vatican_council/documents/vat-ii_const_19631204_sacrosanctum-concilium_en.html.

painkillers on our person so as not to have to endure the least pain. However, while it is good to take care of our bodies, which are temples of the Holy Spirit (1 Corinthians 6:19), any physical benefit we obtain will only be temporary, as all of us will eventually die and most of us will endure sickness before this. When we are confronted with an image of some sick child on television or social media, we might be tempted to change the channel, or scroll on from the post immediately, but we cannot change our ultimate reality. Our medieval forebears were correct when they posted the following reflection in their cemeteries where skeletons were often displayed: 'What you are now, we used to be; what we are now, you will be.' In order to live life to the fullest, it helps to reflect on life's end.

A very legitimate question that we would do well to ask ourselves as Christians, is whether our faith can help us in our struggles with sickness and death. Does someone who believes in Christ face suffering and death differently from a neighbour who does not have a living relationship with Jesus Christ?

St Paul says that what distinguishes those who have Christian faith from others is that Christians do not 'grieve as others do who have no hope' (1 Thessalonians 4:13). St Peter encourages Christians to live differently from the people around them: 'Do not fear what they fear, and do not be intimidated, but in your hearts sanctify Christ as Lord. Always be ready to make your defence to anyone who demands from you an accounting for the hope that is in you; yet do it with gentleness and reverence' (1 Peter 3:14–16).

Christians are not immune from suffering and death, nor are they immune from doubt and feelings of despair. Yet part of the universal call to holiness, which applies to all Christians, is that they have a mission to bear witness to Christ's conquering of death and the existence of heaven. Their faith assures them that God desires to bring to heaven any human person that desires to go there and cooperates with his redeeming grace. So, in answer to the above question, Christians are indeed called by Jesus to suffer in a different way from their non-Christian neighbours.

We can see an example of this in a story from the prophet Daniel in the Old Testament. King Nebuchadnezzar of Babylon has conquered the Holy Land and the city of Jerusalem. As part of his empire building, he commanded that various young men from all over the empire be brought to his capital in Babylon and trained to work in his palace and civil service (Daniel 1:1–6). Three young Jewish men, Hananiah, Mishael and Azariah, have been captured, and now find themselves working in the administration of the empire. They learn the Babylonian language and customs, they are given new names (Shadrach, Meshach and Abednego), yet in the midst of the luxury of the palace in which they are held, they remain true to the God of Israel and their Jewish faith.

At a certain point, others at the court are jealous of the young Israelites and report them to King Nebuchadnezzar for not participating in the state religion. This 'crime' is punishable by death, and King Nebuchadnezzar loses his patience with them and orders them to be executed by burning (Daniel 3:19–20). The furnace is heated to seven times its usual temperature and the flames reach twenty-two metres above the furnace. The strongest soldiers in the army bind the young men and cast them into the midst of the furnace. The flames are so hot that the soldiers who throw them in perish due to the heat. But God does not abandon his servants and sends an angel to protect them with a heavenly wind that drives the heat and flames away from them. The king is amazed to see Hananiah, Mishael and Azariah walking around in the midst of the flames, singing hymns to God and blessing the Lord. He also is amazed to see the fourth figure of the angel in the middle of the furnace. The song of praise sung by the young men is commonly referred to as the Song of the Three Young Men (Daniel 3:52–90), and to this day this song is sung in the Roman Catholic Church's official Morning Prayer of the Liturgy of the Hours every Sunday.[7] Then King Nebuchadnezzar calls the young men out from

---

7   This canticle, translated from the Greek, is found in Catholic editions of Daniel, chapter 3, but it is absent from most Protestant Bibles that follow the Aramaic text here.

the furnace and is amazed to see that 'the fire had not had any power over the bodies of those men; the hair of their heads was not singed, their tunics were not harmed, and not even the smell of fire came from them' (Daniel 3:94).

While this story is no longer familiar to all Christians, it was a staple of the early Christian imagination and there are many portrayals of it in Christian artwork. There is a famous example from the third century on the Catacombs of Priscilla in Rome and, closer to home, another on the eighth-century High Cross at Moone, County Kildare. The example of the three young men teaches us that it is possible to praise God in the midst of the flames. When we face flames in our own lives, including the flames of sickness, our faith promises us not that God will remove these flames, but that he will take care of us in the midst of the flames. Christians face the same problems as everyone else, but through faith they experience the consoling wind of the angel's wings protecting them from the flames. Furthermore, Christians, by virtue of their baptism, possess a calling to act as priests – not as ministerial priests presiding at the sacraments, but as priests who make the divine present to this world where so many people do not know God and his love. If they bear their sufferings and sickness with dignity and trust, this can be a presence of God for those who do not know him.

There is always the danger of thinking that this depends on human effort. Christians are not necessarily strong people or superheroes. Most Christians are very weak in and of themselves. The secret is to have discovered that Christ makes us strong when we are facing trials and tribulations – as St Paul famously explains, 'I can do all things through [Christ] who strengthens me' (Philippians 4:13). A 2018 letter from the Congregation of the Doctrine of the Faith in Rome stresses:

> The salvation that God offers us is not achieved with our own individual efforts alone ... Rather, salvation is found in the relationships that are born from the incarnate Son of

God and that form the communion of the Church. Because the grace that Christ gives us is not a merely interior salvation ... and introduces us into concrete relationships that he himself has lived, the Church is a visible community.[8]

The next paragraph of the document continues to stress that God wishes to save Christians through the sacraments, and that 'the participation, in the Church, in the new order of relationships begun by Jesus occurs by means of the sacraments.'[9]

God can and does help Christians face their sufferings in many ways and his Providence even extends to those who do not believe in him. Yet the Sacrament of the Sick is one of the main ways that he helps Catholics (and other Christians who celebrate this sacrament) in their time of need. This sacrament has two main ritual actions: the laying on of hands and the anointing with blessed oil. These are accompanied by a prayer. Different versions of the prayer have been found over the ages, but in the current form, after the priest has laid hands on the sick person's head, he anoints their forehead and hands with the holy oil of the sick as he prays these words: 'Through this holy anointing, may the Lord in his love and mercy help you with the grace of the Holy Spirit. May the Lord who frees you from sin save you and raise you up.'[10]

According to the *Catechism of the Catholic Church* (1520–23) there are four main effects of this sacrament. The first effect is that it imparts 'a particular gift of the Holy Spirit'. It grants a grace of 'strengthening, peace and courage to overcome the difficulties that go with the condition of serious illness or the frailty of old age.' This particularly helps the sick person to fight against the evil one, who

8   Congregation for the Doctrine of the Faith, *Placuit Deo: On Certain Aspects of Christian Salvation*, 12–13. Available at https://www.vatican.va/roman_curia/congregations/cfaith /documents/rc_con_cfaith_doc_20180222_placuit-deo_en.html.
9   Ibid.
10   *The Roman Ritual: Pastoral Care of the Sick. Rites of Anointing and Viaticum. Approved for use in the Dioceses of Ireland, England and Wales, and Scotland* (Dublin: Veritas Publications, 1983), 124, #124.

tempts every sick person with discouragement and giving up in the face of sickness and death. The strengthening of the sacrament also promotes healing – both healing of the soul and, on occasion, even physical healing, if that be God's will. Finally, the Sacrament imparts the forgiveness of any venial sins the recipient might have committed. This is an important aspect of the sacrament as people who are sick are often tempted to despair, but knowing that God forgives their sins can be a great consolation.

The second effect is 'union with the Passion of Christ'. When we are sick, God invites us to join our suffering to that of Christ in his Passion. There is a priestly aspect to the suffering of every Christian. We are configured to Christ's redemptive Passion (Colossians 1:24). Pope John Paul II wrote a beautiful letter *On the Christian Meaning of Human Suffering*. Here he proposed that 'suffering seems to be particularly *essential to the nature of the human person* ... Suffering seems to belong to the human person's transcendence: it is one of those points in which the human person is in a certain sense "destined" to go beyond themselves and is called to this in a mysterious way.'[11] Later in this letter John Paul, who gave a visible example of his teaching during his own prolonged suffering from Parkinson's disease, even speaks of the 'Gospel of Suffering'. In some ways, his perspective on suffering is vastly different from that of today's civil society. He considers it not as something to be avoided, or a problem to be solved, but as one of the most important aspects of being human:

> It is suffering, more than anything else, which clears the way for the grace which transforms human souls. Suffering, more than anything else, makes present in the history of humanity the powers of the Redemption. In that 'cosmic' struggle between the spiritual powers of good and evil, spoken of in the Letter to the Ephesians, human

---

11 Pope John Paul II, *Apostolic Letter* Salvifici Doloris *on the Christian Meaning of Human Suffering*, 11 February 1984, number 2, https://www.vatican.va/content/john-paul-ii/en/apost _letters/1984/documents/hf_jp-ii_apl_11021984_salvifici-doloris.html.

sufferings, united to the redemptive suffering of Christ, *constitute a special support for the powers of good*, and open the way to the victory of these salvific powers.[12]

The third effect is that this sacrament imparts an 'ecclesial grace'. One of the main temptations that faces us in sickness is the temptation to give in to feelings of loneliness and abandonment, but by this sacrament we are more closely bound to the communion of the saints. This works both ways: on a primary level the prayers and support of the members of the Church help the sick Christian. Then, by the grace of God imparted by this sacrament, the sick Christian is called to unite their suffering to the Passion of Christ and offer it for the good of the people of God. In this way the fruits of Christ's redemption are mediated to the Christians who need it most. This mysterious working of Christ is one of the hardest things to believe in this world, but on a deeper level of faith it can make sense of sickness and suffering and allows each Christian to become a mystic, finding God even in the most difficult level of sickness and death.

The sacrament is a 'preparation for the final journey'. While the sacrament is not reserved to the dying, and our hope is that every sickness will be healed, sometimes sickness will end in death. Additionally, sickness that we recover from ought not to be forgotten. God calls us to learn from every experience in this life. Sickness can help us to live our lives in a right perspective, realising that we will all have to face death one day.

The sacrament is also to be given to those who are dying – indeed it can be administered a number of times during a prolonged illness. By this it also helps to consecrate us for death. The Sacrament of the Sick joins the anointings in the sacraments of baptism and confirmation to prepare the Christian for eternal life. Death is the final enemy to be overcome before we can enter eternity (1 Corinthians 15:26). In a particular way, as the Catechism notes (*CCC*, 1523), 'this last

12   Pope John Paul II, *Salvifici Doloris*, 27.

anointing fortifies the end of our earthly life like a solid rampart for the final struggles before entering the Father's house'.

These reflections might seem a little exaggerated to some. But on the day of our baptism each of us was claimed for Christ. This adhesion to Christ has consequences. As a priest, one of my disappointments is that all too often people do not avail of this beautiful sacrament. Families tend to wait till the very last moment before calling a priest. However, this sacrament can be a great help during sickness, both for the sick and their relatives and friends. This sacrament helps us put our life in its true perspective as 'sometimes a person has to become sick in order to recognize what we all—healthy or sick—need more than anything else: God. We have no life except in him.'[13]

Questions for Reflection and Discussion

1. How does a renewed appreciation of this sacrament as Sacrament of the Sick and not simply Extreme Unction help Christians to receive it?
2. Is sickness a problem that must be overcome, or does it have a role to play in the spiritual journey of this life?
3. Is it correct to say that Christians face sickness and death differently from those who do not know Jesus Christ?
4. How can we help others by our own sickness?

---

13 Christoph Schönborn (ed.), *Youcat English: Youth Catechism of the Catholic Church*, trans. Michael J. Miller (San Francisco, CA: Ignatius Press, 2011), 140, n. 241.

18: 'Go Forth, Christian Soul, from this World': A Theological Commentary on the *Proficiscere*

Andrew Meszaros

It is a theologically necessary and pastorally expedient part of the Christian tradition to pray for what Catholics call a 'happy death'.[1] Some of the most common prayers either call death to mind, or explicitly ask for assistance at death: the Sign of the Cross, the Hail Mary and the Mass are just a few examples. At its core, a happy death is ultimately one that takes place in communion with the Church and, thereby, with God. This is why the Eucharist – the sacrament of our communion with God and each other – is an essential aspect of Viaticum, or the last rites. But more broadly, a happy death involves a death that is adequately prepared for – such that, when the time comes, the Christian is ready to 'let go', to make peace with the world, with their life, and, most importantly, with God.

Another version of a happy death exists by the name of 'euthanasia', which, etymologically, also means a 'good', 'pleasant' or 'happy' death,[2] but refers to the intentional killing of a patient in order to

---

1   *Catechism of the Catholic Church*, 1014. (Hereinafter *CCC*.) Available online: https://www .vatican.va/archive/ENG0015/_INDEX.HTM

2   The word comes from *euthanatos,* where *thanatos* means death and the prefix '*eu*' typically means good or happy. The Greek *eudaimonia,* used in one of Aristotle's famous treatises on virtue ethics, is often translated 'happiness'.

eliminate pain and suffering caused by disease, often incurable. However, rather than engaging directly with the ethics of the direct and intentional ending of human life, this essay will explore one alternative means towards a happy death: namely, the Prayer of Commendation, traditionally referred to as the *Proficiscere*. This Latin name comes from the first word of the prayer, beginning *'Proficiscere, anima Christiana'*, commonly rendered as 'Go forth, Christian soul.' Associating the prayer with a happy death is not without warrant. Indeed, a scholar who has dedicated years of his life to researching the history of the prayer refers to it as a 'euthanastic' prayer because

> the prayer offers itself as a new pastoral aid to 'letting-go' when medicine and society often look on death as 'fail-ure' … it is a means through which a person can have a good death as they are helped to be released from holding on to life. It is the means by which a person can find the strength to let go of this life and find the liberty to die.[3]

While the *Proficiscere* is a prayer meant to assist the dying, the wisdom of the Christian tradition has long held that preparation for a happy death begins *now*. From a Christian perspective, this preparation, at its core, consists of befriending Jesus so as to live by his Spirit. This means living a life of grace, virtues and God-given gifts, which become essential for dying well. For example, one can courageously accept death with fortitude or, with patience, die with 'calm resignation'.[4] Dying with these virtues and others, including charity, forgiveness and obedience to God's will, is exhibited to us perfectly in Christ's own excruciating death. It is something we, in our fallen state,

---

3   John S. Lampard, *Go Forth, Christian Soul: The Biography of a Prayer* (Peterborough: Epworth Press, 2005), xxvi. Lampard's invaluable work – on which I rely heavily here – offers an extensive and detailed history of the prayer, even if some of his commentary on the text is more disputable. For more on the indirect but real Irish imprint on the prayer by Irish pilgrim-missionary monks, see Lampard, op. cit., 36–46.
4   John Hardon, *The Catholic Catechism: Contemporary Catechism of the Teachings of the Catholic Church* (Garden City, NY: Doubleday, 1975), 258.

cannot achieve; we need God's help. To pray for the dying is an act that implicitly acknowledges this need.

History of the Prayer

The first versions of this particular 'prayer of commendation', the *Proficiscere*, originate in the Frankish Empire of the eighth century, and were used by monks on behalf of dying brethren. The name 'prayer of commendation' might come from Christ's words on the cross, 'Father, into your hands I commend my spirit' (Luke 23:46), thereby associating the Christian's death with that of Christ. Alternatively, but not in contradiction, there is the possibility that this prayer of commendation was an extension of the so-called 'commendatory letters' that medieval pilgrims would carry with themselves, without which the reception of the sacraments in foreign lands was often not possible: whether in letter form to a pilgrimage site or in oral form to one's heavenly destination, this commendation was an aid for receiving the sacred.[5]

Monastic in origin, the prayer emerged at a time of religious plurality and – one might say – confusion, when Frankish paganism had not yet been entirely supplanted by Christianity. In addition to the mysteriousness of death itself, uncertainties abounded in the culture, stemming especially from pagan mythology. What happens after death? Is there an afterlife? Are we immortal? What dangers are posed to us in death and after death? To many such questions, the Christian Gospel provided clear answers; they are implicit in the *Proficiscere*. However, these answers were obscured in the tumultuous cultural and religious back-and-forth that the Frankish Church endured in the sixth, seventh and eighth centuries.[6]

The prayer spread rapidly throughout Europe over the centuries, tending towards ubiquity both within the monastery and without. But

---

5   Lampard, op. cit., 48. This latter reading is corroborated by the prayers following the *Proficiscere*. We find in the older *Roman Ritual* (1964) the priest praying, 'I commend you to almighty God … ', and 'O Lord, receive your servant … ', and 'We commend to you, O Lord, the soul of your servant … '.
6   Lampard, op. cit., 36–46.

this expansion ebbed in the localities where the Reformation took hold.[7] In the West, outside the Catholic liturgical tradition, the prayer was re-popularised among English speakers by John Henry Newman's (1801–1890) epic poem, *The Dream of Gerontius*, about a soul's journey to God – later put to music by Edward Elgar (1857–1934) – in which the prayer is recited according to Newman's translation.[8]

The version of the prayer I will comment on is the following:

> Go forth, Christian soul, from this world
> in the name of God the almighty Father,
> who created you,
> in the name of Jesus Christ, Son of the living God,
> who suffered for you,
> in the name of the Holy Spirit,
> who was poured out upon you,
> go forth, faithful Christian.
> May you live in peace this day,
> may your home be with God in Zion,
> with Mary, the Virgin Mother of God,
> with Joseph, and all the Angels and Saints[9]

This pruned version of older, more elaborate versions is the first option for the Prayer of Commendation found in the revised *Roman Ritual* of Pope Paul VI. Some elements of longer (older) versions are included as options in the current *Roman Ritual*.

---

7   Different theologies of death, grace and intercession – ones that viewed any intercession with respect to one's eternal destiny as superfluous – resulted in the *Proficiscere* being scrapped from Protestant prayer books, including, for example, the *Book of Common Prayer*. Lampard, op. cit., xix.

8   The prayer appears, fittingly, at the beginning of the drama as Gerontius is dying. John Henry Newman, *Verses on Various Occasions* (London: Longmans, Green, and Co., 1903), 323–70, at 330–31.

9   *Roman Ritual. Pastoral Care of the Sick. Rites of Anointing and Viaticum* (Dublin: Veritas Publications, 1982), 178–79.

Before the liturgical reforms of Paul VI, the older versions of the prayer included a more extensive litany, invoking not only Mary and Joseph, 'her illustrious spouse', but also angels and archangels, thrones and dominions, principalities and powers, virtues, cherubim, seraphim, patriarchs, prophets, apostles and evangelists, martyrs and confessors, holy monks, hermits and virgins. These invocations are suppressed in the revised version.[10]

Also omitted in the revised version (option B in the new *Roman Ritual*) is the line ' ... so that, when by your dying you have paid the debt to which every man is subject'. Nor does the newer version, unlike the old, petition Christ to free the dying from 'excruciating pain'. Also missing from the newer version are these beautiful lines from the older version:

> May the assembly of the apostles, our judges, welcome you. May the victorious army of white-robed martyrs meet you on your way. May the glittering throng of confessors, bright as lilies, gather about you. May the glorious choir of virgins receive you. May the patriarchs enfold you in the embrace of blessed peace. May St. Joseph, beloved patron of the dying, raise you high in hope and may the holy Mother of God, Virgin Mary, lovingly turn her eyes toward you. And then, gentle and joyful, may Christ Jesus appear before you, to assign you a place forever among those who stand in his presence.[11]

These omitted lines offer us a vivid expression of Catholic hope in our ultimate beatitude that is achieved through Christ and the intercession of all his saints, and which ultimately overcomes the realities of sin, suffering and death. Whether one prays these lines or not,

---

10 Cf. *Collectio Rituum* (Collegeville, MN: Liturgical Press, 1964), 269ff.
11 The newer version also omits the petition to be freed 'from the death that never ends'. The *Libera* petition to be delivered from 'all the dangers of hell, from constraining punishments, and from all distress' (in the older version) is reduced to 'from every distress' (in the new).

highlighting the older form here helps to imbue the new version of the prayer with the same firm hope that is expressed in the old.

Theological Commentary
Our theological commentary on the prayer begins with the first line:

Go forth, Christian soul, from this world …

From the first line, we see an acknowledgment of the doctrine of the immortality of the soul. That is to say, according to Christian anthropology, the soul of the human being, unlike the animating principle of a dog or of even the most advanced of primates, is a spiritual substance whose existence endures even after its separation from the body.[12] This does not mean that the human person is essentially the soul; the human person is essentially body *and* soul united. The grief of those left behind reflects this reality: namely, that the mode of existence by which we have come to know and love someone – an embodied existence – is now absent. At death, the mode of existence has radically altered to a disembodied existence, an existence which, as the resurrection informs us, is an incomplete one.

'Go forth' connotes the dynamism that is inherent in human existence. From its very beginning each human life is on a pilgrimage towards an ultimate destiny. In his *Dream of Gerontius*, Newman avails of poetic licence to insert into his translation the word 'journey': 'Go forth upon thy journey, Christian soul!' Such an insertion makes sense, given common expressions used to refer to one's impending death: a person is described as being 'on his way' or as 'making her journey'. As the prayer teaches us, this journey *does not end* with death, but continues. That death is viewed as only one stop on a longer journey is also corroborated by the phrase commonly used to refer to the last rites: namely, Viaticum, or provision for the way. The soul,

---

12   The 1964 *Roman Ritual* still gave expression to this truth when the priest prayed, 'Then, when your soul goes forth from your body, may the radiant company of Angels come to meet you … '; *Collectio Rituum*, 271.

even after its separation from the body (and with it, the entire material world), continues on its way, on its journey, on its pilgrimage towards its destination which, as the prayer indicates, is 'home with God in Zion'.

The destination, furthermore, transcends or lies beyond this world as we currently know it. The dying person goes forth *from this world* into another. While more will be said below about the destination itself, the line 'from this world' refers specifically to this world's mode of existence: namely, one that is subject to the limitations of space and time, and to the consequences of sin. The next world is a spiritual world, not one that is intrinsically immaterial (for one still expects the resurrection of the body in the next world), but one that surpasses the limitations that the material world imposes on us here and now. The world the Christian is leaving is characterised by deliberation, exertion, struggle, suffering, decay and mortality. The next world is characterised by an eternal and unfathomable peace and joy which is the loving vision of our Creator.

This pilgrimage is undertaken *in the name of* the Trinity:

> in the name of God the almighty Father, who created you,
> in the name of Jesus Christ, Son of the living God,
> who suffered for you,
> in the name of the Holy Spirit, who was
> poured out upon you.

The trinitarian formula here is a dense summary of the Christian Gospel narrative. In it, the trinitarian shape of God's creative, redemptive and sanctifying activity is expressed. The prayer reminds us that it is the Father who brought us into existence and sustains us. However, our relationship with God, initiated by the Father in his creative activity, is damaged by sin. Because God so loved the world, the Father sends us his only Son 'who loved me and gave himself for me' (Galatians 2:20; cf. John 3:16). And together, the Father and the Son send us his Spirit (John 15:26), or, as St Paul expresses it: 'God's love has been poured into our hearts through the Holy Spirit who has been given to us' (Romans 5:5).

The formula *in the name of* is significant. To do something *in the name of* someone, biblically, has multiple meanings. It can mean to act *on behalf of* someone else, or *for the sake of* someone else. Given the liturgical context of this prayer, the more suitable meaning can be garnered from that which we witness in the baptismal formula; when one is baptised *in the name of* the Trinity, one is united to God by the grace that Christ bestows through his human nature. Such a union with God is not a physical union, for we do not become God's arms or legs. Neither, however, is the union merely a moral one; for, by baptism we are not simply sharing the same goals or objectives with God in the same way that members of a club are united by a common cause. In baptism, we are united to God really, truly, ontologically. This union, which is not physical, but more than moral, the Catholic theological tradition has called *mystical*. By it, the Christian truly has a share in God's life.

In echoing the baptismal formula, the prayer alludes to this mystical union, and so rightly addresses the dying one as *Christian*. It is the one who is baptised in the name of the Father, and of the Son and of the Holy Spirit who is going forth, and doing so with the same grace with which the human soul of Christ was filled.

This sharing in God's life we call grace, at the centre of which lie the theological virtues that unite us to God by way of participation. The Christian soul goes forth having a share in God's knowledge of himself and the world through the virtue of faith. The Christian soul goes forth with a share in God's own love through the virtue of charity. In desiring God and clinging to his promises, the Christian soul goes forth with the virtue of hope.

When the Christian soul goes forth 'in the name of' the Trinity, then, it is going forth on the basis of, or with the strength of, or with the power of, a union with God,[13] but this union will be completed and brought to fulfilment at the beatific vision (when we are at 'home with God in Zion'). Thomas Aquinas called this life of grace the 'beginning of glory'.[14] It is a partial and imperfect but real participation in God's life. The Christian soul completes its journey in the consummation or perfection of this glory. It is, in essence, a journey from the beginning of glory to its perfection. Faith gives way to the vision of God; hope is fulfilled in the possession of God's promise; and the love that one had for God in this life is brought to perfection such that 'a person's whole heart is always actually borne towards God'.[15]

Returning to the question of our ultimate destination, the prayer commands:

> Go forth, faithful Christian. May you live
> in peace this day,
> may your home be with God in Zion …

These lines refer to our ultimate destiny, the consummation of the glory we are already enjoying partially through grace. The peace that the prayer speaks of is eternal peace which, as St Augustine observed, is the only real peace; any peace that will eventually expire is no real peace.[16] Is there any other goal worth pursuing? Augustine asks, 'For what other end do we set for ourselves than to reach that kingdom of which there is no end?'[17]

Our eternal peace is dwelling or living with God. The domestic imagery of the home alludes to Christ's promise: 'In my Father's house there are many dwelling places. If it were not so, would I have told you that I go to prepare a place for you? And if I go and prepare a

---

13 This interpretation of the prayer coheres also with older versions that exhort the soul to go 'in the name of' various saints and martyrs, for the power of the saint lies in the same grace of Christ shared by all the righteous.
14 Thomas Aquinas, *Summa Theologica,* II–II, q. 24, a. 3, ad. 3.
15 Ibid., a. 8, cor.
16 Augustine, *The City of God against the Pagans*, trans. R. W. Dyson (Cambridge: Cambridge University Press, 2015), XVII.13; XIX.17.
17 Ibid., XXII.30.

place for you, I will come again and will take you to myself, so that where I am, there you may be also' (John 14:2–3).

The prayer's additional allusion to Zion gives this dwelling place an aura of sublime transcendence. In the Old Testament, Zion is synonymous with Jerusalem, the city of God's temple and kingship. But the use of Zion, primarily in Isaiah and the Psalms, means that this Zion is something that has been taken away, something that stands in need of restoration (Isaiah 49:14; Psalm 137:1). In this respect, Zion is a gift, not something owed. Its absence is a real possibility. In the same way that Adam and Eve were driven out of Eden – out of their paradise, now lost – the Jews were driven out of Jerusalem. So, too, the Christian soul goes forth to Zion, a destination given, not owed.

The allusion to a paradise lost makes sense only if there is a real possibility of eternal loss. Implicit in the fact that the Church prays this at the time of impending death is the fact that the Church believes that the dying person is in need of assistance and that this prayer, indeed, assists the dying in reaching that heavenly city,

> … with Mary, the Virgin Mother of God,
> with Joseph, and all the Angels and Saints.

As a city, this divine dwelling is the home of many. Its citizens, as Augustine says, are united by their love of God.[18] While all angels and saints are mentioned, the explicit reference is not only to Mary, but also to Joseph – those who shared the most years of God the Son's pilgrimage on earth. Such a reference is suggestive of Christ's own death, resurrection and ultimate inhabitation of the City of God. Jerusalem, conceived of as a restoration of a once-lost communion with Christ at its centre, is given concentrated expression by St Bernard of Cluny, whose Latin poem is translated for us by hymnist John Mason Neale (1818–1866) in the hymn 'Jerusalem the Golden'.

---

18 Ibid., XI.1; XIX.24.

They stand, those halls of Syon,
conjubilant with song;
and bright with many an angel,
and all the martyr throng:
the Prince is ever in them,
the daylight is serene;
The pastures of the blessed
Are decked in glorious sheen.[19]

Conclusion

The Christian liturgical tradition and, in particular, the *Proficiscere*, are by no means 'solutions' to the problem of suffering. Their purpose is neither to eradicate suffering nor even to lessen it, but rather to offer the consolation of divine assistance at a person's most crucial moment in this world. By its invocation of Christ 'who suffered for you', the prayer calls to mind the excruciating agony undergone by the Son who became flesh for us and for our salvation. In this way, the prayer serves to assist the dying by uniting their agony with that of Christ, and thereby offering those graces necessary for a death that leads to life abundant (John 10:10). The contents of the prayer reveal a wider panorama of human existence that extends beyond this world. Suffering is not mitigated, but it can be ameliorated by this eternal perspective.

The *Proficiscere* is pregnant with theological depth. Naturally, the recitation of this prayer *in situ* on behalf of someone who is dying is not the time to recall all of its theological contents. Reflecting now on the meaning of the prayer, however, helps cultivate in us a habitual recollection of the dynamic purpose of life that God has revealed to us. In fact, cultivating a habitual awareness of this eternal perspective is crucial for preparing for death. Regular participation in the sacramental life is the best way of cultivating this habit, for through it we strengthen

---

19 From 'The Rhythm of Bernard de Morlaix', John Mason Neale, *Collected Hymns, Sequences and Carols of John Mason Neale* (London: Hodder and Stoughton, 1914), 210. While these last two lines evoke Christ the good shepherd, the alternative rendering of the last two lines evokes Christ the new Adam who restores Eden: 'the tree of life and healing / has leaves of richest green.'

the virtues of faith in God's word and hope in God's promises. These revealed truths (e.g. that we have immortal souls, that we are destined for heaven and that we are in need of God's grace to achieve our end) serve as the foundation for an *Ars Moriendi*, or the art of dying well. The practice of this art for everyone begins now.

Nor is it necessary to use the prayer exclusively for someone dying. Rather, we can recite the prayer regularly, even daily, not necessarily at the bedside of someone *in extremis*, but for all those in the world who are dying at that time. The theological rationale behind such intercessory prayer, even on behalf of those unknown to the petitioner, is the mystical union alluded to earlier in this essay: because Christians have in common that grace which unites each to Christ, together they constitute a corporate unity whose constitutive parts mutually affect each other. In this regard, St Paul teaches us: 'If one member suffers, all suffer together with it; if one member is honoured, all rejoice together with it' (1 Corinthians 12:26). By extension, the Church, in her liturgical life, intercedes on behalf of the entire world.

The uncertainties and fears surrounding death today are not entirely unlike those in the Frankish Empire of the first millennium. The unequivocal Gospel promise of our heavenly Father's house with many rooms is preached in the context that is full of uncertainty and amid alternative or agnostic views on the subject. In the context of such uncertainty, such a didactic response needs also to be paired with a liturgical one. Christians are responsible not only for proclaiming our heavenly destiny, but also for praying for its fulfilment.

Questions for Reflection and Discussion

1. What difference, if any, could praying the *Proficiscere* make in preparing for death?
2. 'Grace is nothing else but a certain beginning of glory in us' (Thomas Aquinas). What are some of the ways in which your life now is a foretaste of the happiness that God promises?

3. What concrete steps can we take to begin preparing for a happy death?
4. Do you think sufficient attention is given to death and our eternal destiny in the Church's preaching?

19: From Death to Eternal Happiness

Thomas G. Casey SJ

Each of us can be sure of two things – we are going to die, and our death is getting closer each day. Death is not merely something that happens to other people. It befalls each one of us, on a particular day (one of the seven days of the week) and at a specific time (one of the twenty-four hours of the day). Although the fact of death has been unavoidable for thousands of years, humanity has also been trying to dismiss, ignore or minimise it for millennia. In his *Letter to Menoeceus*, Epicurus (341–270 BC) stated, 'That most fearful of bad things, death, is nothing to us, since when we are, death is not, and when death is present, then we are not.'[1] This statement of Epicurus appears to make sense, but only if we accept his claim that death is the end of us. It is true that if there is no kind of existence after death, there is no longer a self or soul to feel anything, either positive or negative, and so death is not to be feared.

However, even before we turn to the Christian view of these things, it can be shown that non-existence is not as benign as Epicurus implies. Thomas Nagel, the American philosopher, has argued against the position of Epicurus by asking us to imagine an intelligent person who suffers an injury to the brain, and as a result is reduced to the

---

1   *Epicurus: The Extant Remains*, with short critical apparatus, translation and notes by Cyril Bailey (Oxford: Clarendon Press, 1926), 85.

condition of a happy infant.[2] This person is content in their new state and moreover receives excellent medical care. However, the family and friends of this person are profoundly saddened; not because there is anything regrettable about being a contented infant, but for the simple reason that the person in question has lost so much, above all their adult capabilities and their future. In a similar way, it is because death robs us of so much that it is so undesirable.

Given the loss inflicted by death, it seems excessive to suggest that we are destined to partake of a happiness beyond any happiness we can possibly imagine. Even believers are liable (unintentionally) to dampen down the ecstatic reality of heaven. A number of years ago a priest was preaching at the funeral Mass of his own mother. After explaining that she enjoyed a good glass of wine every so often, he surmised that she was now enjoying several bottles of her favourite wine in paradise. It was an appealing image, and the congregation received it as such. At the same time, it fell far short of the wonderful reality. Heaven isn't about quantitative change – enjoying a greater amount of your favourite wine. Heaven is about qualitative change – enjoying a celestial drink compared to which the best vintage wine tastes like dishwater.

This priest was not alone in his failure to appreciate fully the huge dimensions of eternal happiness. Even when we are intellectually aware of the grandeur of the Christian notion of paradise, our spontaneous images can lag far behind the truth in our minds. We sometimes imagine heaven merely in terms of ethereal angels plucking harps atop white fluffy clouds, or as a congregation in a vast church singing hymns all day long. The secular culture around us also finds it difficult to believe that heaven could entail pure joy. We can get a flavour of how heaven is pictured in our Western culture by briefly turning to a couple of recent novels that deal with the topic. These books reflect an

---

2   Thomas Nagel, 'Death', in Thomas Nagel, *Mortal Questions* (Cambridge: Cambridge University Press, 1979), 1–10.

inability on the part of our culture to depict heaven as anything more than a moderately improved version of our present world.

The Lovely Bones, a bestselling novel by Alice Sebold from 2002, starts like this: 'My name was Salmon, like the fish; first name, Susie. I was fourteen when I was murdered on December 6, 1973 … It was still back when people believed things like that didn't happen.'[3] When Susie arrives in heaven, there is no God to welcome her, and there is no angel or saint in sight. Susie is helped to adjust to this new space by a guidance counsellor named Franny. It turns out that each person is given their own personal heaven, and Susie is glad that hers is so like the life she was forced to leave behind: it has the kind of buildings she remembers so well, a school where she is only required to read favourite magazines such as *Vogue* and *Glamour*, and the peppermint-stick ice cream of which she is particularly fond.

Tim Thornton's *Felix Romsey's Afterparty* (2018) portrays heaven as a celestial rock festival.[4] Some of the most iconic singers of our age appear at this musical extravaganza – John Lennon, Kurt Cobain, Whitney Houston, Michael Hutchence and Serge Gainsbourg. Yet for all that, there is no qualitative change – this heaven does not have a higher kind of music. There is simply quantitative change – the rock festival has the same music we are used to hearing on earth, only it brings the best of this music together in a spectacular line-up.

These two novels reflect the tendency to visualise heaven as the intensification and enlargement of earthly satisfactions and joys. The fictional characters undergo change by virtue of being in heaven, but they do not experience genuine transformation. What is appealing about these fictional portrayals of heaven is that they are basically good; what is disappointing about them is the mediocrity of their goodness. They represent a cheap counterfeit compared to the richness of the real thing.

3   Alice Sebold, *The Lovely Bones* (London: Picador, 2002), 1.
4   Tim Thornton, *Felix Romsey's Afterparty* (London: Unbound, 2018).

Yet something in us wants to believe that eternal happiness is infinitely more wonderful than anything we experience in this life. My wager is that our innate desire for eternal happiness corresponds to a state of bliss that really exists. I base my wager on the difference between two kinds of desires we have: inner and outer. We naturally desire things such as food, drink, friendship and goodness. These desires are innate: they come from our nature, and there is always something real out there corresponding to these natural desires. We also desire things such as driving a Ferrari, winning the lottery and being Superman. These desires come from outside of us, and simply because we desire these things does not mean that they actually exist: there are Ferraris, but (spoiler alert!) there is no Superman. By contrast, the objects that we naturally desire are objects that time and again have been found to exist.

The desire for heaven is innate. This doesn't mean that we are necessarily conscious of it. And when we do become (often dimly) aware of it, we often prefer to ignore it. As C. S. Lewis once said: 'Our Lord finds our desires not too strong, but too weak. We are half-hearted creatures, fooling about with drink and sex and ambition when infinite joy is offered us, like an ignorant child who wants to go on making mud pies in a slum because he cannot imagine what is meant by the offer of a holiday at the sea. We are far too easily pleased.'[5]

We cannot identify this object called 'heaven' in a precise way because it is always greater than any concept or image that we can form of it. St Paul describes it in words that indicate how ineffable and mysterious it really is: 'what no eye has seen, what no ear has heard, and what no human mind has conceived – the things God has prepared for those who love him' (1 Corinthians 2:9). My contention is that this longing to live for ever is not something we acquire accidentally. This helps explain why even people who reject the very notion of an afterlife are often eager to see themselves remembered by posterity for their philanthropy, their children or other contributions

---

5   C. S. Lewis, *The Weight of Glory* (San Francisco, CA: HarperCollins, 2001), 26.

to society. They may dismiss any talk of eternal life, but they still put huge energy into assuring some kind of immortality for themselves. By engaging with such energy in immortalising themselves, they unintentionally witness to this innate desire that God has planted in each one of us. Our longing for eternal happiness is not pointless, but has a point that makes a lot of sense, precisely because it is an innate and natural longing for something that exists, and consequently it is a longing that can be fulfilled.

Despite all this talk of eternal happiness, it is the case that our flesh rots and decomposes after death. At first glance, the very thought of this is repellent, but, on reflection, it turns out not to be as macabre as it initially appears. After all, we shed and regrow our outer skin cells every four weeks, and so many body cells are renewed each year that every seven years we receive a completely new body. In other words, in the course of the average lifespan, the body has already 'died' many times. Although the ancient Greeks didn't have sophisticated technology at their disposal, they were nevertheless aware of this truth. Quoting the priestess Diotima, Socrates says: 'Even while each living thing is said to be alive and to be the same – as a person is said to be the same from childhood until he turns into an old man – even then he never consists of the same things, though he is called the same, but he is always being renewed and in other respects passing away, in his hair and flesh and bones and blood and his entire body.'[6]

What then survives death? Not the body, which is visible, but something that is invisible, and yet of decisive importance. Let's turn once again to the Greeks for inspiration. Plutarch, a Platonist philosopher of the first century after Christ, was intrigued by the well-known Greek legend concerning the ship of Theseus, the renowned king of Athens. Theseus sailed on this ship to the island of Crete. There he slew the dreaded Minotaur. He rescued a number of Athenian prisoners and brought them home. The Athenians preserved the ship and

---

6   Plato, *Symposium*, 207d-e, trans. Alexander Nehamas and Paul Woodruff, in Plato, *Complete Works*, edited, with introduction and notes, by John M. Cooper, associate editor, D. S. Hutchinson (Indianapolis, IN: Hackett, 1997), 490.

sailed it each year. However, over time, the ship steadily began to fall apart. They removed the rotten planks, replaced them with new timber, installed new parts, and so on. In his work *Life of Theseus*, Plutarch explains:

> The ship on which Theseus sailed with the youths and returned in safety, the thirty-oared galley, was preserved by the Athenians down to the time of Demetrius Phalereus. They took away the old timbers from time to time, and put new and sound ones in their places, so that the vessel became a standing illustration for the philosophers in the mooted question of growth, some declaring that it remained the same, others that it was not the same vessel.[7]

Here Plutarch raises a thorny question to which such renovations give rise: if the material that makes up the ship is replaced, is it still the same vessel?

It is reasonable to suggest that the ship is the same to the extent that it still fulfils its intended purpose, even if some or all of its material parts have been replaced. We could apply this in an analogous way to the human being. To be a human being is not to be formed of never-changing material – after all we know that the material making up the human body changes many times during an average lifespan. Instead, to be a human being is to have a particular configuration or structure, so that the bodily material is organised into a functioning system.

The human soul gives a specific configuration to the body that enables it to exist and function as the body that it is. The soul is the animating principle of the body. If there is no soul, the body would have no more life than a corpse. It is the soul that gathers and

---

7   Plutarch, *The Parallel Lives*, Volume 1, translated by Bernadotte Perrin (Loeb Classical Library; Cambridge, MA: Harvard University Press, 1914), 49.

organises the body, enabling it to exist and function as a living body. Although invisible, the soul is the inner and unifying principle of the body.

The life of the body comes to a temporary end at death, while the life of the soul continues. Of course, although body and soul are separated at death, which is the reason that human life ceases, Christians believe that body and soul will be reunited in the world to come. The doctrine of the resurrection of the body gives grounds for tremendous hope, since it emphasises the value of the body and promises that *all* of human existence will be renewed and transformed. This future hope redounds in turn upon our present lives, since it underlines the sacredness of the body, which is not merely an instrument or appendage, but expresses the whole self.

Can we detect the life of the soul within us? Our thoughts offer an example of this invisible life at work. Animals can communicate, and some animals are capable of transmitting messages in complex ways, but only human beings are able to think in such a way that they can express their thoughts with words. A number of years ago, there was a telling story in the British newspapers that expressed this difference between animals and human beings in a comic – and sad – way.[8] A computer programmer called Chris was sharing a flat with his girlfriend Suzy. They had a pet parrot called Ziggy. Chris felt thoroughly at ease in Suzy's company, and his only regret was that she wasn't at all as fond of their parrot as he was. The parrot used to make Chris laugh, especially because Ziggy screeched 'Hiya Gary' every time Suzy's mobile phone rang. Chris laughed even louder on hearing Ziggy make kissing noises when the name 'Gary' was mentioned on television. One day, as Suzy was about to kiss Chris, Ziggy imitated her voice and screeched, 'I love you, Gary'. Suzy broke down, and admitted she had been having an affair with a man called Gary for the previous

---

8   See for instance: 'How Talking Parrot Spilled Beans on Owner's Cheating Girlfriend', *The Guardian*, 17 January 2006, https://www.theguardian.com/uk/2006/jan/17/samjones.uknews2. Accessed 7 April 2021.

four months. Her confession brought her two-year relationship with Chris to an abrupt end.

Now, the parrot had no idea that Suzy had been having an affair. Neither had it any notion that it was disclosing her secret. That was because the parrot had no idea what it was talking about. Unfortunately, Chris felt compelled to part with Ziggy soon after his break-up with Suzy, because the parrot kept repeating Gary's name over and over again. Of course the parrot had no intention of hurting Chris's feelings and putting him through this torture: it was simply mimicking the sounds it had heard Suzy make. By contrast, when we speak, we express our thoughts.

Although advanced imaging technology has made it possible for us to detect when a person is thinking, this technology is incapable of identifying specific thoughts. It can indeed detect the kind of mental activity that occurs in the brain when we think in a certain way. It can detect the brain signals or brainwave patterns that accompany certain categories of thought. But as for identifying a specific thought taking place at a particular moment, that's not possible – at least for now! Mind-reading software can see *that* we are thinking; but it cannot see *what* our thoughts are. In a similar way, the body reveals to others the kinds of feelings we are experiencing, but not the exact nature of those feelings. For instance, if we get angry, our heart rate typically increases, our breathing becomes quicker and we start perspiring because of an overall rise in body temperature. People can safely say that we are angry, but as for identifying the exact nature and object of our anger, that is another matter. All they can see are the physical effects of the feeling of anger, and not the feeling itself, which remains invisible.

The soul – this invisible, intelligent and immortal divine gem – is uniquely equipped to give us access to heaven, because the soul enables us to love in the best sense of the word. We can love in ways that go far beyond instinct, by laying down our lives for those with whom we have no blood relationship. Interestingly, in Dostoevsky's novel *The Brothers Karamazov*, the holy monk Zosima recommends love as the gateway to full life. Zosima is approached by a woman whose faith is faltering. He encourages her to walk along the path of active love in order to strengthen her faith in God and in the immortality of her soul: 'Strive to love your neighbour actively and indefatigably. Insofar as you advance in love you will grow surer of the reality of God and of the immortality of your soul. If you attain to perfect self-forgetfulness in the love of your neighbour, then you will believe without doubt, and no doubt can possibly enter your soul. This has been tried. This is certain.'[9]

Love gives us confidence because 'perfect love casts out fear' (1 John 4:18). Joseph Ratzinger, later Pope Benedict XVI, maintained that what makes us distinctively human is our capacity for dialogue with God, a dialogue of love that death cannot destroy, a dialogue that will continue forever: 'All love wants eternity, and God's love not only wants it but effects it and is it.'[10]

Since eternal life is a relationship of love with God, this relationship can start on earth. And this eternal now is not boring, because it is not the satisfaction of desire, but its continual expansion. A parable about a medieval monk illustrates this truth. The monk had problems believing that there was such a thing as eternal happiness. Whenever he tried to picture it, all he could imagine was a large congregation packed into a huge church singing hymns all day and night. One day as he walked through the forest, a blackbird burst into song. The monk was so captivated by the mellow, flute-like singing of the bird that he stood still and listened for a long time. When he walked back to the monastery, things looked different. None of the monks recognised him. He looked for his abbot, but when he gave the monks the name of this man, he was told he had died three hundred years earlier!

This legend evokes the ecstatic nature of eternal happiness: time stops in its tracks, and our hearts bask in wonder. Yet this time beyond time surpasses anything we can imagine. But the monk in the story

9   Fyodor Dostoevsky, *The Brothers Karamazov*, trans. Constance Garnett and revised by Ralph E. Matlaw (New York, NY: W. W. Norton, 1976), 48.
10 Joseph Ratzinger, *Introduction to Christianity*, trans. J. R. Foster (San Francisco, CA: Ignatius Press, 1990), 271.

was also greater than he thought, because he grasped the fact that eternity is truly timeless. When it comes to eternity – and to ourselves – we need to be freed from a suffocating smallness in our desires and aspirations. We need to be bold enough to believe that God promises this unimaginable gift of salvation to us, and confident enough, despite the disintegration of the body after death, to trust that this prospect more than fulfils our deepest hopes and longings.

Questions for Reflection and Discussion

1. Within your daily life, where have you found sources of wonder – e.g. gazing at a beautiful sunset, listening to sublime music, catching the scent of a rose?
2. How can you tap into more of these moments, so as to expand your imagination and realise that you are more than a citizen and a consumer, that you are in truth a child of God with an eternal destiny?
3. Do you only want to live longer, or do you want to live a different *kind* of life? A life bigger than anything you can dream of or wish?
4. If cleaning your room cannot compete with going on holiday, how could this world possibly compete with heaven?
5. If eternity includes all time, could heaven include excitement at the newness of an endless future, together with gratitude for an ecstatically happy past?

20: Facing Life's End: The Life of the World to Come

Declan Marmion SM

One of the earliest, and most potent, Christian symbols during the time of Roman persecution was the anchor. That anchor, of course, was Christ. For the Christian martyrs, hope in him and in his resurrection was 'a sure and steadfast anchor of the soul' (Hebrews 6:19). Epitaphs on believers' tombs in the catacombs displayed anchors alongside messages of hope in anticipation of heaven. Where Jesus had gone, they hoped to follow.

While the anchor symbol has fallen out of fashion today, it offers us a framework for considering what Christianity has traditionally called the 'last things': death, judgement, heaven and hell. The framework is one of hope. Christians live in the hope and expectation of communion with God – beginning in this life and culminating in the next. *Spe salvi* – 'in hope we are saved' (Romans 8:24).

Hope – as 'a trustful and confident movement toward the future'[1] – assumes there is a meaning and purpose to life. Christian life cannot simply be equated with transience and despair. Faith and hope go together. 'The one who has hope lives differently' (Benedict

---

1   Anthony Kelly, *Eschatology and Hope*, Theology in Global Perspective Series (Maryknoll, NY: Orbis, 2006), 1.

XVI), whereas living without hope renders life meaningless.[2] Faith is thus future-directed – 'the assurance of things hoped for, the conviction of things not seen' (Hebrews 11:1). At the same time, faith gives us *even now* something of the reality we are waiting for, drawing the future into the present and providing us with a sure foundation, a living hope.[3]

The foundation of hope for the Christian is the resurrection of Jesus. St Paul, possibly the greatest witness to the resurrection, put it starkly: 'If Christ has not been raised, then our proclamation has been in vain and your faith has been in vain' (1 Corinthians 15:14). The resurrection is thus pivotal for Christian faith. As we profess in the Creed, 'we look forward to the resurrection of the dead' — where 'we shall be with the Lord for ever' (1 Thessalonians 4:17). Communion with Christ and with one another is the central idea, a communion that becomes more intense after death.

The resurrection of Jesus not only vindicated the disciples' belief that he was the Messiah; it had a transformative effect on their outlook and way of life. It convinced them that God had acted in an ultimately decisive manner. The Crucified One lives. God's transformative love has triumphed over evil. It brought into being a community of witnesses to the resurrection who proclaimed Jesus as 'both Lord and Messiah' (Acts 2:36).

When the disciples claimed they had 'seen the Lord' (John 20:25), they insisted on the bodily nature, or physicality, of his resurrection. He was not a disembodied spirit or a ghost. He walks with the two disciples to Emmaus and eats with them (Luke 24:30). He has been raised up in his total physical reality – body and spirit – and with his whole history.

The disciples' encounters with the risen Lord were totally unexpected. At first, they had difficulty recognising him. His is a new mode

---

2   *Spe Salvi. Saved in Hope*, Encyclical Letter of Pope Benedict XVI (Dublin: Veritas Publications, 2018), 2, https://www.vatican.va/content/benedict-xvi/en/encyclicals/documents /hf_ben-xvi_enc_20071130_spe-salvi.html.
3   Ibid., 7–8.

of presence to the world. He appears and disappears at will. He is transformed, yet his body still bears the marks of his passion. There is both continuity and discontinuity between the body that died and the body that was raised. Paul speaks of an earthly 'physical body' and a heavenly 'spiritual body' (1 Corinthians 15:44). But the latter is still a body, rather than some ethereal entity, a transformed being totally suffused by the life-giving Spirit of God.

So, for Paul, resurrection meant resurrection of the body. 'The body will be *transformed*, not abandoned' (N. T. Wright).[4] Paul calls Christ the 'first fruits of those who have died' (1 Corinthians 15:20), implying that Christians can hope to have the same experience as Christ did. Just as he was completely transformed, so will they be. It is the *whole* person, our entire life history, who is raised and redeemed, and not only our spirit. Bodily resurrection is to be understood not so much physiologically, but personally. 'The resurrection of the body means the resurrection of the life that has been lived, with all its good and evil' (Romano Guardini).[5]

Yet Christianity has often been accused of being anti-body and other-worldly – more concerned about the next life than this one. This has been a serious challenge to Christianity from the beginning. Some early groups of Christians believed salvation consisted in escaping the material world and history to enter a life beyond. In their view, we are imprisoned in our bodies within an alien world and long to escape and return to the divine realm. Here there is no redemption '*of* the body' but only '*from* the body'. Such a mentality overlooked the corporality of Christ, who retained a body in his resurrected life. It gave rise to a denigration of matter and of creation, and even of the need to engage in the struggles of daily life.

Against this, Christianity proclaims the goodness of the material world as created by God (Genesis 1:31). We are not redeemed *from* the world but *with* it. 'Human and cosmos, spirit and world belong

---

4   N. T. Wright, *The Resurrection of the Son of God* (London: SPCK, 2012), 230.
5   Romano Guardini, *The Last Things: Concerning Death, Purification After Death, Resurrection, Judgment, and Eternity* (Notre Dame, IN: University of Notre Dame Press, 1965), 69.

inseparably together' (Gerhard Lohfink).[6] Just as there is human death and resurrection, there is a parallel process of death and resurrection on the part of the entire cosmos. There will be a final transformation of the world following the model of the resurrection – a 'new heaven and a new earth' (2 Peter 3:13). In this new creation, 'death will be no more' (Revelation 21:4).

If the *how* of the final resurrection ultimately exceeds our imagination and understanding, Scripture and tradition also underline the continuity and identity between our earthly and risen body. The personal life history of each person will be manifested and perpetuated – 'their works follow after them into [God's] kingdom' (Teilhard de Chardin).[7] Of our human endeavour in this life, 'nothing will be lost or have been in vain' (Pope John Paul II).[8] Rather than positing a dualism between this life and the next, it is more in line with the New Testament to see 'death as a transition to a greater and more perfect form of life' – eternal life.[9]

Resurrection, therefore, is not only corporeal but also collective or universal. Paul speaks of 'a resurrection of the righteous and the unrighteous' (Acts 24:15), and in the Creed we declare: 'he will come again to judge the living and the dead'. The notion of judgement developed alongside that of resurrection. The Church believes that judgement takes place in two stages: a particular or individual judgement, at death, where we are judged by God for the lives we have led; and a final, or universal, judgement of all humanity at the end of time. In Jesus' great parable of judgement – the parable of the sheep and the goats (Matthew 25:31–46), the criterion of judgement is charity. We will be judged according to our deeds: 'As you did it to one of the least of these my brothers and sisters, you did it to me' (Matthew 25:40). Our

---

6   Gerhard Lohfink, *Is This All There Is?: On Resurrection and Eternal Life* (Collegeville, MN: Liturgical Press, 2017), 185.
7   Pierre Teilhard de Chardin, *Hymn of the Universe* (New York, NY: Harper & Row, 1965), 133.
8   Pope John Paul II, *Sollicitudo Rei Socialis*, 48, https://www.vatican.va/content/john-paul-ii/en /encyclicals/documents/hf_jp-ii_enc_30121987_sollicitudo-rei-socialis.html.
9   Terence Nichols, *Death and Afterlife. A Theological Introduction* (Grand Rapids, MI: Brazos, 2010), 54.

charity on earth will be the measure of our sharing in the life of God in heaven. Or, as St John of the Cross put it, 'In the evening of our life we will be judged on love'.[10]

The prospect of rendering an account of our lives after death, however, has often filled Christians with a sense of fear and foreboding. Yet we hope that the love and mercy God shows us in this life will not cease in the next. God's love is always ready to meet the returning prodigal. The doctrine of purgatory is a sign of this infinite mercy of God who wants all people to be saved (1 Timothy 2:3). Since we are neither wholly sheep nor wholly goat, judgement might not only be 'a retrospective assessment of what we have been', but 'includes the prospective offer of what we might become. Perhaps judgement is a process rather than a verdict' (John Polkinghorne).[11] It is not about appearing before a vengeful God, but of seeing ourselves as we really are, a process of coming into the truth, all in the context of God's love.

Thus, judgement can become an object of hope because it is related to the justice of God. As the *Catechism of the Catholic Church* puts it, 'the Last Judgement will reveal that God's justice triumphs over all the injustices committed by his creatures and that God's love is stronger than death' (*CCC*, 1040). The injustices of history do not have the last word. Pope Benedict XVI said something similar: 'there can be no justice without a resurrection of the dead ... There will be an "undoing" of past suffering, a reparation that sets things aright ... God is justice and creates justice. This is our consolation and our hope' (*Spe Salvi*, 42, 43 and 44).

If judgement is primarily manifestation – manifestation of the truth about ourselves and the removal of all our masks – rather than verdict, there is another, more threatening strand running through the Bible that depicts judgement in terms of retribution. Even Jesus, in the parable of the last judgement, says that those who act without compassion for the poor and needy will be subjected to 'eternal

---

10 St John of the Cross, *Dichos* 64 (quoted in *CCC*, 1022).
11 John Polkinghorne, *The God of Hope and the End of the World* (New Haven, CT: Yale University Press, 2003), 130.

punishment' and sent 'into the eternal fire prepared for the devil and his angels' (Matthew 25:41).

How can we reconcile a picture of God who appears at once loving and stern? Firstly, salvation and damnation, good and evil, are not on a par. God's love and God's wrath are not simply two sides of the same coin. Jesus' words and actions were primarily acts of salvation, not of judgement. He did not come 'to judge ... but to save the world' (John 12:47). 'The truth which judges [humanity] has itself set out to save [humanity]' (Benedict XVI).[12] Secondly, salvation is offered to all; yet, at the same time, God takes us seriously and does not usurp or bypass our freedom. Judgement is an image that evokes responsibility: 'In the final analysis man becomes his own judgement. Christ does not allot damnation.'[13] Our eternal destiny, therefore, depends on our decision and response to God's offer of salvation in Jesus.

Nowadays, in contrast to previous eras, one rarely hears a sermon on hell. Some feel that fear about hell has given way to a banal optimism about salvation that renders Christianity superfluous. Both extremes are to be avoided. All stand under divine judgement, yet 'the Church has never once declared the damnation of a single person as a concrete fact'.[14] The biblical messages of judgement are best understood as words of warning and an invitation to repentance. Hell, as separation from God and refusal to love, remains a real possibility, not due to God's anger, but to human freedom. It is not simply a threat coming from the outside but a consequence of the human capacity to close oneself off from God. 'The one who irrevocably refuses love condemns himself' (Hans Urs von Balthasar).[15] Moreover, as alluded to above, hell is linked with the question of justice and the ultimate

---

12 Joseph Ratzinger, *Eschatology: Death and Eternal Life* (2nd ed.) (Washington, DC: Catholic University of America Press, 2007), 206.
13 Ibid., 207.
14 International Theological Commission, 'Some Current Questions in Eschatology' (1992), 10.3, https://www.vatican.va/roman_curia/congregations/cfaith/cti_documents/rc_cti_1990 _problemi-attuali-escatologia_en.html.
15 Hans Urs von Balthasar, *Dare We Hope: "that All Men be Saved"? With, A Short Discourse on Hell* (2nd ed.; San Francisco, CA: Ignatius Press, 2014), 131.

triumph of God's love over evil. The power of evil will be negated once and for all. As Pope John Paul II put it:

> There is something in [the human] conscience that rebels against any loss of this conviction: Is not God who is Love also ultimate Justice? Can he tolerate these terrible crimes, can they go unpunished? Isn't final punishment [hell] in some way necessary in order to re-establish equilibrium in the complex history of humanity?[16]

While judgement may be ominous for those who have acted without mercy, it is not a question of putting mercy and judgement on an equal footing, for 'mercy triumphs over judgement' (James 2:13). Hence Walter Kasper declares: 'The human being's "no" of refusal cannot be an equally powerful possibility alongside the unconditional "yes" that God has spoken to humankind. The prior reality of divine mercy must have the first as well as the last word.'[17] Jesus' prayer for forgiveness for those who were responsible for his death (Luke 23:34) reveals mercy as the other face of justice. 'God loves the sinner because this is his nature' (Maximus the Confessor).[18] Although Jesus is both Judge and Saviour, we may hope for the salvation of all. It is not for us to put limits on God's mercy but, rather, to hope that he is a gracious judge.

In sum, the biblical testimony about the afterlife is complex and multifaceted. Both Scripture and the tradition of the Church exhibit a certain reserve or reticence when it comes to describing the realities to which they witness. Paul writes, 'What no eye has seen, what no ear has heard, and what no human mind has conceived [are] the things God has prepared for those who love him' (1 Corinthians 2:9). The various images and similes for hell – from the 'eternal fire' to the 'weeping and grinding of teeth' (Matthew 25:30, 41) – are not literal

---

16 Pope John Paul II, *Crossing the Threshold of Hope* (London: Jonathan Cape, 1994), 186.
17 Walter Kasper, *Mercy. The Essence of the Gospel and the Key to Christian Life* (New York, NY: Paulist Press, 2013), 108.
18 Maximus the Confessor, *First Epistle*; quoted by Balthasar, op. cit., 203.

descriptions of a place, but rather underline the permanent possibility of suffering the loss of God.

If the general or final resurrection at the end of history is still to come, does this mean the dead exist in a kind of interim or intermediate state? The Church affirms the existence of a spiritual element in the human person that 'survives and subsists after death, an element endowed with consciousness and will, so that the "human self" subsists'.[19] This element has traditionally been called 'spirit' or 'soul'. Separated from the body at death, 'it goes to meet God, living with the Lord, while awaiting its reunion with its glorified body' (*CCC*, 997). There is a certain duality, deficiency and provisionality here, in that the human soul (without a body) is not the entire person. The assumption is that, while the 'holy souls' after death enjoy communion with God, their bodies will be raised up only on the last day.

Critics of an interim 'disembodied' existence (such as Gerhard Lohfink) feel it is dualistic and devalues the resurrection of the body, while the soul already enjoys the vision of God.[20] Such critics put forward, instead, the idea of 'resurrection in death', i.e. at the death of each individual, rather than an event on the last day. They oppose not so much the continuance of the soul after death in line with the Christian tradition, but rather they develop a concept of soul connected with the body, a soul that has shaped and internalised the entire history of the person, giving him or her a personal identity. They want to show that the distinction between body and soul presupposes a more fundamental unity, i.e. that the person is a psychosomatic unity: she 'not only "has" a body but "is" body, and not only "has" a soul but "is" soul' (Gerhard Lohfink).[21] In this view, the immortality of the soul and the resurrection of the body can only be grasped as *being one* (Karl Rahner).[22]

19 Sacred Congregation for the Doctrine of the Faith, 'Letter on Certain Questions Concerning Eschatology', 17 May 1979, https://www.vatican.va/roman_curia/congregations/cfaith/documents/rc_con_cfaith_doc_19790517_escatologia_en.html.
20 Lohfink, op. cit., 175.
21 Lohfink, op. cit., 175.
22 Karl Rahner, *Theological Investigations*, vol. 17 (New York, NY: Crossroad, 1981), 121.

Notwithstanding the concerns and merits of the above theory, Scripture speaks of the resurrection not at the time of death but at the final coming of the Lord, the Parousia. Even in the case of Jesus, death and resurrection do not coincide in time but 'on the third day' (1 Corinthians 15:4). Thus, the Church retains the twofold phase of Christian hope for the resurrection, namely, the continued existence of the soul after death as 'intermediate' or 'transitory', but 'ultimately ordered to the resurrection' at the end of time.[23] If Catholic spirituality tended to privilege the former, the point, as the above-mentioned theory underlines, is that the immortality of the soul and the resurrection of the whole person belong together inseparably.

For most of us, the intermediate state will likely entail a process of purification whereby we are 'purged' from the remains of sin. This final stage of our maturation and sanctification – traditionally known as purgatory – is a process rather than a one-off event. We are not instantly perfected at the moment of death – there is also penance and purification in the next life. But purgatory is not a boot camp for the mediocre, nor is God a divine bookkeeper – so many years for so many sins. Rather, purgatory is that 'inwardly necessary process of transformation' (Joseph Ratzinger)[24] where we grow in our love of God, while being liberated from the obstacles that hinder this process, however painful it might be. And we are assisted in this by the prayers and penance of fellow believers. The liturgical practice of praying for the dead, especially at the Eucharist, can be traced back to the second and third centuries. It gave rise to the notion of the 'communion of saints'. The faithful departed are not separated from the Church; rather, a living communion and solidarity exists between us (the living) and our departed brothers and sisters. We pray for them, and they pray for us.

If purgatory is heaven's 'antechamber', our gradual incorporation into God, what of eternal life? Some find the prospect of an 'eternal'

23 Ibid.
24 Ratzinger, op. cit., 230.

life unattractive – uninterrupted boredom! Another way of seeing this, however, is to say that we are made for immortality. We are beings with an infinite horizon – continuously searching for meaning and fulfilment, yet never entirely satisfied with the finite or transient. This reflects our dynamism towards God, who alone can bring about a definitive realisation of our deepest desires and hopes. And this dynamism, this orientation to God, continues after death.

The person is more than a biological entity; on the contrary, our capacity for relationship with God constitutes what is deepest in the human being. This is what we mean by 'soul' – a subject in relation to God – 'not an extrinsic "thing" waiting to be inserted into a body'.[25] It is the abiding element of my personal identity, the essence of what makes me a human person. Personhood and relationality do not end in death. Indeed, Scripture and tradition underline how eternal life means a sharing in God's intimate life, where 'we will be like God, for we shall see him as he is' (1 John 3:2). Heaven, eternal life and salvation are terms that designate the fullness of life for which all people yearn. Rather than speaking of the immortality of the soul, perhaps we should speak instead of the immortality or indissolubility of our relationship with God.

Human life beyond the grave, therefore, must be understood 'dialogically' (Joseph Ratzinger). 'Eternal' does not necessarily mean something interminable but

> something more like the supreme moment of satisfaction, in which totality embraces us and we embrace totality ... It would be like plunging into the ocean of infinite love, a moment in which time – the before and after – no longer exists. ... such a moment is life in the full sense, a plunging ever anew into the vastness of being, in which we are simply overwhelmed with joy.[26]

---

25   Nichols, op. cit., 131.
26   Pope Benedict XVI, *Spe Salvi*, 12.

The social aspect of humanity, therefore, does not disappear in heaven. Rather, our love of God goes hand in hand with the joy of communion with others. In the consoling words of St Cyprian of Carthage: 'What glory, what a pleasure it will be when you are admitted to see God … There await for us the multitude of our loved ones, our parents, brothers and sisters, children, who are sure of their safety, yet solicitous for our salvation.'[27]

If God is the 'end' or goal of all human life, then, in heaven, in the contemplation of God, all our desires for communion will be ultimately fulfilled. We cannot equate our experience of time in this life with time after death. Rather, we are using the concept in an analogous sense – where the dissimilarity is greater than the similarity. Eternity is not endless time but rather the fulfilment and transcending of time, a dynamic process of growth in knowledge and love. Joseph Ratzinger describes 'the image of hands encircling time, and in so doing becoming contemporaneous with it' as an apt way 'to depict God's relationship to time and, at the same time, God's superiority over time'.[28] Theologians speak of the 'always now' of God: God is pure Act, pure giving and receiving, into whose life we are drawn. Such a 'homecoming' begins in this life and culminates in the next.

We began this chapter with a reflection on hope – 'the one who has hope lives differently'. And we saw how this hope is not confined to the individual but includes the entire cosmos. Today science speaks of an 'unfinished universe', of a cosmos still unfolding. While some believe the universe will end badly in a kind of cosmic catastrophe, the Christian has a more anticipatory and hopeful vision for the universe, grounded in a God who calls creation towards a new future. St Paul speaks of his hope 'that the creation itself will be set free from

27 St Cyprian of Carthage, *On Death*, Treatise 7.26, trans. Robert Ernest Wallis, *Ante-Nicene Fathers*, Vol. 5, Alexander Roberts, James Donaldson and A. Cleveland Coxe (eds),(Buffalo, NY: Christian Literature Publishing Co., 1886); revised and edited for New Advent by Kevin Knight, http://www.newadvent.org/fathers/050707.htm.
28 Joseph Ratzinger, 'The End of Time', in *The End of Time? The Provocation of Talking about God*, Tiemo Rainer Peters and Claus Urban (eds) (New York, NY/Mahwah, NJ: Paulist, 2004), 11.

its bondage to decay and will obtain the freedom of the glory of the children of God' (Romans 8:21). Such cosmic hope awaits not the destruction but the transformation of the universe. It refuses to define itself deterministically, or in terms of what has been, but rather in terms of what is to come and what God has promised. If the cosmic narrative is still unfinished, the appropriate Christian stance is one of patient but hopeful expectation.

Questions for Reflection and Discussion

1. What images of the afterlife do you find helpful or unhelpful? Explain your choice.
2. How can faith help us to 'prepare' for death?
3. Do you think faith and science can be reconciled?
4. What are your hopes and fears about dying?
5. 'In the evening of our life we will be judged on love' (St John of the Cross). Is this a good starting point for reflection on the afterlife?

Frequently Cited Sources

Catechism of the Catholic Church, https://www.vatican.va/archive/ENG0015/_INDEX.HTM

Pope Benedict XVI, *Message for the Fifteenth World Day of the Sick, 11/2/2007*, https://www.vatican.va/content/benedict-xvi/en/messages/sick/documents/hf_ben-xvi_mes_20061208_world-day-of-the-sick-2007.html

Pope Benedict XVI, *Deus Caritas Est*, https://www.vatican.va/content/benedict-xvi/en/encyclicals/documents/hf_ben-xvi_enc_20051225_deus-caritas-est.html

Pope Benedict XVI, *Spe Salvi*, https://www.vatican.va/content/benedict-xvi/en/encyclicals/documents/hf_ben-xvi_enc_20071130_spe-salvi.html

Pope John Paul II, *Apostolic Letter Salvifici Doloris on the Christian Meaning of Human Suffering*, https://www.vatican.va/content/john-paul-ii/en/apost_letters/1984/documents/hf_jp-ii_apl_11021984_salvifici-doloris.html

Pope John Paul II, *Sollicitudo Rei Socialis*, https://www.vatican.va/content/john-paul-ii/en/encyclicals/documents/hf_jp-ii_enc_30121987_sollicitudo-rei-socialis.html

Pope John Paul II, 'Life-Sustaining Treatment and the Vegetative State: Scientific Advances and Ethical Dilemmas', https://www.vatican.va/content/john-paul-ii/en/speeches/2004/march/documents/hf_jp-ii_spe_20040320_congress-fiamc.html

Pope Francis, *Fratelli Tutti*, http://www.vatican.va/content/francesco/en/encyclicals/documents/papa-francesco_20201003_enciclica-fratelli-tutti.html

Congregation for the Doctrine of the Faith, *Samaritanus Bonus: On the Care of Persons in the critical and terminal phases of life*, https://www.vatican.va/roman_curia/congregations/cfaith/documents/rc_con_cfaith_doc_20200714_samaritanus-bonus_en.html

Congregation for The Doctrine of the Faith, *Declaration on Euthanasia*, https://www.vatican.va/roman_curia/congregations/cfaith/documents/rc_con_cfaith_doc_19800505_euthanasia_en.html

Vatican II, *Gaudium et Spes*, https://www.vatican.va/archive/hist_councils/ii_vatican_council/documents/vat-ii_const_19651207_gaudium-et-spes_en.html

Vatican II, *Constitution on the Sacred Liturgy: Sacrosanctum Concilium*, https://www.vatican.va/archive/hist_councils/ii_vatican_council/documents/vat-ii_const_19631204_sacrosanctum-concilium_en.html

HSE Pregnancy and Infant Loss website, www.pregnancyandinfantloss.ie

St Mary's University, London, The Art of Dying Well website, www.artofdyingwell .org

Spiritual Health Victoria, *Spiritual Care in Victorian Health Services: Towards Best Practice Framework*, https://www.spiritualhealth.org.au/download/Guidelines-4-Qual -Spir-Care-Health-2020-5-310120-Web.pdf

World Health Organization, *WHO Definition of Palliative Care* (2013), http://www .who.int/cancer/palliative/definition/en

World Health Organization, *WHO Fact Sheets - Palliative Care* (2020), https://www .who.int/news-room/fact-sheets/detail/palliative-care

List of Contributors

Bairbre Cahill is a facilitator and writer on the spirituality of everyday life, based in Donegal.

Thomas Casey SJ, Rector of the Jesuit Community at Milltown Park and chaplain at Gonzaga College in Dublin, is the former Dean of Philosophy at St Patrick's Pontifical University, Maynooth.

Pádraig Corkery lectures in moral theology at St Patrick's Pontifical University, Maynooth.

Brendan Corkery is a palliative medicine registrar in Dublin.

Jeremy Corley lectures in Sacred Scripture at St Patrick's Pontifical University, Maynooth.

Sinéad Donnelly is a palliative medicine and internal medicine physician in Wellington, New Zealand.

Dermot Farrell is Archbishop of Dublin and a former President of St Patrick's College, Maynooth.

Anne Francis is an adjunct lecturer in pastoral theology at St Patrick's Pontifical University, Maynooth.

Philip John Paul Gonzales lectures in philosophy at St Patrick's Pontifical University, Maynooth.

Chris Hayden is Spiritual Director at the National Seminary, St Patrick's College, Maynooth.

Gaven Kerr lectures in philosophy at St Patrick's Pontifical University, Maynooth.

Luke Macnamara OSB lectures in Sacred Scripture at St Patrick's Pontifical University, Maynooth.

April MacNeill is Clinical Pastoral Education Educator, Interdisciplinary Professional Supervisor and Director, Rockpool Supervision, in Newcastle, NSW, Australia.

Declan Marmion SM is Professor of Systematic Theology at St Patrick's Pontifical University, Maynooth.

Aoife McGrath is Director of Pastoral Theology at St Patrick's Pontifical University, Maynooth.

Andrew Meszaros lectures in systematic theology at St Patrick's Pontifical University, Maynooth.

Daniel Nuzum is Clinical Pastoral Education Supervisor and Healthcare Chaplain at Cork University Hospital and Cork University Maternity Hospital.

Neil Xavier O'Donoghue lectures in systematic theology at St Patrick's Pontifical University, Maynooth.

Salvador Ryan is Professor of Ecclesiastical History, St Patrick's Pontifical University, Maynooth.

John-Paul Sheridan is Director of Education Programmes, St Patrick's Pontifical University, Maynooth.

Michael Shortall lectures in moral theology at St Patrick's Pontifical University, Maynooth.

Liam M. Tracey OSM teaches liturgy at St Patrick's Pontifical University, Maynooth, and is a parish priest in Dublin.

Select Index